The Great Northwest

The Great Northwest

THE SEARCH FOR REGIONAL IDENTITY

&

EDITED BY

William G. Robbins

Oregon State University Press
Corvallis

Dedication

⤫

This book is dedicated to
Mike Malone (1940-1999)

Distinguished Historian,
Western Regionalist,
and Consummate Storyteller

The paper in this book meets the guidelines for permanence and durability of
the Committee on Production Guidelines for Book Longevity of the Council
on Library Resources and the minimum requirements of the American
National Standard for Permanence of Paper for Printed Library Materials
Z39.48-1984.

Library of Congress Cataloging-in-Publication Data
The great Northwest : the search for regional identity / edited by
William G. Robbins.-- 1st ed.
    p. cm. -- (Culture and environment in the Pacific West series)
Includes bibliographical references (p.   ) and index.
  ISBN 0-87071-492-9 (alk. paper)
  1. Northwest, Pacific--Civilization. 2. Regionalism--Northwest,
Pacific. 3. Northwest, Pacific--Social conditions. 4. Northwest,
Pacific--Economic conditions. 5. Human geography--Northwest, Pacific.
6. Group identity--Northwest, Pacific. I. Robbins, William G., 1935-
II. Culture and environment in the Pacific West.
  F852.3 .G737 2001
  979.5--dc21
                                                    00-012037

Oregon State University Press
101 Waldo Hall
Corvallis OR 97331-6407
541-737-3166 • fax 541-737-3170
OREGON STATE
UNIVERSITY   http://osu.orst.edu/dept/press

Series Editor's Preface

Not long ago commentators on the relevance of region in American culture had little good to say about the idea. At best, some suggested, region and place had become commodities that could be peddled as something "southern" or something "western," but there was no genuine content. That view has changed. Today historians and geographers freely discuss the "Old West" and the "New West" as legitimate descriptions of region. There really is something to the ideas of place and region, they admit, but it is still unclear what is meant by the terms. There are, perhaps, many Wests, as one historian has suggested, but clearly the current focus on regionalism is timely and important during this era of rapid and profound cultural changes.

For these and other reasons, the ideas of place and region are central to the purpose of this series of books on *Culture and Environment of the Pacific West*, which study the relationships between human experience and the natural world west of the Rocky Mountains. The dimensions and meaning of place are fundamental to our ongoing discussions in this series. Cultural geographer E. V. Walter describes place as a "location of experience . . .[and] the work of the imagination," which emphasizes the overlap of human experience and human creativity. Walter argues that places are actually intersections between culture and the environment, or spaces where the real and the ideal coexist. By extension, a region can be understood as a place writ large, in effect a broader conception of location where nature and human perception intersect. This said, however, it is daunting to address the ideas of place and region because they are so inexact. Stating them even generates frustration, for it tends to just beg other questions about the origins and meanings of place and region. How can we understand these seemingly tenuous or even ethereal descriptions of the location of experience?

We can begin by admitting that place and region are inherently complex, that they are messy ideas that resist easy characterizations. Region is perhaps the most untidy, for nearly any description includes nagging exceptions and obdurate contradictions. Nothing seems to stay neatly packaged or bounded. The Pacific Northwest, for example, might be described as everywhere salmon can reach. But that definition leaves out large pieces of landscape, and what about the areas once hospitable to salmon but now bereft of those great fish? Even if agreed-upon definitions were handy, the idea of globalization threatens to make the idea of region look almost oxymoronic. A world dominated by globalization seems to disdain and diminish things regional and local. But humans act and react in contrarian ways, so it is also true that many resist the ideology of globalization by holding the particularism of their backyards dear and by forsaking identification with a generalized world. Regionalists, it turns out, find themselves resisting globalization while they define a geography of frustrating complexity.

In *The Great Northwest*, historian William G. Robbins walks straight into this complicated discussion. He does it by introducing readers to a group of insightful commentaries on the Pacific Northwest that document the intrinsic appeal of regionalism and provide evidence of its content. For some, there is a material basis for this region. It might be described, for example, as the corner of North America demarcated by the Rockies on the east, the Pacific on the west, the Alaskan and Yukon tundra on the north, and the edge of the Great Basin and redwood forests on the south. Other descriptions with much different boundaries might compete with this one, and still others might break free of material limits and define the Pacific Northwest as a state of mind. It might be understood in the iconography of salmon, or it might be described as a cultural region dominated by a characteristic ecological perception of the world.

Many scholars agree that a fair portion of regionalism's content is a matter of consciousness. Put differently, we imagine our corner of the world in a self-referenced way. We claim the region as our place, and thereby we create a means of connecting individuals and groups to the landscape. It goes without saying that regional consciousness is multiple, that there are many versions and many viewpoints. It depends on who is doing the imagining and what angle of vision they use. Robbins embraces this reality and lets the essayists in *The Great Northwest* smartly investigate the idea and reality of the Pacific Northwest in their own ways.

Specific places and the iconography of particular geographies have a lot to do with how we understand this region. The language we use to describe a place like Celilo Falls on the Columbia River, for example, can tell us surprising things about what we think is especially Northwest. Descriptions of such distinct places as Alaska, interior British Columbia, and the reforested Tillamook Burn in Oregon inform a larger idea of the Pacific Northwest, but each includes information that forces us to revise our uncomplicated explanations of the region. Even the well-known and accepted characterization of the Pacific Slope section of the region as perennially soggy—the quintessential regional distinction most often lampooned by non-Northwesterners—is not what we think it is. Recognition that the region is seemingly divided between wet and dry climates, between rural and urban cultures, and between older natural resource and newer high technology economies underscores the importance of attaching Walter's "location of experience" to a variety of landscapes. It is in the connection between culture and environment, the essayists in *The Great Northwest* suggest, that we can best understand this region.

The stories and analyses in this volume do not define the Pacific Northwest, but they document how certain experiences connect with specific parts of the broader landscape. They argue for a Pacific Northwest region that is not imposed on the place or its people. The idea emerges from lived experience in real locations. If it is genuine, it rings true in politics, in economics, and in perceptions, but it is also clear that the ideas of region and place are creatures of history and imagination. This book embraces these complexities, as William Robbins explains in his introduction, to define the "local and unique," while avoiding a romantic attachment to the "quaint and anachronistic." The business of understanding the Pacific Northwest is messy but important. Knowing what we think about our place and our region offers opportunities to understand ourselves, our communities, and our relationships to a larger world.

William L. Lang

Contents

Acknowledgments

The credits for this book are many and varied, extending from the creative generosity of the contributors, to the sponsors of the conference in which the essays originated, and finally to Mecila Cross of the Dean's Office in Oregon State University's College of Liberal Arts. Mecila gracefully and efficiently arranged travel agendas for conference participants, coordinated the various symposium events, and prudently watched over budget matters. Through two major conferences, participants have appreciated her patience and understanding. A bouquet of flowers to you, Mecila!

I am especially indebted to the major sponsors of the February 1999 conference, *The Pacific Northwest: A Region in Transition:* the College of Liberal Arts at Oregon State University and Dean Kay Schaffer and the Oregon Council for the Humanities and Director Christopher Zinn. The Horning Endowment in the Humanities and the Department of History at Oregon State University also provided generous support. I also extend my appreciation to the university's Department of English and the Center for the Humanities for their assistance.

The lively discussions, brainstorming, and contributions of a loosely structured steering committee vastly helped to shape the final program. My special thanks to Sarah Greene, an ecologist with the U.S. Forest Service; Ron Doel, of our Department of History; Bill Lang, Department of History at Portland State University and director of the Center for Columbia River History; and Robert Frenkel, Professor Emeritus of Geography at Oregon State University. Barbara Arnold, who has moved beyond the life of a graduate student, constructed the conference web site and designed the program brochure. Finally, I extend my special thanks to two friends: Kay Schaffer, again, for her enthusiastic support and for providing me with the time to organize the conference, and Paul Farber, chair of the History Department, for his endless curiosity of all things historical.

Complexity and Regional Narratives

William G. Robbins

⮾

TO STUDY A PLACE is to come to some understanding about the intimate connections between people and their earthly surroundings. Kathleen Dean Moore, one of the contributors to this book, contends that we humans have hearts and minds, we remember particular sounds, and we have memories of smell. "We recognize landscapes the way we recognize faces." Our notions about regions and regionalism, therefore, have geographical and material reference points. As mentally bounded places, regions rest at the borders between geography and history. But to speak of the essence of a region is to address much more than an intellectual construction tailored to meet literary fashions of the moment. Because the term *regionalism* implies geographical and spatial dimensions, we should give special attention to material, tangible, even objective realities. Regionalism is best appreciated if its perspective is centered in the dynamics of social, economic, cultural, and biological change. Such an approach provides the best means to understand the persistent and increasing ability of humans to direct and control the forces of nature, the centerpiece to some of the best regional studies.[1]

Although our descriptions of places are fraught with ambiguity and sometimes blur the boundaries of culture and nature, scholars writing about the Pacific Northwest have usually defined the region in terms of the extensive Columbia River system, the vast North Pacific watershed that provides a physical description for a people with a passion for geographic bounding. Referred to during the early years of European American penetration of the region as the Oregon Country, imperial policymakers eventually negotiated the political boundaries of the Pacific Northwest that we know today. But the greater transborder region represented more than a simple, politically circumscribed geography, because common cultures, resources, and economies often transected the international boundary. In rough chronology, the Northwest's written narratives have featured Indian-white relations, the fur trade, subsistence agriculture, fishing, wheat farming in the interior, logging and lumbering, and the eventual industrialization of all forms of economic endeavor. Through more than 200 years of history, the more enduring and constant theme has centered on relations between the original occupants of the land and those who came to dominate the region.

For more than 150 years, Pacific Northwest writers have sought out the region's shared stories and traditions in an attempt to explain the common features of its places and people. They have also pursued larger questions about geography and the temporal nature of regions: "Where does a region begin?" Jeremy Mouat asks. "*When* does a region begin?" In the more conventional regional studies, it has been customary to look to contemporary political boundaries to define spatial limits, lines of demarcation that reflected geopolitical and geometrical convenience rather than cultural or ecological reality. Such boundaries meant little to aboriginal people, Mouat points out, because they possessed "their own sense of identity and region." Even more significant, he suggests, are the boundaries between nation states such as the forty-ninth parallel, a line "born of Euclidean geometry and geopolitics" that imposed an imperial agreement between England and the United States across the Northwest landscape. What Mouat and several other contributors to this volume offer is a framework of inquiry that embraces observable and empirical ways to assess changes in population, production, perception, the cultural interface with the natural world, and a host of other issues.

Since World War II, the revolutionary forces of an increasingly aggressive global economy have threatened to undermine regional culture and what had once been deep-rooted local traditions. Postwar affluence, the growing mobility of the professional classes, and the accelerating movement of capital around the globe have posed ever-greater challenges to the efficacy and meaning of regionalism. By the late twentieth century, placeless (and faceless) business people, many of them rooted in the world of information technology, were remaking former resource-dependent communities into gentrified and gentile homelands, a reflection of a sudden investment of new wealth and new values. Escalating real estate prices and a rising tax base increasingly threatened long-time residents in many rural settings. But gentrification has also crept into the working-class districts of major metropolitan areas such as Portland, Oregon; Seattle, Washington; and Vancouver, British Columbia endangering in the process an older, deeper-rooted Northwest with its own complex and fascinating stories.

❧

Michael Malone, the historian to whom this book is affectionately dedicated, believed that any fresh approach to understanding the American West should be multifaceted and that it should recognize the region's significant features: its abiding aridity; the presence of the federal government; the importance of its extractive industries; and the persistent integration of the West with the global economy.[2] Although those criteria fit the Pacific Northwest only imperfectly because of the marine climate that prevails from the Cascade Mountains to the Pacific Ocean, the writer David Laskin notes that much of the humid Northwest has less annual precipitation than New England, the middle Atlantic, most of the Midwest, and almost all of the Southeast. But still, he argues, the "damp myth" persists in regional lore and literature and is intimately associated with the region's identity. It should also be said that the most productive agricultural area in the Northwest in terms of dollar return is Oregon's Marion County, where irrigation water during the dry summer months makes possible an incredibly diverse bounty of fruit, vegetable, and grain crop production. The maritime Northwest, Laskin contends, has the greatest seasonal fluctuation between wet and dry of any region in the United States.

The second trademark that Malone identifies for the American West is an appropriate fit for the Pacific Northwest. The heavy presence of federal authority in Alaska and its equally important role in the economic and political life of Oregon, Washington, Idaho, and the mountain counties of western Montana is apparent to everyone. If the American public is fascinated with the West as a unique place, then federal lands in the *greater* Northwest hold some of its most attractive treasures. The region's magnificent national parks, huge public ownerships in forests and rangelands, and an extensive and spectacular seacoast extending from the Columbia River to Alaska's southern coastline speak to a profound federal influence.[3] The interests of the U.S. government in the far western reaches of the continent, Keith Benson indicates, appeared early and ultimately proved to be an enduring phenomenon. The imperial-minded Thomas Jefferson's directive to send Lewis and Clark to the Columbia River was one of the first examples of "federal expenditure in support of basic or applied science in the United States." The great railroad reconnaissance missions of the mid-1850s and the land surveys of the same period heralded similar federal activities in the region. Of course, the 1846 Oregon boundary treaty itself, reflecting the collective ambitions of empire builders in Washington, D.C., and London, will continue to attract our attention as foreign border crossings in the Far West between Canada and the United States become points of controversy.

The federal presence in the greater Northwest is especially apparent in the long-running political battles over government control of sizable portions of the region's land base. Nowhere is this more obvious than in Alaska, where the federal government owns 60 percent of the state's land base in conservation, military, and natural resource reserves. As Alaska historian Stephen Haycox indicates, "the federal government was the biggest employer and biggest spender in Alaska between 1940 and 1970," and today the state continues to rank very high in per capita federal spending. With its economy heavily dependent on natural resource extraction, Alaska's modern story is very much at one with the history of the other Pacific Northwest states. But with the state's burgeoning tourist economy now bringing in more than 1 million people a year, the time may be ripe for crafting what economist Thomas Michael Power calls new environmental/ economic stories.

Gail Wells indicates the complexities of those stories in her account of the different meanings that rural and urban Oregonians attach to the state's Tillamook Forest, a vast timbered area that was repeatedly burned over in a series of dramatic fires between 1933 and 1951. When public-spirited Oregonians replanted the more than 350,000 acres in the 1950s, Wells describes the collective effort as "a deep attachment and affection for their landscape." The new stands of Douglas fir that eventually carpeted the old Tillamook burn represented a kind of human power over nature, and, Wells argues, the replanted forest "became an icon of Oregon's cultural identity." But the utility of the new Tillamook has been the subject of contentious debate between local interests who want access to the fresh stands of timber and urban communities in the state who want the forest preserved for its amenity values. What is needed most in this dispute, Wells contends, is a fresh narrative about the forest that is more complex, reflects our own personal ambiguities toward nature, and suggests the need for some sort of compromise between the those who want to preserve the spiritual values of our forests and those who believe in the necessity of using them.

Thomas Michael Power suggests that it is time to move beyond the region's traditional economic stories, folk tales that have "become cultural beliefs unrelated to current economic reality." Power argues that today's new economic wisdom also suggests the need for new environmental stories, the "forces that are actually transforming our economy rather than focusing on the past." These new economic realities are vested in amenity values and nourishing the region's scenic splendors, the very features that attracted Connecticut investment analyst William Smith and his family to Bend, Oregon, for its mountainous vistas and access to outdoor recreation. "Now we're living where others are fortunate enough just to visit," he told the Eugene *Register-Guard*. "This business is portable—we can live anywhere we want."[4] As such, William Smith is representative of what John Brinckerhoff Jackson has called the "landscape of the temporary," people who are weakening place as a central experience in everyday life. Such free-floating mobility and placelessness presents a new set of challenges to sustaining a regional identity. According to the writer William Leach, Smith and others like him are undermining the notion that people have a civic responsibility to act as caring stewards for the places they call home.[5]

With demise of the Soviet Union and the full-blown emergence of global capitalism, there is abundant evidence that the historically migratory character of the Northwest population may be accelerating in recent years. Those developments have heightened the spirit of placelessness that seems to pervade the thinking of many newcomers to the Northwest. A few years ago, the *Wall Street Journal* referred to migratory business professionals such as William Smith as the "footloose soldiers" of "history's mightiest cultural and commercial empire," a floating population rooted seemingly everywhere and nowhere at once. In his angry but provocative study, *Country of Exiles,* William Leach contends that such attitudes are "subversive of the notion of place" and promote the idea of placelessness as a ruling presence in our lives.[6]

Thomas Friedman of the *New York Times,* an otherwise unabashed admirer of globalism, points to the high risks for regional cultural and economic autonomy in his best-selling book, *The Lexus and the Olive Tree: Understanding Globalization.* His argument followed the reasoning of the conservative economist, Joseph Schumpeter, who described the essence of capitalism as "the process of 'creative destruction,'" in which innovation supplants tradition and the present and future replace the past. The current era of globalization, Friedman warned, has caused widespread fear in traditional communities because of its capacity "to destroy the environment and uproot cultures." Seattle's Microsoft, Boise's Micron, and other manufacturers of cyber stuff are providing the infrastructure for the vastly accelerating pace of change in the nation's business culture that is weakening the meaning of place in citizens' lives.[7]

The transformation of former resource-based communities such as Bend, Oregon; Coeur d'Alene, Idaho; and Leavenworth, Washington are part of the continuing integration of the regional with the global economy (Bend added nearly 3,000 new residents in the last six months of 1993 alone).[8] Alaskan coastal ports selling themselves to visiting cruise ships are certainly part of the new emerging globalism along with the influential tourist bureaus in every Northwest state and in British Columbia, each in their own way in the business of promoting their spectacular outback regions to make money. It is fair to point out, however, that Alaska has loudly protested the discharge of polluted water by cruise ships in the Inside Passage. Affirming a sense of regional identity and renewing the ties of affection that bind people to places can provide a powerful counterforce against placeless globalism.

In the introduction to *Regionalism and the Pacific Northwest,* a collection of essays published in the early 1980s, I observed that the study of regions was fraught with ambivalence and irony and that the intellectual confusion associated with such an activity might well be a lasting condition.[9] One of the contributors to that volume, Richard Maxwell Brown, pointed out that scholars had never been able to agree on a singular approach to regionalism because of the inherent ambiguity and lack of precision involved. He concluded that fluidity and change, which was true for all scholarly inquiry, appeared to be the hallmarks of regionalism.[10] But there was common agreement among most of the volume's contributors that the best regional studies were predicated on geographic and social reality and enjoyed some association "with loyalty to and sense of place."[11] For scholars working the ground of environmental history, the reference to physically bounded places has special significance. A decade ago, historian William Cronon advised those specializing in the interface between humans and the environment to pursue "the tasks of finding subtler tools for building bridges among ecosystems, economies, and the cognitive lenses through which people view the world." Cronon believed that those tools were most apparent at the local and regional level.[12]

Although "*regionalism* and *regional identity* are frustratingly slippery terms," as William Lang's essay indicates, the importance and meaning attached to such references pervades our thinking. Writing in the immediate aftermath of World War II, Roy Bessey, a planner and Interior Department field coordinator, reflected that some of the best thinking about regional problems was found in the Pacific Northwest. For Depression-era policymakers seeking a way out of the social chaos of unemployment and hardship, the best approach was to view the region "as an economic, political, and cultural unit. We in this area," Bessey told a Reed College audience, "are bound together geographically, physically, and psycho-logically." According to Bessey, formerly with the National Resources Planning Board, metropolitan influences and the transportation and hydropower potential of the Northwest's great river system bound the region together as a coherent unit. In the world of public affairs, especially among practical-minded planners, the Northwest was a distinct place with unbounded potential for improvement.[13]

Bessey's reference points, of course, were bureaucratic and addressed to the efficient development and administration of natural resources. Such singular and focused approaches to regionalism were devoid of ambiguity, speculation, and local nostalgia. In an essay published a decade ago, Michael Malone warned scholars to avoid that which was "romantic, antiquarian, and . . . irrelevant to achieving a true regionalism." For the greater American West to achieve a sense of itself, Malone suggested, the real challenge for scholars was to take advantage of public affection for the past to advance a convincing argument.[14] To carry out such a task, writers should use their expertise as public intellectuals to examine myths and engage audiences in a dialogue about the meaning of the symbols and traditions that drive regional discussions. Historical understanding (and museum exhibits that strive to confront the complexities of culture and place) offer a way to enhance self-awareness about valuable local knowledge. In fact, the most attractive feature of the *best* Northwest writing has been its presentist impulse, scholars who have served as moral and ethical voices for a responsible civic conscience. My purpose here is not to survey such literature, but to remind readers of the important function provided by those who have written with compassion about the region and who provide a moral compass through their writing.

Katrine Barber, whose chapter takes readers on a narrative tour of the federally sponsored Columbia Gorge Discovery Center (The Dalles, Oregon) and the Yakama Nation Cultural Heritage Center (Toppenish, Washington), illustrates persuasively the social responsibility of that enterprise. Those who monopolize museum narrative presentations, she reminds us, stifle alternative viewpoints and otherwise sanitize what is presented to the public. Quintard Taylor tells a parallel account of the hitherto silent stories of two African American women social activists who fought for social justice and racial equality in the region. In bringing these remarkable lives to public attention, he provides us with a powerful reminder that in matters of racial tolerance and racial equality, the Pacific Northwest shared much with the rest of the nation. Susie Revels Cayton and Beatrice Morrow Cannady, Taylor argues, are striking examples of two people whose experiences illustrate that the struggle "for social justice transcends racial, gender, and regional boundaries." Their lives also remind us that "standard" stories about the Northwest have a different meaning to its African American residents.

Roberta Ulrich's recent book, *Empty Nets: Indians, Dams, and the Columbia River,* is yet another reminder about the sixty-year collective struggle of a people in search of justice, the effort of mid-Columbia River Indians to gain replacement sites for their traditional fishing areas flooded in the Bonneville pool. Ulrich, a journalist who worked for United Press International and then the *Oregonian,* was the first reporter to regularly cover Native American issues for the Portland newspaper. In *Empty Nets,* she tells with passion and conviction the story of the River Indians' long and agonizing fight to assert their treaty-guaranteed right to fish "in their usual and accustomed places." But while they jousted with the Army Corps of Engineers, the river that coursed through their ancestral lands changed, the water grew warmer as the number of upstream dams increased, and the once abundant salmon runs, the lifeblood of aboriginal populations and arguably a regional icon for us all, continued to diminish. Finally, the National Marine Fisheries Service listed three species of salmon for protection under the Endangered Species Act. *Empty Nets* is a millennial story, linking 10,000 years of the region's human history with the twenty-first century.[15]

The essays in this book remind us that we pass through an ages-old, storied, and always changing landscape in our travels about the Northwest: the physical environment itself; Native American ecosystems; the early white settler regime; the industrialized landscape; and the modern "built" environment of cities, suburbs, and tourist destinations in our recreational back country.[16] Although most people in the greater Pacific Northwest now live in urban corridors—the Puget Lowlands, the Willamette Valley, the Spokane and Boise Valleys, lower British Columbia, and metropolitan Anchorage—the spacious countryside beyond those settings continues to fascinate and otherwise occupy our thinking. It can be said with some truth that the region's sense of well-being has been centered on celebrating the big outdoors. Long before Gore-Tex, Northwest residents looked to the sea, the Cascade Range, the Northern Rocky Mountains, the fjordlike northern Pacific Coast, and Alaska's amazing geography for recreational and spiritual nurture. For many in the Northwest, that affection for coastal waterways and the great outback beyond reflects the growing affluence of its population since World War II. It also suggests an attachment to the region's magnificent physical iconography, to a less layered landscape bereft of the effects of the built environment.

But the contributors to this volume make clear that regional narratives are never crisp, certain, and unequivocal. The stories about many of our places, Katrine Barber suggests, are highly contested: "We wage battles to determine dominant narratives because it is through stories that we build an understanding of place and of ourselves in connection to that place." We live, after all, in a long-inhabited region, one that traces its earliest human inhabitants to at least the late Pleistocene. The setting for Celilo Falls on the Columbia River, Barber suggests, is a multilayered landscape with a richly textured culture and history. Presently inundated in the reservoir behind The Dalles Dam, the site was once the location of numerous wooden scaffolds built on basalt outcroppings and extending over the roaring water falls; adjacent to the falls were the drying sheds of a native fishery that dates back several millennia. Thus, the new regional identity associated with the Columbia River is literally an engineered phenomenon, a reminder that regions are often created through the destruction of other representations of place, including indigenous ones.

In the years following World War II, the busy working river at Celilo Falls ultimately gave way in 1957 to the vast stillness and sluggish waters that welled up behind The Dalles Dam. Where dozens of fishermen once deftly walked the scaffolding and where cables once crisscrossed the river, the area now lives on only in memory and in fading black-and-white photographs in historical museums. The ancient fishery at Celilo Falls fell victim to burgeoning economic and demographic growth in the Pacific Northwest, a boom that rolled out across the countryside, bringing good wages to the traditional lumber and agricultural sectors and beyond. Augmented by money flowing into defense and aerospace industries, especially around Puget Sound, federal funding attracted new people, additional capital, and fresh ideas. The Cold War rhetoric of those years created a sense of crisis, an atmosphere in which opposition to the big projects on the Columbia and its tributaries was deemed unpatriotic, un-American, and opposed to progress.

Fueled by the Soviet threat and fears of an energy shortage, policymakers and engineers in the nation's capital and a host of regional developers and politicians joined together to push through the last of the giant dam projects on the Columbia River system. When the work was done, the huge concrete structures turned generators, helped bring arid lands into cultivation, and provided convenient and cheap ship passage upstream.

Further upriver, postwar development plans embroiled the United States in transborder negotiations with Canada and the province of British Columbia. Again, the issue centered on controlling the flow of the great waterway and the allocation of waters between the two nations. With the signing of the Columbia River Treaty of 1961, Canada and the United States appeared to have resolved the issue of apportioning development of the river. However, when British Columbia posed objections to the agreement made in Ottawa, all came unraveled. Control over the province's resources lay at the center of the haggling between the federal capital and provincial leaders in Victoria. Finally, with the 1963 election of Liberal Party candidate Lester B. Pearson as prime minister, matters moved to a close. Pearson, who believed the United States would get most of the benefits under the existing agreement, called for an immediate resumption of negotiations. President Lyndon Johnson and Prime Minister Pearson signed the second Columbia River Treaty and Protocol in September 1964, an agreement that ended twenty years of bitter wrangling over allocating water and hydropower between the two countries. Under the terms of the treaty, Canada agreed to complete three dams by 1973 that would provide 20.5 million acre-feet of storage; in return, the United States would finance most of the construction costs and purchase the hydropower.[17]

Those international protocols further advanced the ability of the greater Northwest to produce cheap hydropower and provided an additional attraction to investment capitalists. The inexpensive kilowatts and industrial rate fees proved a boon to the energy-consumptive aluminum industry, provided cheap electrical power to the Boeing Company, and lay the infrastructure for the eventual emergence of the high-tech sector. While metropolitan sprawl was extending further from Seattle, Portland, Spokane, Boise, Anchorage, and Vancouver, British Columbia, some rural counties (especially east of the Cascade Range) actually lost population as agriculture, mining, and logging activity became increasingly mechanized. Like much of the rest of the nation, the postwar Northwest was comprised of a people in motion, many of whom were losing their provincial commitments and connectedness to place. "Our migratoriness," Wallace Stegner observed, was increasingly hindering us "from becoming a people of communities and traditions."[18] Those new globalist threats to localism, traditional economic activity, and place-centered cultures and the influx of professionally mobile people from outside the Northwest threaten to weaken further regional autonomy. The important question for civic-minded regionalists, in my view, is to develop appropriate strategies to cope with the corporatization and homogenization of what we deem to be local and unique without, at the same moment, indulging in the defense of the quaint and anachronistic.

Notes

[1] See Donald Worster, *Dust Bowl: The Southern Plains in the 1930s* (New York: Oxford University Press, 1979); Richard White, *Land Use, Environment, and Social Change: The Shaping of Island County, Washington* (Seattle: University of Washington Press, 1980); and William Cronon, *Changes in the Land: Indians, Colonists, and the Ecology of New England* (New York: Hill and Wang, 1983).

[2] Michael P. Malone, "Beyond the Last Frontier: Toward a New Approach to Western American History," *Western Historical Quarterly* 20 (November 1989): 417.

[3] Michael P. Malone, "The 'New Western History,' An Assessment," in *Trails: Toward a New Western History,* ed. Patricia Nelson Limerick, Clyde A. Milner II, and Charles E. Rankin (Lawrence: University Press of Kansas, 1991), 100-102.

[4] Eugene *Register-Guard,* 16 August 1998.

[5] William Leach, *Country of Exiles: The Destruction of Place in American Life* (New York: Pantheon Books, 1999), 6, 16.

[6] Ibid., 28-29, 65. For the *Wall Street Journal* quotation, see p. 65.

[7] Thomas L. Friedman, *The Lexus and the Olive Tree: Understanding Globalization* (New York: Farrar, Straus, Giroux, 1999), 9, 11, 27.

[8] Bend *Bulletin,* 5 November 1993.

[9] William G. Robbins, Robert J. Frank, and Richard E. Ross, eds., *Regionalism and the Pacific Northwest* (Corvallis: Oregon State University Press, 1983), 1-9.

[10] Richard Maxwell Brown, "The New Regionalism in America, 1970-1981," in Ibid., 62.

[11] Ibid., 1.

[12] William Cronon, "Modes of Prophecy and Production: Placing Nature in History," *Journal of American History* 76 (March 1990): 1130.

[13] Bessey's remarks are in Ernest Haycox, "Is There a Northwest?" in *Northwest Harvest: A Regional Stocktaking* (New York: Macmillan Company, 1948), 51n.

[14] Malone, "The New Western History," 99.

[15] Roberta Ulrich, *Empty Nets: Indians, Dams, and the Columbia River* (Corvallis: Oregon State University Press, 1999), see especially 216-29.

[16] These ideas are borrowed from Edward Countrymen, *Americans: A Collision of Histories* (New York: Hill and Wang, 1996), 109.

[17] Paul C. Pitzer, *Grand Coulee: Harnessing a Dream* (Pullman: Washington State University Press, 1994), 338-40.

[18] Stegner is quoted in Leach, *Country of Exiles,* 28-29.

Holdfast

Kathleen Dean Moore

⌘

THE SEA OTTERS AT THE COAST AQUARIUM drifted slowly in the currents, floating on their backs with their eyes closed and their hands clasped across their bellies. One bumped against a kelp, then gently rotated and drifted away. Another floated around the tank until its feet bumped into the wall. It ran a hand over its face and went back to sleep, peacefully pivoting across the bay. I made my way to where my daughter was watching the otters from an underwater viewing window. Silhouetted against white fog, the otters appeared as dark shapes drifting unmoored. I wondered how they ever got to sleep, resting on something as insubstantial as salt water. To slide unconscious on a shifting surface that carries you out to sea——it's a human's nightmare. Do the otters wake up startled in an unknown place, with no home port and no influence on the direction of the tides, with only the entangling kelp to keep them from drifting down the coast or washing up on rocks?

I wanted to gather the otters in my arms, bring them to shore, and wrap blankets around them. A sleeping otter, a sleeping child, moves me deeply, dim light spreading from the open door on the face of a child kept only by some miracle from falling through the surface of the Earth.

I looked over at my daughter, who had just turned twenty-four. "What are you thinking about?" I asked.

"My carburetor," she replied.

⌘

I didn't like the idea of getting in one car while she got in another, waving good-bye at some gas-station crossroad, and simply driving off in different directions. But Frank and I were leaving for a camping trip along the Pacific Coast, and Erin was heading for Boston. She had given herself two weeks to cross the country, move into her new apartment, and start her first job. Already her car was pinging under the weight of what she thought she would need for her new place: books, music, a rack of spices, binoculars, a giraffe lamp, and a pet scorpion named Buddy.

"This will never work," I had said. If we all cut our connections to home, how can we keep our connections with each other? Erin assured me there was nothing to worry about; our answering machine wasn't going anywhere. Each day she would call to check in, and we could call the machine to pick up her messages. As long as there was a message, we would know she was safe for another day. We could take comfort at least in that, imagining the dark shape of her car drifting slowly across the continent, windows open, heater jammed to high, tape deck pouring country-western music into currents of cold air.

That first afternoon, we called our message machine from a pay phone at the Dairy Queen in Reedsport. "Hi. I'm in Richland at Aunt Nancy's," Erin's voice said. "So far so good. The wind was fierce in the gorge, but you should have seen the eagles!" I called her aunt's house, but no, she had gone out, her uncle said. "But hey, she ate a good dinner, so don't worry."

Frank and I drove on and set up camp next to an island of shore pines in the dunes. All that night, wind gusted in the trees and sand rained on the tent. By morning, the dunes had moved a few inches inland, uncovering old driftwood and burying beach grass in loose sand. I walked the beach to see what the storm tide had left behind. Windrows of by-the-wind sailors. Clumps of mussels, blue and stony. The torn body of a common murre, its head drawn back, throat exposed, feathers touched with foam. Herring gulls pecked at detritus tumbled in the high-tide line. Sand fleas popped and clicked, snapping up and falling back, making the sand tremble. At the highest reach of the surf, I found a stranded bullwhip kelp, a rope thirty feet from its flat fronds and air bladder to the holdfast at the end of its stem. The holdfast clung to a broken chunk of bedrock.

I turned the holdfast over in my hand. Each winter, mature kelp plants shed thousands of spores that drift off in the currents and gradually settle on the ocean floor. Wherever a spore lands---on a cobble, a pile of broken shells, or bedrock---it grows strong green fingers that hold on tight, while the plant grows quickly toward the light. In this narrow subtidal zone, where ebbing tides pull the kelp toward the dark sea and storm tides threaten to toss it onto shore, holding on is everything. But what can you cling to, when even bedrock gives way to the tide? What will connect my daughter to a place where she belongs, this daughter who is driving east, holding tightly to the steering wheel of her car?

Carefully over algae-slicked rocks and mussel beds, I picked my way among tidal pools, stopping to pry at a patch of crustal algae spreading across stone like pink paint, an alga reduced to nothing but the capacity to stay in place. A green anemone flinched when I touched it, and suddenly I understood that all the plants and animals at my feet, the periwinkles, the urchins, the acorn barnacles, and rock-wrack, all of them have evolved ways to hold against the surf---thousands of tube feet on a single starfish, suction-cup stomachs for gastropods, tufts of black hairs to hold the mussels, bony tubes, sticky feet, calcified plates. What chance do we have, we humans, born with two feet and an imagination light as a bird?

❧

When I was a child, I couldn't bear to leave home. If our family went for a week's vacation---to a cabin in a beech-maple woods or the shore of Lake Erie—-it was always the same. I would lie in the backseat of the car, feverishly, desperately homesick. Even now, I sometimes get that same feeling when I am away from home. It's a kind of emptiness, as if my ribs have sprung a leak, and when I try to breathe, there's nothing to hold in the air. Back then, I tried to stay overnight at my friends' houses, settling myself on the floor in a roll of blankets, but it was no use. Late at night, when the other children started to slide into sleep, I would get up, holding the blankets around me, awaken whatever mother was nearby, and tell her I had to go home. "Are you sick?" she would ask, a startled mother's standard response. "No," I would answer, "I just have to go home." My house was always locked, and I rang the doorbell so my parents would let me in. While I waited, I leaned my cheek against the white siding of the only place I belonged and listened to the screen door open with a squeak I knew by heart.

But our children dart from one continent to another, changing time zones and airplanes as easily as they change their clothes. Our son was in Mexico, but he's on his way to Australia. Erin has just returned from Greece. Sometimes, I don't know where they are for days. I look at the constellations and try to imagine what the stars look like from the Southern Hemisphere. Our house has the worn edges of a turnpike motel.

"Give our kids roots, and let them have wings," urges the poster on the inside of my kitchen cabinet, and I read the admonishment with increasing horror, imagining a winged and rooted chimera, an osprey, its overgrown talons grotesquely entangled in rocks and root balls, its wings reaching for air, struggling to be skyborne but held to the ground by all the connections, flapping desperately, almost tearing itself apart with the effort—this creature rooted firmly to the ground and capable of great flight. Sometimes I don't even know what to hope for my children.

❧

"Hi. This is me. You won't believe this. My car conked out in the Rockies and these guys from the park towed me to Bear Lodge. There are no rooms because tomorrow is opening day of deer season, but the waitress says if worse comes to worse, I can sleep on the couch in the bar, so I really lucked out. It's gorgeous here—you can smell the aspens—and the hunters are buying the beer. So, don't worry. Love you. Bye."

✦

I sat on driftwood and imagined sea otters in deep dusk, washing their faces, getting ready for bed on the sea. An otter reaches for a single strand of kelp and lays it across its stomach. In this unreliable embrace, it goes to sleep.

When Erin was learning to walk, we went on penny hikes around our neighborhood, flipping a coin at each corner to decide which way to go, coming home in late afternoon sun that flared through sweet-gum trees and caught in her hair. She learned east from west at the corner where Jackson Street points to the sun falling behind Mary's Peak. She learned to read a map driving red-cinder roads through lodgepole pines at night. But on five-lane, inbound Boston highways, will she know where she is? Will she remember what she's made of—the minerals from lava flows that strengthen her bones, the salmon, the winter rain that pushes through her heart? Will the salty smell of Boston Harbor remind her of the times she sat in blowing beach grass, leaning against her father's back?

This much I know: Humans don't have holdfasts or suction-cup stomachs, but we do have hearts and minds. We have strong memories of smells that have held meaning for us since we were small, smells that fill us with joy or bring us to our knees with sorrow and regret. Certain sounds go straight to our hearts—seagulls, wind over water, a child's voice, a hymn. We recognize landscapes the way we recognize faces we haven't seen for many years and greet them with the same embrace and grieve for them when they are gone. You can put down roots by staying in one place. But my hope for my daughter is that there is another way to be deeply and joyously connected to the land even while she's on the move, a way for Erin to feel at home in the natural world, no matter where she is. It's a kind of rootedness that has to do with noticing, with caring, with remembering, with embracing, with rejoicing in the breadth of the horizon and taking comfort in the familiar smell of rain. In the sliding, shifting world my daughter lives in, this may be the closest thing to bedrock.

✦

Somewhere south of Tillamook Bay the next day, we pulled into a gas station on the east side of a little lake. There was fog along the coast, muffling the sunset, but between there and where we stood, the lake lay calm, a watercolor of clouds disturbed now and then by rings like raindrops on the water. At the edge of the lake, a little girl waded in a shallow bay. Pink light reflected off the plane of her cheek. Ordinary people in baseball caps, people with dogs snuffing around their feet, people with children of their own, stood around on the boat ramp while my daughter slept in a motel someplace in Ohio or Pennsylvania or New York, while the lights of passing trucks swept across her face. In a phone booth littered with broken glass, I pressed the telephone number of Erin's new apartment to leave a message that would be there when she arrived. "Welcome home," I said, and I had trouble finding air enough for two simple words.

Reprinted from *Holdfast: At Home in the Natural World*, published by the Lyons Press (www.lyonspress.com)

How to Create a Forest

Gail Wells

⤇

The Tillamook Story

O NCE UPON A TIME, there was a beautiful, ancient forest, soft-floored, light-dappled, draped across the rugged canyons of the Tillamook country, in Oregon's northwestern corner. Its trees—Douglas fir, hemlock, and cedar—were immense, 3 to 7 feet thick.

Then one day there came a big fire. It burned the trees down to ashes and gray, dead sticks. A few years later came another fire, and then another, and another. The beautiful forest lay in ruins. What was once a moist, green-cloaked landscape of ridges and canyons now looked like valley upon valley of dry bones. There was nothing but ashy earth, ghostly snags, and an eerie silence where once the air was filled with the songs of birds.

There were people living in the towns on the edges of the ruined forest. They were angry at the fires for stealing their beautiful trees—angry that the fires had wasted 12.5 billion board feet of clear, fine-grained timber, top-quality wood that now lay useless on the ground, a feast for the insects. Telling the story in their newspapers, the people accused the fires of "killing" billions of board feet of timber—as if a board foot of timber were a living thing. Which in a sense it was, because timber was their economic blood, their staff of life. That "dead" timber could have been turned into houses, ships, furniture, paper, paychecks from the sawmills, and money to run the cities, the counties, and the schools.

So the people got together and resolved to put the forest back, to replace the timber the fires had stolen. It was a difficult and complicated job. Most of the burned land sat heavy on the tax rolls of Tillamook and Washington Counties. The owners, timber companies and other private parties, had simply walked away from it after the fires. Why pay taxes on worthless land? So the state forestry department made a deal with the counties: Give us your land, and we will make it grow trees again. When the new trees get big enough to log, you, the counties, will get most of the money from selling the timber.

The people of Oregon agreed to tax themselves to accomplish the reforestation. And then the hard work began. Men felled the snags that poked up from the burned earth, worked knee-deep in ash with chainsaws and axes, and came home looking like chimney sweeps. Then crews surveyed the burned hillsides, built roads, planted seedlings, scattered tree seed from helicopters and airplanes. They poisoned the mice that ate the seeds. They killed the brush that competed with the tender new trees. It was a hard, long, dirty job, but they succeeded. The young trees grew taller, sturdier. The canyons were cloaked in green again.

The people of Oregon promised themselves that the new forest would be a gift of *timber forever* to their children, grandchildren, and great-grandchildren, who would enjoy the blessings of prosperity to the end of their days. The Tillamook would become a perpetual tree farm, thanks to their effort and their vision.

A Created Forest

I wanted to start with this story to explain why I titled my book *The Tillamook: A Created Forest Comes of Age.* The story I just told is, of course, the story of the Tillamook Burn, four notorious fires in 1933, 1939, 1945, and 1951, which together burned 355,000 acres of mostly virgin forest in northwestern Oregon.

The Tillamook Burn has become inscribed in Oregon folklore. Everybody of my generation who grew up in Oregon knows it by heart. The burn's reforestation is sometimes cited as an example of the state's vaunted progressive spirit. Oregonians feel a thrill of pride at being the first to come up with a visionary solution to a vexing public problem. The Tillamook reforestation was a big point of pride for Oregon. Nobody in any other part of the country had ever tried a project of this magnitude before. Even the Forest Service declined to tackle this one; the country was too rugged, too huge, and it had been burned too badly.

The greening of the Tillamook Burn become an emblem of the virtues for which Oregonians have traditionally prided themselves: a cooperative spirit, a can-do attitude, a progressive vision, and a deep attachment to and affection for their landscape.

When I chose the subtitle, "A Created Forest Comes of Age," though, I felt I was taking a chance, reaching a little. What might a "created forest" be? I felt uncertain about taking the notion of "creating" and applying it to an entity, a forest that in many people's minds is wholly natural. Yet one of the things that got me started on my Tillamook journey was my fascination at how the people of the region took it for granted that they *could* do such a thing, that they had that kind of power over a landscape. On the face of it, that taken-for-granted attitude seems justified. Here, after all, was a landscape that seemed to force a rethinking of what *forest* means. Burned four times over, stripped of its cloak of Douglas firs, cedars, and hemlocks, the steep hillsides stood naked. Had the area ceased to be a forest then? But the people planted it like a garden, sowed it like a wheat field, and the new trees took root, flourished, and became another forest, a created forest.

The story encourages us to take the word *create* in a quite literal sense. The forest was gone; nature itself had taken it away. It was up to the people of the Tillamook to put it back. And because they had created this forest with their own hands, they felt the obligation to settle in their minds the question of what this forest was for: to provide *timber forever* for their children and to generations yet unborn.

I learned in elementary school that only God can make a tree. Later I learned that the Coast Range has been a forested landscape for as long as perhaps 14,000 years. The type of forest has shifted through time, in response to shifts in climatic conditions and the occurrence of large fires and other events, but the land has, so far as we know, remained in a forested condition. Trees have been sprouting out of the ashes of forest fires for a long, long time, millennia before humans arrived on the scene.

All this made me ponder again what it might mean to "create" a forest, to "create" one's landscape. And I came to agree with the Tillamook storytellers that humans had indeed created this forest, but perhaps in a more powerful sense than even they realized. By planting and tending trees on treeless mountainsides, the people of Oregon created a forest on the ground. And by telling the Tillamook's story over and over, until it became an icon of Oregon's cultural identity, they created a forest inside their heads.

This chapter is about how people reach for understanding of their landscape by telling stories about it. These stories tell us not only how to think and feel about our landscape, but what to do about our landscape. In this chapter, I will talk about the one big story that we Westerners have traditionally told ourselves about our landscape. I will show how this story no longer provides the understanding it once did—it is no longer functional.

It is painful to be in a situation where your stories do not work for you any longer. But finally, I hope to show that being in this situation is a good thing, because it offers an opportunity to create a new story, a new forest inside our heads, and perhaps a new one out on the ground, too.

About Story

In struggling to tell the Tillamook's story, I came to see that "story" is a far richer and more complex notion than I had initially thought. In his essay, "A Place for Stories: Nature, History, and Narrative," the historian William Cronon draws on literary theory to show that stories are human inventions that help us make sense of our experiences. They are "a peculiarly human way of organizing reality," and, in the end, "our best and most compelling tool for searching out meaning in a conflicted and contradictory world."

But using stories as a framework for the facts raises a dilemma for storytellers, namely how to interpret human actions within "a network of relationships, processes, and systems that are as ecological as they are cultural." When environmental historians describe human activities within an ecosystem, Cronon says, "we seem always to tell *stories* about them." Yet how do you honor the nonnarrative, cyclical, and stochastic character of natural events within the context of the narrative form?

I understand what Cronon means. In the case of the Tillamook, juxtaposing a human narrative on landscape processes poses some problems. Telling a forest's story is a complicated business. It does not exactly lend itself to an opening like, "Once there was a king who had three beautiful daughters. One day there came into the castle a mysterious knight all in black." This sort of opening sets up an expectation of a beginning, a middle, and an end, with cause-effect relationships drawn for everyone to see, and all the loose facts neatly woven back in—a story.

But a forest is not a story; there's no beginning, middle, or end. A forest is a collection of processes, a complex dynamic of events that precede and follow other events, layers of cause and effect with multiple feedbacks and short circuits and, sometimes, catastrophic interruptions. People describe these processes in terms of stories all the time, because that is how our minds work. But it is a lumpy fit, and it points up a big disadvantage of stories: they can never tell The Truth. They can get pretty close, and some get closer than others. But the very authority that stories have in organizing our reality is gained by leaving out or distorting the chunks of reality that don't fit the story. A good story has a coherent plot, it can make what happened seem like an inevitable unfolding of events according to plan or destiny. But it achieves this coherence by leaving out the role played by accident, contingency, and pure dumb luck.

So we should be suspicious of any narrative about a landscape that purports to tell The Truth. One such narrative that has aroused much retrospection in recent years is frontier progress—what I call simply the frontier story. This narrative has shaped American understanding of, and attitudes toward, the Western landscape perhaps more than any other. The Tillamook story with which I began this chapter is woven through with its strong threads.

The most famous teller of the frontier story was, of course, Frederick Jackson Turner, who told it in this way: The transformation of the American West recapitulates human progress from a simpler to a more-complex social organization, and this upward process produces in the end a more democratic and egalitarian American society. The frontier story has taken a beating in the past couple of decades from a new school of historical interpretation. These critical historians—Cronon, Donald Worster, Richard Slotkin, Richard Drinnon, Patricia Nelson Limerick, Donald Meinig, William Robbins, and others—are forcing a reinterpretation of the history of the West by challenging the story that, for almost a century, gave it shape and form.

These historians use the notion of story in the sense Cronon does, as a device for framing the events of history in a way meaningful to human beings. They describe the power of a story to mold, for better or for worse, our interpretation of reality. Richard Slotkin uses the word *myth* to describe the sort of story that imposes a timeless set of meanings on temporal events and shapes them to fulfill some ideological purpose. Slotkin defines a myth as "a set of persistently recurring structures" that make the present "metaphorically equivalent to the past" and reduce both past and present to a law or principle that exists outside of time. Patricia Limerick offers an example of this process in her "myth of innocence," a recurring story in Western political discourse, in which the plot turns on federal heavy-handedness in managing public lands and the ensuing economic troubles of independent-minded rural Westerners. Nancy Langston uses story in the same sense in her description of the confusion and denial of foresters in the Blue Mountains as it became increasingly clear that their best-intentioned efforts were unraveling the ecosystem. "Each time, when faced with complexity, foresters eventually denied it and retreated into their certainty," not because they were greedy or stupid, but because "they needed to hold onto a story that made their lives make sense."

In sum, stories are essential tools for human understanding, but a simplistic or ideologically charged story has great power to distort reality. Knowing this helps us understand how the Tillamook Burn story draws its ideological power from the frontier story. Simply put, the smaller narrative is the larger one in a nutshell. The stories share a particular set of convictions about the place of humans in nature and particular attitudes that flow from those convictions. According to the frontier story, humans are supposed to tame nature to their own ends, in the service of their own upward progress toward egalitarian democracy. Humans are supposed to be masters of nature; we are entitled to its fruits and entitled to use whatever technology is necessary to extract those fruits. Nature is matter, not spirit. The frontier story celebrates optimism, progress, human inventiveness, physical prowess, courage, endurance, daring, and hard work.

Many people critical of the frontier story—including those critical historians I mentioned earlier—have pointed out a flip side to these sturdy attitudes: a callousness toward the suffering of those who got in the way of progress (for example, the Native Americans who hindered the colonizing efforts of white European-Americans across the continent) and an indifference to environmental damage. These points are well taken, but the fact remains that the frontier story is the story we Americans, especially those of us in the West, have told ourselves, for better or for worse, for a couple of hundred years.

And so the frontier story played itself out on the Tillamook. "We're a can-do bunch, we progressive Oregonians," said the people who reforested the burn. They did not have much patience with fatalistic, deterministic, or pessimistic notions. Thinking of them, I'm reminded of a scene in the movie *Lawrence of Arabia,* which you will remember is about T. E. Lawrence, the English soldier who goes to help the Arabs in their revolt against the Turks in the early 1900s. Throughout the movie, Lawrence's Arab comrades preface every other comment with, "It is written . . ." Finally losing his patience, Lawrence turns to one of them and thunders, "*Nothing* is written!" This sentiment very aptly distills American frontier values, which owe a lot to their British heritage.

Nothing is written. We do the writing ourselves. A writer friend of mine, Chris Anderson, introduced me to the idea of the landscape as text, as something that we literally write on through the effects of our actions on the land. You can read our writing across the whole of America: in its highways, bridges, dams, farms, cities, suburbs, shopping malls. We write on the land, its animals, its plants, its geologic forms.

We also write on the land by telling stories about it. Stories tell us not only what is, but what ought to be. They provide a scheme of meanings that presents certain actions as logical and reasonable and other actions as unthinkable, immoral, or stupid. Stories can be limiting or liberating because they are *functional,* they inform, guide, and rationalize action. The frontier story informed, guided, and rationalized the actions that created the Tillamook Forest. And as we've seen, the notes of the Tillamook story play the melody and the counterpoint of the frontier.

A Different Story

Within the time and place in which the Tillamook was reforested, the frontier story made sense. But it has been challenged in recent years by another story, the one I am calling the arcadian story. This is a story in which nature, not man, is the main character. It is a story of nature as primarily a source of aesthetic and spiritual meanings, even a story of nature as a living being with which humans may enter into an I-Thou relationship.

The arcadian story is not new. It is formed of the collected strands of thought of many writers and thinkers over the past two centuries. It may seem new to some, though, because it has achieved a very high profile on our contemporary political scene.

The arcadian story articulates the meaning and the values of the environmental community. The environmental movement's primary mission is to validate the arcadian story and make it a part of the political mainstream, and in this effort they have largely succeeded. As a result, the frontier story is becoming eclipsed. Nobody talks about conquering nature any more, unless it's in an ironic, jesting tone. In much of the popular discourse about forestry, whether encountered in newspaper stories, magazine articles, or casual conversation with friends, it is assumed at the outset that modern forest management amounts to rape of the landscape. Everyone simply *knows* that.

The arcadian story is creating a new forest inside our heads: a forest that is a living thing, a sacred whole, an entity composed of the workings of living organisms; a forest in which any extraction of material goods is a necessary evil at best; a forest from which the human presence ought to be severely restricted or banned altogether; a forest with civil rights—the right to exist on its own terms, with no interference from humans.

The rise of this story in the American culture has been accompanied by (which is not to say it's entirely responsible for) an existential pessimism about the consequences of human actions on nature, and indeed about every aspect of life. I think it's significant that the environmental movement's ascension coincides with the coming of the Age of Anxiety, or what some people call the postmodern age. The dropping of atomic bombs at the end of the most destructive war in history, the periodic alarums about world overpopulation and massive famine, the dawning awareness of limits on the productivity of natural systems, the shifting of scientific models away from assumptions of fundamental order and toward assumptions of fundamental chaos, the overturning of traditional social and moral taboos, the increasing intrusion of (usually unpleasant) global happenings into our breakfast-table consciousness—all these have contributed to a widespread feeling that life is whirling out of control.

As we have seen, human beings tell stories to make meaning out of their experience. Stories arise in response to the human need for meaning. When the old stories cease to provide the meaning people crave, people tell themselves new ones. The frontier story offered meaning in a world that depended on extraction of goods from nature for simple physical survival. We no longer live in that world—those of us fortunate enough to live in the developed countries do not, at any rate. We live in a world where we have material blessings in plenty. There is still a depressingly long list of threats to life and limb—cancer, terrorist bombs, mad shooters on the freeway—but most of us will not starve or freeze to death.

What many in the developed world experience instead, I think, is *spiritual* hunger, craving in the midst of plenty. We are disturbed about the present, pessimistic about the future, alienated from traditional spiritual sources of comfort. The arcadian story about forests offers a set of meanings that feeds this spiritual hunger.

This is a very rich and complicated issue. It would be a mistake to conclude that the arcadian story is mere misplaced religion. Environmentalism has offered a powerful and, in many ways, justified critique of forestry philosophy and practice. And in response, the timber industry has changed its ways for the better. But in sum, the arcadian story is eclipsing the frontier story today because the frontier story no longer serves all its former purposes.

A Collision Course

Now, what does all this mean for the Tillamook State Forest? It means these two stories are on a collision course right out there on the ground. Let me sketch the situation. The trees planted back in the 1950s and 1960s are getting big enough to be interesting to loggers. The management philosophy of the Oregon Department of Forestry, which has responsibility for the Tillamook and all state forests, is that these trees were planted for timber, the counties are expecting the money, and a deal's a deal.

However, say the state foresters, the forest ought to be managed—*will* be managed—in a way that does not impair the forest's productivity or its ecological functioning, now or ever.

These foresters have proposed a long-term management plan that they say will protect the Tillamook's streams, soils, and wildlife, and at the same time permit a substantial level of timber harvest. Their plan calls for an innovative approach called structure-based management, or SBM. SBM is drawn from ideas that have shaken up the forestry academy and profession in the last couple of decades, generally collected under the rubric of New Forestry. One of the main principles of New Forestry is that a forest is, first of all, a set of biological systems interacting with a landscape. New Forestry says that whatever else foresters do, their first mission ought to be to maintain the biological integrity of the forest.

That is exactly what the state's foresters say SBM will do. This management scheme is complicated, but essentially what it boils down to is this: The Tillamook Forest will be managed so as to create a "dynamic balance" of five forest types across the landscape, in perpetuity. The five forest types are, in order of ascending age and complexity: (1) regeneration stands: newly planted clear-cuts or open patches; (2) closed, single-canopy stands: young stands of trees that are starting to compete with one another for light and nutrients; (3) understory stands: stands of older trees in which an understory layer (that is, the community of shrubs and plants the grow underneath the trees) is starting to develop; (4) layered stands: stands of still older trees with a highly developed understory layer; and (5) older forest structure: stands of old trees that resemble old growth in appearance and in some aspects of ecological functioning. (Just for the record, there is virtually no old growth left on the Tillamook—the fires pretty much took care of it.)

Foresters will work to develop a balanced pattern of these stand types across the landscape. Stands of each type will exist in different places at different times in the life of the forest. The forest will thus become what one of the Tillamook's forest planners calls a "traveling mosaic" of forest structures "flowing" into and out of different locations.

For example, a 90-year-old stand with two or more ages of trees might be clear-cut, with live trees and snags left for the wildlife, and planted with seedlings. It would thus become a regeneration stand. Within the same decade, a closed, single-canopy stand might be thinned to hasten it on its way to developing a complex understory, while a stand of 10-year-old trees might be left to grow into a closed-canopy condition. A 120-year-old stand might be thinned to create the openness characteristic of older forests, or it might be left the way it is for another several decades.

The harvest rate under SBM would be slower than under plantation-style forest management, and the timber volume removed would be lower, at least in the beginning decades, while the promised "dynamic balance" is being achieved. Because the Tillamook Forest is mostly young and even-aged, most of the harvesting for the next several decades would be accomplished by thinning, to accelerate the development of more-complex forest structures. Within seventy or a hundred years, if all goes as planned, the Tillamook would achieve its dynamic balance, with adequate wildlife habitat and a relatively even rate of timber harvest.

SBM calls for using all the tools of conventional forest management: clear-cutting, thinning, spraying competing vegetation, and planting genetically improved seedlings. But its philosophy, say the state's foresters, is very different from that underlying most timber-focused forest plans. The principal difference is that SBM is driven by a desired forest structural pattern across the landscape, not by a desired revenue or board-foot target.

The diversity of structural features that is expected to ensue from SBM should, say the foresters, provide enough of the right kind of habitat for wildlife. At the same time, the forest would afford a substantial level of timber harvest, as long as it is done within the context of the "traveling mosaic." The plan also calls for regular monitoring to ensure that the management is actually creating the forest structures as expected and that wildlife are actually living in them.

SBM is an innovative and audacious idea—as audacious as the idea of reforesting the burned landscape in the first place. SBM relies on tested forestry principles and draws on a lot of scientific research about how forests and wildlife respond to various manipulations. But the fact remains that, as with the initial reforestation, nobody has tried such a long-term plan over such a large area before.

Developed and refined over the past six or seven years, the SBM focus of the state's plan has drawn heavy protest from the environmental community. Environmentalists argue (correctly) that SBM is unproven. They argue that the state should put the forest into reserves, in whole or in part, to protect the fish and wildlife. The Sierra Club and others are mounting an initiative campaign to turn the whole 364,000-acre Tillamook State Forest into a state park.

A New Story?

This all has an old, familiar ring: environmentalists versus loggers, preservation versus management, owls versus jobs, etcetera, etcetera. Is there really anything new here? Or is it just more of the same endless wrangling that's taken place over the federal forests? Is SMB really a better way to run a forest? Or is it just a kinder, gentler version of production-driven timber management?

I've said that the state's management proposal for the Tillamook draws heavily on frontier ideals and values. This is not necessarily a bad thing. The frontier story may be out of fashion in some quarters, but I don't think it has completely outlived its usefulness. We should not disdain the positive qualities it celebrates, even as we stay mindful of the environmental and human costs of that period in our country's history. Courage, inventiveness, energy, strength, confidence, hard work: These are values that can serve our modern life well, and I hope those who are charged with carrying out the sustainable stewardship of Oregon's natural resources in this new century will have them in abundance.

More to the point, though, is that the Tillamook's management plan also draws on key elements of the arcadian story. Most importantly, it is founded on the central idea of New Forestry, that forests have an ecological integrity that ought to be preserved. SBM is ecosystem-centered, at least in principle, and the successful practice of it will require a landscape-wide perspective, another important tenet of New Forestry.

The forestry department has embraced the principle that anybody with any stake or interest in the forest has a right to help shape its future. This is another key arcadian idea. Oregon state forester Jim Brown talks about a forest's "community of place," those who live in and near the forest and take their material livelihood from it, and its "community of interest," those who do not live in the forest but value it for its recreational, aesthetic, and spiritual attributes. The state's foresters have invited both these communities, and indeed anybody who wants to be there, into the Tillamook planning process right from the start. They have held dozens of public meetings, poured gallons of coffee, photocopied tons of documents, collected reams of comments, and patiently answered a million questions. In this public outreach we hear the echo of a subtler arcadian idea: that the race should not always go to the swift, nor the battle to the strong; that the whole range of ordinary people, not just those who own the land, ought to have a say in what happens to it.

The Tillamook's foresters have invited the scientists in, too. The wildlife provisions of the management plan (contained in a habitat conservation plan for northwestern Oregon's state forests) have been given a thorough working-over by a twenty-six-member independent panel of botanists, wildlife experts, biologists, ecologists, hydrologists, geologists, and others. The scientists recommended important changes, and the state's foresters are now revising the wildlife part of the plan.

The foresters also pledge "adaptive management," keeping track of what happens on the forest as the plan unfolds and making midcourse corrections as necessary. "There are ways of living on the land that pay attention to the land, and ways that do not," says the historian Nancy Langston, "The land is full of information." The Tillamook's foresters are promising to pay attention to the information from the land and not only to the stories inside their heads.

In sum, the Oregon Department of Forestry professes a commitment to ecological principles, public and scientific participation, and adaptive management. This commitment can be verified: we can watch what they do. We can conduct a little adaptive management of our own. We can go to the public meetings, read the annual reports, walk out into the forest, check and see whether the actions are matching the words.

In his *A Conspiracy of Optimism,* the historian Paul Hirt accuses the Forest Service of embracing a "cult of cornucopia" in which heavy logging on national forests during the 1950s, 1960s, and 1970s continued to be blessed in the face of mounting evidence that it was both unsustainable and damaging to the environment. The conspiracy, Hirt says, was fed by pressure from Congress and timber lobbyists, abetted by the agency's own institutional blinders, and tacitly approved by the American people, who did not want to look too hard at what all this timber-fueled prosperity was costing them.

The Tillamook foresters, in contrast, are operating in a fishbowl, in full view of a skeptical public that is demanding a hard look. Hirt's "cultural milieu of techno-optimism" in which the Forest Service of the postwar years operated does not exist today. There is hardly a cultural milieu of *anything* in this country, least of all optimism, which seems in generally short supply.

Today, managers in public land agencies face a much more divided and dissentious constituency. The rise of the arcadian story has been a trial for many in these agencies, but on the whole it has been a bracing development, because it has forced foresters to examine their own professional culture, acknowledge their blind spots, and open the door to other, conflicting, but ultimately enriching, values.

A Land Ethic

It is not my intention here to argue for or against the SBM plan proposed for the Tillamook Forest. What I want to do is point out how, by opening the frontier story to arcadian ideals, the process of planning for the Tillamook's next hundred years is opening the possibility of a third story, one that could serve the needs of both the forest and ourselves better than either of the others has done until now.

In a famous 1949 essay, Aldo Leopold set forth a prophetic vision that he called the *land ethic*. A land ethic, he said, "changes the role of *Homo sapiens* from conqueror of the land-community to plain member and citizen of it." According to Leopold, for us humans to embrace our role as citizens of a land community, we must begin to see the relationship between ourselves and the land in a new way. The way to do that is to tell ourselves a new story.

In looking for guidance on how to devise a new story, we could do worse than Aldo Leopold. Trained as a game manager, his outlook at first firmly utilitarian, Leopold over the course of his life came to a more complex, inclusive, and paradoxical understanding of the relationship between humans and nature. I sense that Leopold embraces the fundamental moral imperatives of both the frontier and the arcadian stories and brings them together in his concept of *community*, which advocates an ethical treatment of land that does not leave human needs behind. Leopold's idea of community implies that an ethic that ignores human welfare for the sake of the land or ignores the land's welfare for the sake of humans is no ethic at all, for it fails on both the moral and the practical level.

Leopold articulates the stirrings of a consciousness that elevates the land to a community of which we humans are a part—an essential part, but no more important than any other part in light of the integrity of the community. His idea of a land community extends and enriches the idea of the human community. It invites a new way of thinking not only about the land, but about ourselves and about one another. Leopold's land ethic provides a framework for a new story.

Why is it important to tell a more complex, ambiguous, and open-ended Tillamook story? Why is it important to think about the Tillamook, about all forests, in a new way? I offer you two good reasons. On the practical level, a more complex story will help us imagine a range of actions in between the two extremes of "log it off" and "lock it up." We in the Northwest have witnessed painfully the battles in the federal forest arena, a conflict that has left everybody exhausted. It is a conflict between factions informed by incomplete and flawed views of reality. Telling a different story would reveal a different set of choices.

Perhaps an even better reason is that a new story can help us put our fragmented selves back together. Both the frontier and the Arcadian stories suffer from a one-sidedness about human nature. The frontier vision masks one essential human dimension, the aesthetic and spiritual; the Arcadian vision masks the other, the material. But just as we are more than the sum of our body's appetites, we are more than the sum of our soul's yearnings. A new story invites us to reach past this matter-spirit split and acknowledge that our material and spiritual selves are as thoroughly interwoven as a river is with its banks. Telling a new story might help us better express the duality and paradox of our own being.

So, how do you create a new forest? By telling a new story, or rather, by telling the old stories in a new way. Right now on the Tillamook, I think we're seeing an opportunity to do just that.

Sources

Ackerman, Sybil. Interview by Gail Wells, tape recording, Portland, OR, 9 September 1997.

"Arsenal out of Ashes: Tillamook Burn Salvage," *Sunday Oregonian Magazine,* 4 October 1942, 5.

Balfour, Ric. Interview by Gail Wells, tape recording, Forest Grove, OR, 1 September 1994 and 24 February 1995.

"Big Tillamook Burn May Again Be Green," *Sunday Oregonian Magazine,* 31 March 1946.

Brooks, David J., and Gordon Grant. *New Perspectives in Forest Management: Background, Science Issues, and Research Agenda* (Corvallis, OR: USDA Forest Service Pacific Northwest Research Station, 1992).

Clary, David A. *Timber and the Forest Service* (Lawrence: University Press of Kansas, 1986).

Cronon, William. "A Place for Stories: Nature, History, and Narrative," *Journal of American History* (March 1992): 1237–1376.

Fick, Larry, and George Martin, *The Tillamook Burn: Rehabilitation and Reforestation* (Forest Grove: Oregon Department of Forestry, 1992).

Fick, Larry, and George Martin. Interview by Gail Wells, tape recording, Forest Grove, OR, 8 September 1993.

Fox, Stephen. *John Muir and His Legacy: The American Conservation Movement* (Boston, MA: Little, Brown & Co., 1981).

"From Ruin to Rejuvenation," videocassette (Salem: Association of Oregon Counties, 1978).

Hayes, John. *An Independent Scientific Review of Oregon Department of Forestry's Proposed Western Oregon State Forests Habitat Conservation Plan* (Salem: Oregon Department of Forestry, 1998).

Hirt, Paul. *A Conspiracy of Optimism: Management of the National Forests since World War Two* (Lincoln: University of Nebraska Press, 1994).

Huntington, Charles W., and Christopher A. Frissell. *Aquatic Conservation and Salmon Recovery in the North Coast Basin of Oregon: A Crucial Role for the Tillamook and Clatsop State Forests* (Portland: Oregon Trout, 1997).

Labhart, Mark. Interview by Gail Wells, tape recording, Forest Grove and Tillamook State Forest, OR, 24 August 1994.

Langston, Nancy. *Forest Dreams, Forest Nightmares: The Paradox of Old Growth in the Inland West* (Seattle: University of Washington Press, 1995).

Levesque, Paul. *A Chronicle of the Tillamook County Forest Trust Lands.* Vols. 1 and 2 (Tillamook, OR: Tillamook County, 1985).

Levesque, Paul. Interview by Gail Wells, tape recording, Independence, OR, 17 August 1994.

Limerick, Patricia Nelson. *The Legacy of Conquest: The Unbroken Past of the American West* (New York: W. W. Norton, 1987).

Lucia, Ellis. *Tillamook Burn Country: A Pictorial History* (Caldwell, ID: The Caxton Printers, 1983).

Lyon, Thomas, ed. *This Incomparable Lande: A Book of American Nature Writing* (New York: Penguin Books, 1989).

Meinig, D. W. *The Shaping of America: A Geographical Perspective on 500 Years of History.* Vol. 2, *Continental America 1800-1967* (New Haven, CT: Yale University Press, 1993).

Office of the Attorney General. "Oregon Board of Forestry Forest Lands: An Historical Overview of the Establishment of State Forest Lands," unpublished report (Salem, OR: Office of the Attorney General, 1997).

Oliver, Chadwick. "A Landscape Approach: Achieving and Maintaining Biodiversity and Economic Productivity," *Journal of Forestry* 90 (1992): 9.

Oregon Department of Forestry. *Long-Range Timber Management Plan, Northwest Oregon Area State Forests* (Salem: Oregon Department of Forestry, 1984).

Oregon Department of Forestry. *Tillamook Burn to Tillamook State Forest* (Salem: Oregon Department of Forestry, 1993).

Oregon Department of Forestry. "Northwest Oregon State Forests Management Plan," draft (Salem: Oregon Department of Forestry, April 1998).

Oregon Department of Forestry. "Western Oregon State Forests Habitat Conservation Plan," draft (Salem: Oregon Department of Forestry, April 1998).

Power, Thomas M. *Lost Landscapes and Failed Economies: The Search for a Sense of Place* (Washington, D.C.: Island Press, 1996).

Rice, Teresa A., and Jon A Souder. *Managing Oregon's Chapter 530 Lands: Report to the Oregon Board of Forestry* (Salem: Oregon Department of Forestry, 1997).

Robbins, William G. "Western History: A Dialectic on the Modern Condition," *Western Historical Quarterly* 20 (1989): 429-449.

Shindler, Bruce, and Lori Cramer. "Changing Public Values: Consequences for Pacific Northwest Forestry" (paper presented at workshop "Forests and Society: Implementing Sustainability," Triangle Lake, OR, 5-6 December 1997).

Slotkin, Richard. *The Fatal Environment: The Myth of the Frontier in the Age of Industrialization, 1800-1890* (New York: Atheneum, 1985).

Smith, David M. *The Practice of Silviculture.* 8th ed. (New York: John Wiley & Sons, 1986).

Spies, Thomas, David Hibbs, Janet Ohmann, Gordon Reeves, Rob Pabst, Fred Swanson, Cathy Whitlock, Julia Jones, Beverly C. Wemple, Laurie Parendes, and Barbara Schrader. "The Ecological Basis of Forest Ecosystem Management in the Oregon Coast Range," in *Forest and Stream Management in the Oregon Coast Range* (Corvallis: Oregon State University Press, in press).

Tappeiner, John C., II, David Hibbs, and William H. Emmingham. "Silviculture of Coast Range Forests," in *Forest and Stream Management in the Oregon Coast Range* (Corvallis: Oregon State University Press, in press).

Taylor, Bob Pepperman. *Our Limits Transgressed: Environmental Political Thought in America* (Lawrence: University Press of Kansas, 1992).

"The Terrible Tillamook Fire," *Sunday Oregonian,* 24 August 1941, 1-7.

White, Richard. *"It's Your Misfortune and None of My Own": A History of the American West* (Norman: University of Oklahoma Press, 1991).

Worster, Donald. *Nature's Economy: A History of Ecological Ideas* (Cambridge, U.K.: Cambridge University Press, 1994).

Susie Revels Cayton, Beatrice Morrow Cannady, and the Campaign for Social Justice in the Pacific Northwest

Quintard Taylor Jr.

❧

I N 1920, NEARLY 6,000 AFRICAN AMERICAN WOMEN called the Pacific Northwest home. Although they could be found in towns and cities across the region including Helena, Montana; Pendleton, Oregon; Pocatello, Idaho; and Spokane, Washington, approximately 40 percent of these women lived in two cities, Seattle and Portland. Despite their long residence in the Pacific Northwest, the voices of these women have remained silent because of their small communities, the paucity of documentary sources on their lives, and because regional historians have only in the past few years shown interest in their lives and roles in shaping the social, cultural, and political history of the region.[1]

Among those African American women, however, were two remarkably gifted social activists, Susie Revels Cayton of Seattle and Beatrice Morrow Cannady of Portland. As wives, mothers, and working women employed outside the home, the lives of Cayton and Cannady paralleled those of many Pacific Northwest working-class women. As college-educated newspaper editors, however, both women were part of a small African American middle class. Yet, Cayton's background as daughter of the first African American senator in the nation and Cannady's as the first black woman to practice law in Oregon ensured that each would hold a revered place of civic and social leadership in their respective communities. Despite their similarities, these African American women followed distinctly different paths, Cayton as a Communist Party organizer and Cannady as an official in the National Association for the Advancement of Colored People (NAACP), in their campaigns for social justice and racial equality in the Pacific Northwest.

Cayton and Cannady were migrants to the region, arriving in Seattle and Portland in 1896 and 1910, respectively. Much like the other thousands of newcomers streaming into the Pacific Northwest from elsewhere in the United States as well as Asia and Europe, their views on race and region remained inchoate, evolving and subject to periodic reassessment. Both Cayton and Cannady espoused the widely shared idea that the Pacific Northwest offered greater freedom to African Americans than the South or much of the eastern third of the nation. Yet, given their own often painful experiences with bigotry in Washington and Oregon, they, and probably most other African American women of the era, were clearly not ready to declare, as had NAACP founder W. E. B. DuBois in his 1913 visit to the Pacific Northwest, that "the [regional] fight against race prejudice has been . . . triumphant."[2]

If both women identified with the Pacific Northwest, their respective ages, health, and politics influenced their ability to disseminate their messages beyond Seattle and Portland. Susie Cayton, who became an activist only in her sixties, focused her energies almost exclusively on working-class issues in Seattle. The combination of advancing age, diabetes, and her Marxist message precluded Cayton's extensive travel throughout the region in the 1930s. Cannady, twenty years younger and in much better health, easily moved through the region and traveled to small cities and towns across Oregon and Washington as well to New York, Chicago, Philadelphia, and Los Angeles to promote her regional campaign for racial equality. Regardless of their mobility within the region, Cayton and Cannady's combined activities were a powerful reminder that in the matter of race, regional exceptionalism did not apply to the Pacific Northwest.

There is little in Susie Revels Cayton's background that suggested the political path she would eventually follow. Born Susie Sumner Revels in 1870, she was the daughter of Hiram Rhoades Revels, the first African American U.S. senator in the nation's history. Revels, a minister in the African Methodist Episcopal Church and the first president of Alcorn University, was elected senator by the Mississippi legislature the year his daughter was born.[3]

Susie Revels Cayton spent her first two years in Washington, D.C. and the next decade on the campus of Alcorn in Lorman, Mississippi. She became a teacher at the age of sixteen, working in a one-room, rural Mississippi school while attending Rust College. Following a courtship by correspondence, Susie Revels traveled to Seattle to marry Horace Cayton on July 12, 1896. Ten years her senior, Horace Cayton was a fellow Mississippian who had studied with her father at Alcorn. He arrived in Seattle in 1889 after working in Nicodemus, Kansas, and Ogden, Utah. The Caytons had much in common: both were college graduates, teachers, writers, intellectuals, and evolving journalists.[4]

Horace Cayton worked briefly as a political reporter for the Seattle *Post-Intelligencer* before founding the Seattle *Republican* in 1894. Unlike other African American newspapers of the period, the *Republican* carried political news for the entire city and by 1900 had the second largest circulation in Seattle. In 1903, the Caytons were residing in a spacious Capitol Hill home with a Japanese servant and were the wealthiest, most prominent African American couple in the Pacific Northwest.[5]

By the beginning of the twentieth century, Susie Revels Cayton was the associate editor of the *Republican,* where she responsible for articles on religion and women's features. Cayton also wrote the newspaper's editorials and published the *Republican* when her husband was away from Seattle. Her views, as reflected in the editorials during this period, were virtually identical to those of her husband, who considered himself a Theodore Roosevelt Republican. In 1909, Horace Cayton acknowledged on the front page of the *Republican* his debt to Susie when he said the newspaper's success was "not partially due, but . . . sometimes . . . wholly due" to her efforts.[6]

True to her gender and social class, Susie Revels Cayton engaged in social uplift work designed to educate and morally reform African American, working-class women or provide services to the community. It was the latter ideal that prompted Cayton in 1906 to found the Dorcus Charity Club, one of the longest-lived uplift organizations in black Seattle. The club was formed in response to an urgent request for assistance in placing two abandoned African American twin baby girls inflicted with rickets. Unable to find a private home to place them and unsure of what subsequent action to take, Children's Home officials released the girls to the King County Hospital, which in turn sent them to Medical Lake, an institution for the mentally ill. As a last resort, Medical Lake officials contacted Susie Revels Cayton. She and three other black women, Letitia A. Graves, Alice S. Presto, and Hester Ray, recognized this as one of a number of such cases and organized the Dorcus Charity Club. The twins were placed with a foster home located by Cayton and three years later the club continued to provide their full support, "until a suitable home can be found for them."[7]

Susie Cayton's own life took a precipitous change when in 1913, the Seattle *Republican* failed. Whether the paper's demise came because of shifting consumer tastes that the Caytons failed to anticipate or because a grisly account of a Southern lynching drove away white readers, the Cayton's lifestyle declined dramatically and quickly. For the next three decades, they lived on the on the edge of poverty. The Caytons vacated their Capitol Hill home for an apartment in the Central District rooming house they owned. Despite their meager resources, Susie Cayton, at the age of forty-three, withdrew from her business and social activities to care for her four children, who were between the ages of six and sixteen. By 1919, she reentered the employment market only to find that despite her college education, the only work available to her was as a domestic. In the summers, she and her children gathered berries to sell. Cayton watched her daughter, Madge, work as a waitress in small Seattle restaurants, despite Madge's degree in international business, which she earned from the University of Washington in 1925.[8]

The family's declining fortunes had the unintended consequence of liberating Susie Cayton from her husband's vision of class relations and social progress. Unlike Horace, who insisted on maintaining proper class boundaries even after the family's fall from prosperity, Susie Cayton challenged social pretense. The treatment of working-class people in the Cayton employ suggests one such example. Horace Cayton felt their Japanese servant, Nish, and Mr. Fontello, the garbage collector at the family's rooming house, should be "kept in their place." Susie argued that Nish was a source for learning Japanese, and she described Mr. Fontello as "one of the most intelligent men I have ever met," defiantly declaring, "and I will continue to talk with him for as long as I please." Moreover, unlike her husband, Susie had what her biographer called "a love and democratic acceptance of blackness," which allowed her to be much more comfortable around dark-skinned African Americans than Horace.[9] Susie Cayton revealingly wrote of how she could continue to support her spouse with whom she often had significant disagreement: "Since it was impossible to fully unite my efforts with my husbands' . . . I would join him wholeheartedly whenever the opportunity presented itself, steelhandedly pushing my own project yet comforting him when he wished it and loving him always."[10]

Throughout the 1920s, Susie Cayton came into contact with working-class Seattleites—white, Asian American, Native American, and black—and heard their grievances. She also eagerly followed the political conversion of her youngest son, Revels, who, after intense reading during his year-long convalescence from a life-threatening illness in 1925, embraced Marxism, declaring: "By the time I got off that porch I was a socialist. . . . I found it reasonable and sensible . . . that the only way Blacks were going to get free would be in conjunction with the working class." On the day of his graduation in 1929, Revels spent that night not with his class, but on Pioneer Square listening to speakers indicting capitalist exploitation of the working class.[11]

By the early 1930s, Susie Cayton openly differed with her husband in her reaction to political events in Depression-era Seattle. As Horace Cayton looked longingly backward at the individual freedom represented by Seattle's frontier past, Susie looked forward to a more egalitarian future in an industrial democracy. At some point in the mid-1930s, around the time of her sixty-fifth birthday, she followed her son into the Communist Party, declaring, much to the consternation of her husband, "we are now an international family."[12]

Although slowed by age and diabetes, Susie Cayton became more politically active in the 1930s than at any other period in her life. She assisted Revels in organizing a Madison Street branch of the Committee to Free the Scottsboro Boys. For some time she was the only woman member of the Skid Road Unemployed Council and served as its secretary, earning the name Mother Cayton from the organization's mostly white male workers. On another occasion, she formed a sewing circle among African American women that produced quilts for the homeless, while providing a forum for political discussions. Cayton called this process "educating the neighborhood."[13]

Cayton became well known to leading African American leftist intellectuals such as Langston Hughes and Paul Robeson. Her introduction to Robeson was directly attributable to her growing reputation in Communist Party circles. One day, the famed concert singer and political activist arrived at the Cayton's Seattle home unannounced to an astounded household and declared "I'm Paul Robeson, and I'm on a concert tour here, and so many people have told me about you that I just wanted to come up and see you."[14]

In a December 1936 letter to her daughter, Madge, Susie revealed both an active schedule and her ideological commitment to the cause of Marxism. She wrote:

> I will give you some idea of my activities and nothing but shortage of car fare ever keeps me from pursuing them. Monday night: P.W.U. Local, A.F. of L. . . . meets in one of the Minor School portables (walking distance). Tuesday night: The Negro Workers Council, meets in a portable at the Horace Mann School. I'm Vice President and our President is out of the city at this time. Wednesday night: stay in and read late. Thursday: Party Unit always meets. (Some times walking distance, some times not.) Friday night: Stay home or visit in the neighborhood. Saturday: The Harriet Tubman Club meets. . . . Sunday night: The Worker's Forum, 94 Main Street. Besides I try to attend the Legislative Council which meets every first and third Monday in the month, also the P.T.A. at Garfield, which meets every third Thursday in the Month. Of course, there are mass meetings, dances and what not that come in at times. I'm having the time of my life and at the same time making some contribution to the working class, I hope.[15]

Susie Revels Cayton continued to work for the causes of the Communist Party throughout the remainder of the 1930s in Seattle and then in Chicago, where she relocated in 1942. In one of her last acts, Cayton held court in her bed as Richard Wright, Langston Hughes, and other celebrities came to see the seventy-three-year-old daughter of the first black U.S. senator. On the night of her death, July 28, 1943, dozens of Chicagoans joined the Communist Party in her honor. Unlike her husband, Horace, who never deserted the Republican Party, but became increasingly disillusioned just before his death in 1940, Susie Cayton Revels died a proud member of the Communist Party. Susie Revels Cayton's ashes, like those of her husband, were spread over the waters of Puget Sound.[16]

Beatrice Morrow Cannady also envisioned a new world of social justice. Her instrument for effecting that justice, however, was the NAACP. Beatrice Hulon Morrow was born in Littig, Texas on January 9, 1890, one of fourteen children. She attended Wiley College in Marshall, Texas and after graduation became a teacher in Oklahoma. After a brief period at the University of Chicago, where she studied music, Beatrice Morrow arrived in Portland, Oregon in 1910. Two years later she married Edward Daniel Cannady, a waiter at a downtown hotel. By World War I, Beatrice Cannady was a respected member of Portland's small African American community. She was listed as an "active patriotic worker" who served as president of the Colonel [Charles] Young War Savings Society. Cannady was also developing a national reputation. She was invited to speak at the National Association of Women's Clubs convention in Denver, where she proposed resolutions be sent to President Woodrow Wilson asserting the national organization's "whole hearted cooperation and support to the United States and their [sic] allies."[17] In 1919, with two sons, George and Ivan, at home, Cannady enrolled in the Northwestern College of Law in Portland. Three years later, she became the first African American woman to graduate from the law school and was one of two women in the class of twenty-two. Cannady was the first African American woman to practice law in Oregon, having been admitted to the Oregon Bar in 1922. Recalling her graduation ceremony, Cannady "was asked to take her friends away so as to avoid embarrassment." She later bitterly described her reaction to the request: "For the first time during the whole course of study I was reminded of my color. Of course, I do not forget such experiences, and no one can fully appreciate the distress unless they have suffered in the same way."[18]

Cannady was one of 165 founding members of the Portland NAACP in December 1914, however, she quickly emerged as its most powerful voice. When in 1916 D.W. Griffith's controversial, anti-black film, *The Birth of a Nation* was slated to be shown in Portland, Cannady and other representatives from the local NAACP appeared before the city council to protest its showing in local theaters. In response, the Portland City Council enacted an ordinance that prohibited showing any film that, in its view, provoked racial hatred. The ban made Portland one of a handful of cities in the nation to respond decisively to black protests concerning the film. Subsequent attempts to circumvent the law and show the film in 1922, 1926, and 1931 were similarly unsuccessful after Cannady and other black and white community leaders objected. Eleanor B. Colwell, secretary of the Portland Board of Motion Picture Censors, wrote in 1929, "it was entirely due to [Cannady's] effort that *The Birth of a Nation* and similar films were refused exhibition here."[19]

The Portland NAACP's campaign against *The Birth of A Nation* earned Cannady a high profile in Los Angeles in 1928 during the organization's nineteenth national convention, the first held on the West Coast. Personally invited by NAACP Executive Secretary James Weldon Johnson, Cannady was the only major convention speaker who did not hold a national NAACP office. Cannady's address, "Negro Womanhood: A Power in the Development of the Race and Nation," followed W. E. B. DuBois's convention keynote address. Cannady was also selected along with DuBois, Robert Bagnell, William Pickens, and Mary White Ovington to address selected Los Angeles-area churches on the work of the organization and race relations in the United States.[20]

Beatrice Cannady shaped local black community opinion through her role as editor of the city's leading African American newspaper, the Portland *Advocate,* founded in 1903 by three Portland African Americans, Edward Rutherford, McCants Stewart, and Edward Cannady. Beatrice Cannady became assistant editor in 1912, eventually became its editor and owner in 1929, and remained affiliated with the paper until 1934. Cannady used the *Advocate* to challenge the discrimination routinely practiced in Portland during the 1920s and 1930s by restaurants, hotels, and movie theaters and to lobby for state civil rights legislation. Her efforts were not always confined to written protests. In 1928, Cannady was able to obtain seats in the main section of Portland's Oriental Theater after refusing to be relegated to the segregated balcony. She described the anguish of these constant and intermittently successful challenges of segregation in an editorial titled, "Some of the Joys of Being Colored."[21]

Such victories were partial consolation for the continuous difficulty the African American community faced in obtaining state civil rights legislation. Cannady knew that frustration when in 1919 she helped craft the first civil rights bill to be presented to the Oregon state legislature. The bill would have provided for full access to public accommodations without distinction based on race or color. After intense debate, the measure was defeated on the last day of the legislative session.[22]

Beatrice Cannady was successful, however, in her efforts to repeal the notorious black laws of Oregon. The discriminatory measures, which were embedded in the first state constitution enacted in 1858, prohibited African Americans from settling in Oregon and denied voting rights to "blacks, Chinese and mulattoes" already resident in the state. Although both measures were technically voided by the post-Civil War Fourteenth and Fifteenth Amendments to the U.S. Constitution, their continued presence in the state constitution was viewed by Oregon's African Americans, and by many white Oregonians opposed to discriminatory laws, as symbols of the European American populace's attitudes toward black Oregonians. Statewide ballot measures that would have repealed the black laws were narrowly defeated in 1893, 1900, and 1916.[23]

In the winter of 1925, Cannady mounted a fourth campaign to repeal the measures. Urging her black and white fellow citizens to inform themselves about the laws and declaring the campaign "a splendid opportunity for some missionary work," she called on churches, fraternal societies, women's clubs, and other civil and social organizations to become active on behalf of the repeal.[24]

For six weeks before the election, the *Advocate* ran pro-repeal editorials and urged sympathetic white organizations to support its efforts. The highly publicized campaign of the *Advocate* prompted other newspapers including the Corvallis *Gazette-Times,* the Albany *Democrat Herald,* and the Eugene *Guard* to support repeal. The *Guard* claimed the measures were "the shame of Oregon." When the statewide ballots were tallied, the vote for repeal of the black laws was 108,332 to 64,954.[25]

Beatrice Cannady dominated the activities of the NAACP through the 1920s. She led the organization in successfully challenging school segregation in Vernonia, Oregon, and Longview, Washington. When black children were denied access to the public schools in these towns, Cannady intervened by organizing chapters of the NAACP to challenge local segregation. Cannady personally interceded with Vernonia town and lumber company officials to ensure the community's African American children would have access to the local public schools. Once they entered the schools, the African American students were quickly incorporated into academic and extracurricular activities. One black student, according to the recollections of a local resident, was soon after elected student body president.[26]

Viewing herself as an unofficial racial ambassador, during what was then known as Negro History Week, Cannady wrote articles and gave lectures (more than one hundred by 1927) on African American history and racial prejudice. Cannady exploited the new medium of radio to spread her message of racial egalitarianism and justice. During Negro History Week in 1927 alone, she gave radio talks on the three leading stations in Portland, KGW, KXL, and KOIN. "What we need is not a history of selected races or nations," she declared in a 1927 broadcast over KGW, "but the history of the world void of national bias, race hate and religious prejudice. . . . Let truth destroy the dividing prejudice of nationality and teach universal love without distinction of race [and] rank." In 1929, Cannady was nominated for the Harmon Award in Race Relations from the Harmon Foundation in New York City for her efforts to promote racial understanding and specifically for persuading the Portland Board of Education to require courses on African American history in the city's high schools.[27]

Cannady lectured in various venues throughout the Pacific Northwest including Salem, McMinnville, Newberg, Corvallis, and Eugene. When she was scheduled to speak at Willamette University in a class on race relations, Clare Jasper, a member of Beta Chi Sorority requested that Cannady stay at their sorority house: "The girls are all anxious to meet you and talk with you. [Please] come in time for dinner the evening before and then spend the night with us. We have to get up early, for our class meets at 7:45." Irene H. Gerlinger, assistant campaign director of the Portland Community Chest, however, had a special assignment for Cannady as guest speaker, which served as a reminder that even those who presumed to support racial equality often harbored attitudes informed by invidious stereotypes. "Probably only a handful of people would come out to meetings," declared Gerlinger, "that were not enlivened by something entertaining, so . . . I am depending upon you and your friends to get singers; for we can get hundreds of people out to our meetings if we can tell them that negro spirituels [sic] will be sung."[28]

When Cannady arrived to speak to 500 students at the Arleta Vacation Bible School in Portland in 1923, at the invitation of Alice Handsaker, Chairman of the Fellowship for Better Inter-Racial Relations, she found the building surrounded by Ku Klux Klan members passing out racist literature. Undaunted, Cannady calmly walked past the protestors and delivered her scheduled address, pleading "eloquently for justice and fair play for her race," according to Handsaker, who then added, "It gives me such pleasure to bear this witness to her achievements and as an Anglo-Saxon of pure blood, I deem it an honor to be associated with her work." Four years later, Cannady's speech before 200 delegates of the Oregon Federation of Women's Clubs meeting in Bend persuaded the statewide group to endorse an antilynching resolution. The resolution noted that one black man was lynched on May 23 in Braggadocia, Missouri during the time the convention was meeting.[29]

Cannady's interracial ambassadorship often entailed direct interaction with individuals throughout Oregon. Maintaining a library of 300 volumes of literature and history by and about African Americans, as well as a complete file of leading black publications such as the NAACP's *Crisis,* the Urban League's *Opportunity,* and the socialist newspaper *The Messenger,* Cannady allowed interested youth and adults to gather by her living room fireplace to read or to borrow items as needed. Word of Cannady's library spread across the state. In 1927, she received requests from high school students in Bend seeking information on the black population in the Pacific

Northwest and from Mrs. P.S. Davidson of Prineville for a copy of Alain Locke's *The New Negro.* Davidson indicated that the volume was not in the state library and wrote, "I thought you might have it." Cannady sent not only *The New Negro,* but Langston Hughes's *The Weary Blues,* James Weldon Johnson's *Anthology of Negro Verse,* and several copies of *Crisis* and *Opportunity,* with an accompanying letter indicating her "special pleasure to furnish you material regarding the Negro." She then asked that the books and periodicals be returned "as soon as they have served the purpose, as I have numerous calls similar to the one from you."[30]

According to Cannady, improving race relations also meant bringing to white Oregon audiences leading African American artists and intellectuals, "to offset the unjust propaganda disseminated . . . by the newspaper press of the country." In 1919, she arranged the speaking engagement of William Pickens, then dean of Morgan College for Negroes in Baltimore and member of the executive committee of the NAACP. Welcoming addresses for Pickens came from Portland Mayor George L. Baker and Oregon Governor Ben W. Olcott, who flew in from Salem in an airplane to greet the NAACP official. Other prominent artists and activists introduced to Oregonians by Cannady included concert singer Roland Hayes, composer and musician J. Rosemond Johnson, Montana-born author Taylor Gordon, opera singer Florence Cole Talbert, newspaper editor and labor union leader A. Philip Randolph, NAACP executive Robert W. Bagnell, and national official with the YWCA Addie W. Hunton.[31]

Cannady's activism extended far beyond the NAACP's quest for African American civil rights. She served at various times as a member of the Oregon Prison Association, the Near East Relief Organization, and the Oregon State Federation of Colored Women. Cannady also served on one national board, the Commission on the Church and Race Relations for the Federal Council of the Churches of Christ in America, headquartered in New York City. Other commission members included its chair, African Methodist Episcopal (AME) Zion Bishop George C. Clement, prominent African American sociologist George E. Haynes, and Dr. Will W. Alexander, executive director of the Council on Interracial Cooperation, a group of white Southern social activists. Cannady's work as a peace activist prompted her membership in the Oregon Committee on the Cause and Cure of War. In 1929, she wrote an open letter to newly elected Oregon Congressman Frederick F. Korell to support his proposal before the Inter-Parliamentary Union in Washington, D.C. calling for the complete embargo of the exportation of arms and munitions.[32]

Interest in Africa's history and future led Cannady to join the Pan African Congress, a group of black intellectuals founded by W. E. B. DuBois in

1919 to work for the liberation of the world's most colonized continent. Cannady joined the organization soon after its inception, and in February 1927 she represented Oregon at its national convention in New York City. En route Cannady stopped in Chicago, where she received a tour of the Chicago *Defender* facilities, the nation's largest African American newspaper, by owner Robert S. Abbott. Nine months later, Cannady organized a miniature Pan African Conference held at the Portland Public Library. Featured speakers included Nettie Ashberry, a leaders of the Colored Women's Clubs in Tacoma, Ken Nagazawa, a Japanese poet and playwright, Charles A. Rice, superintendent of Portland Public Schools, and Mrs. D. A. Graham, the wife of the president of Monrovia College in Liberia. Dr. Norman F. Coleman, president of Reed College, and Marshal Dana, editor of the *Oregon Daily Journal,* completed the list of speakers.[33]

That only one of the conference speakers, Mrs. Graham, had any direct ties to Africa is not necessarily surprising, considering the dearth of students or political leaders from that continent in the Pacific Northwest. What is surprising, however, are the resolutions that flowed from the two-day gathering, none of which specifically addressed the African condition. Marshal Dana set the tone by focusing on interracial cooperation in Portland and the United States. In fact, he used his address to call for a Pan-Pacific Interracial Conference, declaring "the colors, white, brown, yellow and black, must be harmonized before the era of the Pacific can succeed. The races must learn to live together in human brotherhood, common aspiration and peace. There must be understanding and gratitude." In keeping with that theme, the Portland Pan African Congress requested that the Portland School District place volumes of the *Journal of Negro History* in school libraries, opposed racially discriminatory legislation, and commended Connecticut Senator Hiram Bingham for refusing to enter a discriminatory social club. The conference then closed with papers describing internationally famous persons of African ancestry and international problems.[34]

Beatrice Cannady had her critics. Some NAACP members felt she used the association and the *Advocate* for personal advancement. Others cautioned against her individualistic approach to African American grievances, arguing that her actions often precluded a more deliberate, organizational response. As a consequence of these charges, the branch was reorganized in 1923 to curtail her power as branch president and in the following years disgruntled members continued to ask for Cannady's resignation or intervening action by the national organization. The national headquarters, however, refused to take any action against Cannady and, in fact, commended her for organizing branches in neighboring communities and for "bringing to better understanding the two races . . . in that part of the country."[35]

Beatrice Cannady received her sharpest rebuke from community spokespersons, including members of the NAACP, over her criticism of the popular but segregated Portland YWCA. In 1921, the black branch of the Portland YWCA was established in a portable structure on the corner of Williams Avenue and Tillamook Street. Five years later, work commenced on a new, permanent building on the site, funded primarily by a gift of $12,000 from Mrs. E. S. Collins, a white woman active in YWCA affairs. African American opposition to the segregated facility emerged almost immediately, fueled by rumors that the gift originated with the Ku Klux Klan. Some white Portlanders also opposed the facility, fearing the building of a social service institution serving a predominately African American clientele near their homes would depress property values. The white opponents failed, however, in their bid to persuade the city council to deny a building permit after the city attorney reminded council members that they could not deny a building permit simply because of race.[36]

Cannady's objections to the facility stood in contrast to both black and white opponents and reflected the dilemma common to many civil rights activists committed to integration. "Segregation is the root of all evil," she had written in 1926, "for when people do not know one another, they are suspicious and distrustful of one another. Only by contact of the races will ever an understanding be reached." Although she recognized the desperately needed benefits, services, and support the YWCA would provide to African American Portland, Cannady could not, on principle, endorse a segregated facility while calling on the rest of the community to abolish such segregation, even if her position meant alienating significant segments of the African American community.[37]

The Williams Avenue YWCA was constructed and emerged as a center of community activities despite the concerns of the various opponents including Cannady. The facility had a gymnasium and auditorium with a stage, a kitchen, office, lounge, and locker rooms and showers for both boys and girls. Some local black organizations raised $1,300 to furnish the building. The Williams YWCA sponsored clubs for grade school and high school girls as well as classes in Spanish, sewing, Bible studies, musical programs, dancing, games, and exhibits featuring black artists and activities celebrating community holidays and commemorations such as Negro History Week.[38]

Although most of the previous two decades of her life had been devoted to the politics of civil rights, Cannady entered the political arena formally only once in her career. In 1932, she ran unsuccessfully for state representative from District 5, Multnomah County. Two years later, Cannady left Portland permanently for Los Angeles, California.[39]

✦

There is no evidence that Susie Revels Cayton and Beatrice Morrow Cannady ever met. Yet, the Portland activist could have spoken equally for her Seattle counterpart when she declared: "I believe that if we could be allowed to express or to demonstrate our 'human-ness' there would be less prejudice. . . . We want our children educated, we want to feel safe in our homes, we want to be able to worship God peacefully in our churches, and want to be allowed to maintain a standard of life that is an American standard. No one knows how difficult it is to do this under the conditions prevailing in the country."[40]

Susie Revels Cayton and Beatrice Morrow Cannady represent two of many unheralded activists in the Pacific Northwest, who translated their lived experiences into expressions of hope for a better world. Their histories, like those of other African American Northwesterners, illustrate the persistent campaign for racial and social justice. Unfortunately, generations of regional historians have dismissed stories of African American women like Cayton and Cannady as unimportant to the central narrative of the region. Yet, the experiences and activities of these courageous women illustrate the African American contribution to the development of social and political thought in Washington and Oregon. The Cayton and Cannady stories remind us that the quest for social justice transcends racial, gender, and regional boundaries.

Notes

[1] For works on twentieth-century African American women in the Pacific Northwest, see Susan H. Armitage and Deborah Gallacci Wilbert, "Black Women in the Pacific Northwest: A Survey and Research Prospectus," in *Women in Pacific Northwest History: An Anthology*, ed. Karen Blair (Seattle: University of Washington Press, 1988); Evelyn Crowell, "Twentieth Century Black Woman in Oregon," *Journal of African and Black American Studies* 1 (Summer 1973): 13-15; and Kathryn Hall Bogle, "Katherine Hall Bogle on the African American Experience in Wartime Portland," *Oregon Historical Quarterly* 93, no. 4 (Winter 1992): 404. For general African American histories that discuss Pacific Northwest black women, see Esther Hall Mumford, *Seattle's Black Victorians, 1852-1901* (Seattle: Ananse Press, 1980); Elizabeth McLagan, *A Peculiar Paradise: A History of Blacks in Oregon, 1788-1940* (Portland: Georgian Press, 1980); Mamie O. Oliver, *Idaho Ebony: The Afro-American Presence in Idaho State History* (Boise: Idaho State Historical Society, 1982); and Quintard Taylor, *The Forging of a Black Community: Seattle's Central District from 1870 to the Civil Rights Era* (Seattle: University of Washington Press, 1994). For western regional surveys, see Glenda Riley, "American Daughters: Black Women in the West," *Montana: The Magazine of Western History* 38, no. 2 (Spring 1988): 14-27; Lawrence B. de Graaf, "Race, Sex and Region: Black Women in the American West, 1850-1920," *Pacific Historical Review* 49, no. 2 (May 1980): 285-313.

[2] W. E. B. DuBois, "The Great Northwest," *Crisis* 6 (September 1913): 238.

[3] See Richard Stanley Hobbs, "The Cayton Legacy: Two Generations of a Black Family, 1859-1976," (Ph.D. diss., University of Washington, 1989), 44-45.

[4] Ibid., 49-55.

[5] See Taylor, *Forging,* 19-20; Hobbs, "The Cayton Legacy," 25-41, 101, 117-19.

[6] The quotation is from the Seattle *Republican,* 23 July 1909, 1. Locally Cayton was allied with former U.S. Senator John L. Wilson, the King County Republican "boss" who controlled the Seattle *Post Intelligencer* between 1899 and 1910. See Hobbs, "The Cayton Legacy," 110-12.

[7] See "Northwest Negro Prosperity Number," Seattle *Republican,* 15:11 (June 1909), 21; Horace L. Cayton, *Long Old Road: An Autobiography* (Seattle: University of Washington Press, 1963), 6-7. For a description of black social clubs across the nation, see Willi Coleman, "Keeping the Faith and Disturbing the Peace: Black Women from Anti-Slavery to Women's Suffrage," (Ph.D. diss., University of California, Irvine, 1982), 70-77, 83-85; and Julius Nimmons, "Social Reform and Moral Uplift in the Black Community, 1890-1910: Social Settlements, Temperance, and Social Purity" (Ph.D. diss., Howard University, 1981), 77-82. See Karen J. Blair, *The Clubwoman as Feminist: True Womanhood Redefined, 1868-1914* (New York: Holmes and Meier Publishers, 1980), 39-56, for a description of the role of native-born, middle-class white women in creating comparable organizations.

[8] Hobbs, "The Cayton Legacy," 138-41, 183, 209; Taylor, *Forging,* 61.

[9] The first quotation appears in Hobbs, "The Cayton Legacy,"190. See also p. 193.

[10] Ibid., 314.

[11] See Hobbs, "The Cayton Legacy," 233. The quotation appears on p. 231.

[12] Ibid., 251.

[13] Ibid., 250-52.

[14] Ibid, 251.

[15] Susie Revels Cayton to Madge Cayton, n.d., quoted in Hobbs, "The Cayton Legacy," 311.

[16] Ibid., 312-15.

[17] Quoted in Portland *Oregonian,* undated clipping, Beatrice Cannady Scrapbook, p. 61, Cannady Papers, Oregon Historical Society.

[18] See Beatrice Cannady biography, p. 2, Cannady Papers, Oregon Historical Society.

[19] See letter by Colwell in Cannady Papers, Oregon Historical Society. See also McLagan, *A Peculiar Paradise,* 123, 134-35.

[20] See James Weldon Johnson to Cannady, 11 February 1928 and Beatrice Cannady Scrapbook, p. 40, Cannady Papers, Oregon Historical Society.

[21] The Portland *Advocate,* 8 December 1928, 3. See also McLagan, *A Peculiar Paradise,* 111, 131.

[22] McLagan, *A Peculiar Paradise,* 164-65.

[23] Franz M. Schneider, "The 'Black Laws' of Oregon," (master's thesis, University of Santa Clara, 1970), 81-82.

[24] The Portland *Advocate,* 21 February 1925, 4.

[25] See Schneider, "The 'Black Laws' of Oregon," 93-95, 99. For examples of the newspaper campaign for repeal, see the *Advocate,* 31 July 1926, 4; 14 August 1926, 4; 28 August 1926, 4. See also the Eugene *Guard,* 8 October 1926, 4.

[26] McLagan, *A Peculiar Paradise,* 123, 140-41; Schneider, "The 'Black Laws' of Oregon," 72.

[27] The quotation appears in the Philadelphia *Tribune,* 12 March 1927, 1.

Endorsements of Cannady's nomination were advanced by Levi T. Pennington, President of Pacific College in Newberg, Oregon; Sadie Orr Dunbar, the Oregon General Federation of Women's Clubs; Sceva Bright Laughlin, Department of Economics and Sociology, Willamette University; Bernard Mobile, Professor of Political Science, Reed College; Portland Pastors W. R. Lovell, First AME Zion Community Church, and Daniel G. Hill, Bethel AME Church; Millie R. Trumbull, President of the Oregon Prison Association; and Franklin Griffith, President of Portland Electric Power Company. Robert W. Bagnell, National Director of Branches, NAACP, also endorsed Cannady. All letters of endorsement are found in the Cannady Papers, Oregon Historical Society.

[28] For the first quotation, see Clare Jasper to Beatrice Cannady, 19 May 1927. The second is in Mrs. G. T. Gerlinger to Cannady, 25 August 1928, Cannady Papers, Oregon Historical Society.

[29] Alice Handsaker to Cannady, n.d., Cannady Papers, Oregon Historical Society. On the Women's Clubs resolution, see clipping in the Cannady Papers. In 1926, Cannady also persuaded Willamette University students to pass a resolution urging enactment of the Dyer Anti-Lynching Bill following her presentation on campus. See California *Voice,* 7 May 1926, 1. The clipping is in the Beatrice Cannady Scrapbook, Cannady Papers, Oregon Historical Society.

[30] See Mrs. P. S. Davidson to Cannady, 10 January 1927; Cannady to Davidson, 14 January 1927, Cannady Papers, Oregon Historical Society.

[31] The Pickens lecture is detailed in Portland *Oregonian,* 26 July 1919. See also Beatrice Cannady Scrapbook, pp. 78-82, Cannady Papers, Oregon Historical Society.

[32] Cannady to Congressman Frederick F. Korell, n.d., Cannady Papers, Oregon Historical Society.

[33] See Portland, *Oregonian,* 6 February 1927, 10; 19 November 1927, 9.

[34] Ibid. See also Beatrice Cannady Scrapbook, pp. 67-75, Cannady Papers, Oregon Historical Society.

[35] The quotation appears in a letter from Robert W. Bagnell, National Director of Branches, NAACP, to the Harmon Award Commission, Harmon Foundation, New York City, 19 August 1929, Cannady Papers, Oregon Historical Society. See also McLagan, *A Peculiar Paradise,* 123.

[36] Ibid., 121.

[37] The quotation is from Cannady's response to a call for help in combating the creation of a racially segregated school in Maxville, Oregon. See Cannady to J. L. Stewart, 17 November 1926, Cannady Papers, Oregon Historical Society.

[38] Ibid.

[39] On the Cannady legislative campaign, see Portland *Advocate,* 9 April 1932, 1; 30 April 1932, 1; 28 May 1932, 1.

[40] Beatrice Cannady Scrapbook, p. 4, Cannady Papers, Oregon Historical Society.

Narrative Fractures and Fractured Narratives: Celilo Falls in the Columbia Gorge Discovery Center and the Yakama Nation Cultural Heritage Center

Katrine Barber

⤝

IN A PHOTOGRAPH TAKEN by The Dalles, Oregon photographer Wilma Roberts, an unnamed Indian man stands alone at the end of a wooden scaffold that stretches over the roaring falls at Celilo on the Columbia River.[1] His body curves to the work of holding a dipnet steady in the swiftly moving current, the arc of his back revealing the concentration necessary for this dangerous labor. He is in full shadow, silhouetted against a river illuminated by the setting sun. It is a beautifully rendered photograph: the crisp black outlines of the fisherman's body, the pole of his dipnet, and the safety rope that trails behind him contrast with the foaming falls that reflect the orange of the day's last sunlight. The contrast evokes an ancient history of Native fishing at Celilo Falls and the Long Narrows. More importantly, it is a romantic image made possible by placing most of what one would have seen at Celilo when Roberts shot this photo outside the photographer's frame. It is an image created as much by what it omits as what it reveals. In a second photograph, Wilma Roberts presents an entirely different narrative about fishing at Celilo. In this black-and-white image, hundreds of feet of scaffolding cloak the basalt outcroppings of the river bank, drying sheds perch anywhere that is relatively flat and dry, more than a dozen fishers are busy working the river, cable lines crisscross the air, and a railroad bridge spans the river in the distance.[2] The first photograph is artfully composed; the second captures the history of a working river.

Most of the images of Celilo Falls can be placed into two categories. Popular, romantic images are sold in museum gift stores and at the airport as Northwest memorabilia and all too often undergird narratives about Celilo in places like museums. But there is another Celilo as well. It is less popular, but more richly evocative of the area's history. Buried in old Army

Corps reports and in archives, they are photographs of Indian men and women at work on the river. These very different narrative examples provide the people of the Pacific Northwest with two divergent tales about Celilo Falls and its significance to Indians and non-Indians alike. Historian William Cronon insists that "because we use them to motivate and explain our actions, the stories we tell change the way we act in the world."[3] He concludes that our narratives are not passive accounts of what happened in the past, but moral compasses that direct us into the future. Because stories and histories, in particular, produce the foundation for regional identity, it is imperative that we choose our representative narratives carefully and then engage in a continual critique of how effectively they support the communities we hope to create.

Like photographs, history museums narrate the past by framing stories to highlight certain historical circumstances while omitting others. To paraphrase one scholar, history museums generate ways of seeing and of not seeing the past and can help or hinder people from envisioning alternative ways of living with one another in a shared environment.[4] History museums are also the locations where large numbers of people most fully come into contact with a shared history—audibly, visually, and even through touch. Museums organize the past and allow us to interact with it. Moreover, they reflect "judgments of power and authority" that "resolve themselves into claims about what a nation is or ought to be as well as how citizens should relate to one another."[5] Because of this, it is essential that we view museum exhibits critically rather than passively accept the narratives they tell. What do museum exhibits about Celilo Falls, for example, tell us about what it means to be a resident of the Pacific Northwest and how we should relate to other residents of this region? How do these exhibits help or impede our understanding of the impact history has on the present? Ultimately, whose histories do our museums narrate?

This chapter explores how two museums narrate the significance of Celilo Falls.[6] The Gorge Discovery Center, located at Crate's Point just downriver from The Dalles, Oregon, was funded by Congress when it classified the Columbia Gorge as a national scenic area in 1986. Completed in 1997 at the cost of $21.6 million, the facilities include a natural history museum, the Wasco County Historical Museum, and The Dalles Oregon Trail Living History Park. The U.S. Forest Service, Columbia River Gorge Commission, Wasco County, the Wasco County Historical Museum Trust, and Citizens for the Columbia River Gorge National Scenic Area joined forces to launch this ambitious project, raising all but $5 million of the total cost through private donations and fundraisers.[7] The Yakama Nation Cultural Heritage Center, which opened in 1980 at a cost of $6.5 million, is located in south-central Washington on the Yakama Reservation at Toppenish.[8] Agricultural fields surround the buildings that house the center as well as a branch office of the Bureau of Indian Affairs and the offices of the Yakama Nation. Like Roberts's photographs, these two museums produce very different stories about Celilo Falls, and the differences between the two museums are abundant. The Gorge Discovery Center is new and well funded, whereas the exhibits at the Heritage Center are older and naturally do not incorporate current technology. More significant is the fact that the two museums occupy separate, but intersecting, worlds. A major east-west freeway runs through the Columbia Gorge, and the Columbia River itself has long been a water highway for the transportation of goods and people from Lewiston, Idaho to Astoria, Oregon. The Discovery Center is perched between these two busy thoroughfares on the outskirts of The Dalles, Oregon in Wasco County (population 21,683) and seventy-five miles from the Portland metropolitan area (population 1,239,842). In contrast, the Yakama Nation Cultural Heritage Center, while located in the largest town on the reservation, is relatively isolated in the Columbia Basin's Yakima County (population 188,823).[9] Unlike the Discovery Center, it is operated by a tribal, rather than federal or county government, a fact that ultimately has a significant impact on the kind of narratives told there. As a tribally operated museum, the Heritage Center is an institution poised to reclaim the history of the Pacific Northwest from dominant museums like the Columbia Gorge Discovery Center. Even so, neither museum adequately addresses the essential components of Celilo history: poverty, racism, the struggle among tribes and between Indians and whites over access to the river's resources, and the power of the federal government to transform the region's environment.[10]

At Celilo Falls, the environment largely dictated the character and nature of the fishery. The Dalles marks the transition from the wet, mild coast to the arid, semidesert region of the Columbia Plateau in what writer Robin Cody likens to "driving over a Rand McNally road map with different colored states."[11] Abundant salmon runs and the easy access to resources in the Cascade Mountains drew Indians to the region about 11,000 years ago.[12] The riverbank near The Dalles formed a series of turbulent falls—the Long Narrows including Five-Mile Rapids and the better-known Celilo Falls—that trapped traveling salmon in swirling eddies and backwaters where Indians netted them. Dry, hot weather made it possible for the people to preserve their catch by drying salmon on open-air racks. Dried salmon provided Indians with winter protein and with an important trade item in a market that stretched from the interior to the coast.[13] Salmon shaped Native labor practices and its significance was woven into language, ceremony, and story. In turn, native cultures transformed the mute fish into cultural symbols, salmon beings that represented the connections between human cultures and nature.[14]

The First Salmon Ceremony illustrates the importance of salmon in the social, economic, and political lives of Columbia River Indians.[15] The ceremony marked the break of the long winter with its meals of dried food by welcoming the coming of the first salmon runs in the spring. Tribal members distributed morsels of the first salmon as part of a meal of thanksgiving and celebration that was "based on a reverential attitude toward the fish and a desire to treat it in such a manner that it will come in great numbers."[16] Although fishing people once practiced these ceremonies from Alaska to California, the ceremonies became infrequent and even disappeared as non-Native commercial fishing depleted the annual runs of salmon. In contrast, Indians at Celilo held annual public First Salmon Ceremonies throughout the construction of The Dalles Dam and into the present time. The intertwining of the social and economic aspects of the fishery at Celilo prompted Army Corps writers to concede that "the Celilo fishery has some religious significance to the Indians."[17]

Before the U.S. Army Corps of Engineers built The Dalles Dam, Indian fishers worked from scaffolds that hung from cliffs above the roaring water of the falls or on platforms that reached out over the river like pointed fingers. The Wishram and Wasco Indians traditionally lived between Celilo Falls and Priest Rapids on both banks of the Columbia River, adjacent to nearly nine miles of the best fishing grounds on the continent.[18] (Many of the descendants of mid-Columbia fishers now live on the Yakama Reservation in Washington, the Umatilla and Warm Springs Reservations in Oregon, the Nez Perce Reservation in Idaho, or at Celilo Village.) Alexander Ross, an early white visitor, described the topography of the falls as "a broad and flat ledge of rocks that bars the whole river across, leaving only a small opening or portal, not exceeding forty feet, on the left side, through which the whole body of water must pass."[19] The river rushed through the narrows with "great impetuosity; the foaming surges dash[ing] through the rocks with terrific violence."[20] The same rocks that formed the falls also provided the foundation for the dam that inundated this entire section of the river in 1957.

The Dalles represented more than a transition from a wet to a dry environment; it also marked a confluence of cultures. The Dalles was a traditional marketplace where trade extended well beyond material goods to include languages, social systems, technologies, and mythologies. Cultural intermixing, borrowing, exchange, and transformation characterized the region. The height of activity at Celilo occurred between the spring and fall and coincided with three major fish runs during which Indians from all over the Northwest came to trade, socialize, and fish with local residents.[21]   Both women and men traded goods and strengthened their relationships with neighboring tribes through marriages and renewed friendships.[22] According to trapper and explorer Alexander Ross's estimation, 3,000 Indians gathered at the river to trade, gamble, and socialize each year in the early 1800s.[23] In his often-repeated words, The Dalles was "the great emporium or mart of the Columbia."[24] By the 1950s, the Indian fishery at Celilo supported 5,000 Indians who traveled from as far away as Montana and California to harvest salmon at nearly 480 different fishing stations spread out along the banks of the roaring river. During this period, the U.S. Army Corps of Engineers contracted with the U.S. Fish and Wildlife Service in anticipation that local Indians would be compensated for Celilo Falls. The latter agency observed the fishery over four years and finally concluded that it was worth $700,000 annually.

Although planning for The Dalles Dam was initiated much earlier, this mid-Columbia dam was a product of the Cold War. Like other earlier dams, its proponents promised flood control, irrigation waters, and inexpensive electricity, but, most of all, they claimed that it would be a significant wedge against the spread of communism worldwide. Boosters warned that the Northwest was rapidly approaching a serious power shortage that would shrink its ability to contribute to and strengthen national security efforts. Because it would "make a large amount of low-cost power available at a location close to major load centers and defense industries," The Dalles Dam "was an essential unit in present plans for overcoming the existing power shortage in the Northwest."[25] Its power would be used to manufacture titanium, among other metals, a new and promising defense material.

Concerned that Celilo Falls would be destroyed by The Dalles Dam, just as Bonneville Dam had drowned Cascade Falls and Grand Coulee Dam wiped out Kettle Falls, the Yakama, Umatilla, Warm Springs, and Nez Perce tribal councils and the Celilo Fish Committee (an intertribal regulatory committee) all passed resolutions in protest of the proposed dam from 1945 through 1956. Members of each tribe testified before congressional committees about the economic and spiritual loss they would incur when The Dalles reservoir drowned Celilo. Eventually, Congress compensated tribal members a little over $3,750 each for the loss of the fishery and relocated over thirty families from the old Celilo Village. Watson Totus, a Yakama enrollee, complained to a congressional committee in 1951 that, whatever the monetary compensation, "no compensation could be made which would benefit my future generations, the people still to come."[26]

Celilo Falls and the Indians who fished them captivated photographer Wilma Roberts, like many whites who lived in or visited the Columbia Gorge. Roberts explained that she was drawn to Celilo because it could "stop onlookers in their tracks. Everywhere there was a picture—fishers standing on precarious spots, the color of light in the afternoon through the mist, the rainbows."[27] According to Roberts, her intention was not to record the history of the falls but to "take a good photo from the standpoint of composition, an artistic presentation that would generate an emotional response in a viewer."[28] Nonetheless, because Celilo Falls no longer exists, Roberts's photos are part of both the history of the falls and our collective memory of them, whether her art was meant to accurately reveal the place or simply to evoke a response to the beauty of her composition.

Today, Celilo Falls is two places. One is embodied in postcard-like images, transcendent shots of Indians fishing at the end of long wooden platforms, their backs to the sun, spectacular reminders of how growing industrialism and dam building has transformed the Pacific Northwest. The other is less centered on artistic beauty, but is more historically accurate and encompasses the poverty, racism, intertribal conflict, the struggle between Indians and whites, and the remarkable transformation of resources that comprise the history of Celilo. In this second place, Celilo is not simply picturesque scenery, but represents a defining characteristic of Pacific Northwest history and regional identity. Its very landscape, altered by a large public dam, represents the historical and contemporary struggle over natural resources. *Oregonian* staff writer Courtenay Thompson claimed in 1997 that Celilo Falls was "an icon of the Northwest's heritage."[29] As an icon, Celilo Falls is routinely depicted as an ideal, from its wild water landscape now tamed to the generations of Indian fishers who worked there. But, left in its iconic form, Celilo Falls masks some of the most significant elements of our shared history. These idealized falls are most potent when they are deconstructed. Chip away at the romanticized image and revealed are the conflicts and divisions between residents of the region over how to use the river, for what purpose, and to whose benefit.

The Columbia Gorge Discovery Center

> *To be an Indian in modern American society is in a very real sense to be unreal and ahistorical.*

> VINE DELORIA

Completed in 1997, the Discovery Center is divided into two museums. A natural history museum and the Wasco County Historical Museum are on either side of a shared commons area. The Forest Service and its partners sought to design the center as "a recreational and educational hub for the Gorge" that would help visitors locate additional "landmarks, attractions, and activities" in the area.[30] As a tourist destination, the center attempts to balance a boosterism focused on bringing people to the Columbia Gorge with environmental sensibility that acknowledged the drawbacks of settlement. Clearly, the center meant to tap into the number of people already traveling though the gorge and increase those numbers by drawing additional people to the center itself. At the same time, planners understood that one of the major draws of the Columbia Gorge was its dramatic natural beauty. One of its aims, then, is to promote environmental sensitivity as the center highlights the technological developments in the area provided by transportation, irrigation, and the dams on the Columbia. For example, the center buildings incorporate the surrounding natural setting at Crate's Point. The stonework is basalt and both water and light are important design elements. Outside, reintroduced indigenous plants restore the fifty-acre grounds of the center that will eventually include several walking trails and a pond. A basalt fountain of running water greets visitors as they move from the large parking area to the center. Once inside, an enormous window comprising the entire back wall of the commons area looks out onto the Columbia River.

The natural history museum and the Wasco County Historical Museum face one another across the commons like two halves of a circle. Many of the exhibits in both museums incorporate video technology; monitors are everywhere. For nearly every subject there are video images and narrations that accompany the artifacts and dioramas surrounding them, resembling what Mike Wallace calls a "multimedia hybrid," a combination "theme park, movie studio, and learning center."[31] Shortly after its opening, architectural critic Randy Gragg criticized the museum for "cook[ing] up an eclectic buffet of films, dioramas and the occasional artifact that tantalizes but never quite satisfies."[32] The results of the museum's flashy design include often difficult-to-hear narrations, seating that nearly exclusively faces video monitors rather than other kinds of exhibits, and virtual and technologically enhanced experiences of the river while the actual river flows nearby.

The Discovery Center and the Wasco County Historical Museum together present a nearly seamless narrative that incorporates a pride in the progressive elements of settlement in the Northwest tempered by the acknowledgment that progress has displaced Native inhabitants of the gorge and degraded the environment. In the Wasco County Historical Museum, the first exhibit focuses on Indian fishing at Celilo Falls, providing a kind of origin story for the history of the county. One enters the historical museum through a single entrance, a narrow, short hallway dominated by a huge screen upon which black-and-white film footage of Indians fishing at the falls is projected. The entrance is dark and noisy with a recording of the falls. The footage is mesmerizing, stopping visitors for several minutes as they watch Indians walk the slippery planks over the falls to net salmon. It is a profoundly elegant beginning to the rest of the museum. Unfortunately, the exhibits that follow do not fully engage the cultural and political milieu of the film's Columbia River. Recorded just prior to the completion of the dam, these images could speak eloquently to the actuality of competing fishers, threats to treaty fishing rights, and river development. These are the very conflicts that continue to make the Celilo Falls of the past meaningful today.

One of the most acute shortcomings of the museum is the way in which it neglects to trace the historical use and struggle over salmon, one of the most important resources of Wasco County. While The Dalles Dam threatened to end fishing at Celilo Falls at midcentury, struggles over the fishery long preceded the crisis of the 1950s. Throughout the 1930s and 1940s, Indians who fished Celilo fought to keep Earnest Cramer and E. R. Cramer, two white fishers, from fishing Native-owned sites.[33] The battle came to a head in 1946 when Native fishers claimed the Cramers ran Indians off the contested sites with rifles.[34] The Cramers retorted that Indian youths repeatedly removed their gear.[35]

Struggles over salmon were not only relegated to fishing sites. The Seufert Cannery, the dominant processor at The Dalles where most Indians sold their commercial catches, was another site that reveals the divisions of people as they worked side by side on the river. Although the Wasco museum has an extensive exhibit on the cannery's reliance on Chinese male labor, it missed an opportunity to investigate the intersections of labor, race, and the struggle over access to natural resources on the river, all of which were integral to the history of the cannery. Labor that supported the cannery consisted of four principal groups of men until the 1930s: white gillnetters, Indian dipnetters, white men who worked on the canning crews, and Chinese men who flayed and packed salmon into tin cans.[36] In his memoirs, Francis Seufert recalled that racial categories defined labor positions, social activities, and living quarters. In his words, "in those days the relationship between Indians, Chinese and whites was very clear cut. Each man tended to his own business and didn't interfere with the rights of others. The Indians all stayed at the Indian camp, the Chinese all stayed down at the China house, and the whites all stayed at the white bunk house."[37]

Francis Seufert described a segregated workforce in which there was little, if any, interaction between white, Chinese, and Indian workers (except that mediated by white management). Richard White characterizes this kind of system as a "dual labor" or "two-tiered labor" system in which people of color comprise a bottom rank of low-paying and low-skilled positions, while whites have access to the upper rank of skilled and high-paying work. According to White, this system was pervasive in the West and was based on the belief by whites that "minorities were racially suited" to the limited positions available to them.[38] It was a system that limited direct access to resources important in the markets of the Pacific Northwest and beyond to a racial majority. While Francis Seufert observed that Indians rarely worked at the Seufert Cannery, the San Francisco *Chronicle* reported in 1880 that Chinese would-be fishers "never venture on the [Columbia] river, for the [white] fishermen are not the class to tamely submit to such competition."[39]

Seufert claimed that Indians were unreliable and offered this excuse as the reason they were not hired to work inside the cannery. As for the Chinese workers he hired, their hands were "as nimble as a woman's" but as powerful as a man's, physically suiting them to long hours of packing salmon into tin cans.[40] These kinds of assertions indicate the complexities of the intersections of race and gender in labor practices on the Columbia River in the harvesting of its natural resources. Furthermore, they betray a sometimes-violent exclusionary bigotry that influenced the lives of local residents. A druggist in The Dalles told Bureau of Indian Affairs employee H. U. Sanders in 1940 that Celilo Indians (who did not live in homes with electricity or indoor plumbing and who, on average, made half the wages of white residents of Wasco County) were welcomed in his store if they were "clean, well-behaved, and did not 'smell of fish'."[41] A local employee of the Bureau of Indian Affairs complained in a 1944 report that Celilo Indians were "anti-social" and "clannish" because they refused to "mingle with the white man socially."[42]

More recently, in his memoir of canoeing the Columbia River, Robin Cody describes a conversation he had with a white chiropractor and windsurfer at what used to be Celilo. "John" did not hesitate to link his use of the river with the competing uses of local Indians. John complained that, while Indians often made $80,000 each year fishing "they don't manage it well. You see how they live. They buy a new boat and strip it, and scratch it up."[43] The chiropractor's comment illustrates an ongoing cultural conflict between whites and Indians who fish and live around what used to be Celilo Falls. It is a remark that is part of the mythology surrounding the Indians and whites in the Pacific Northwest. Namely, non-Indians accuse Indians of having an unfair and privileged access to resources that they misuse and may not deserve. Whites who compete with Indians for resources have pointed to the supposed neglect of the resources by Indian people—be they boats, cars or fish—time and again in a strategy that positions whites as the rightful owners or guardians of the region's bounty. It is an attitude born of initial Indian–white contact and was utilized by the region's first settlers, who justified the relocation of Native people by arguing that whites "practiced superior methods of cultivation and represented a more advanced civilization."[44] This attitude has pervaded the conflicts between local whites and Indians in the 1940s and into the present day.

When I visited the Discovery Center, I entered at the historical museum and exited through the natural history museum. The first exhibit I saw was the Celilo Falls exhibit I described previously; the last was one on windsurfing the river. This was the most popular of all the exhibits, a windsurfing board people could actually use. As I passed the board cluttered with kids who watched themselves windsurfing virtually via a blue screen and video of the gorge, I wondered how the museum's smooth narrative would change if Indian fishing rights were addressed within the context of recreation. Civic groups and state agencies have encouraged public access to the Columbia River for windsurfers as a way to boost tourism and bring money into the region. According to journalist Blaine Harden, by the 1990s windsurfing was "the dominant industry" in Hood River, Oregon, which lies about thirty miles west of The Dalles. At the same time, access to the river for Indians who want to fish is compromised. Robin Cody recorded the complaints of one Native fisherman regarding windsurfers: "They'll go right into the nets, tangle them up or slice a cork line. Lose a net, you've lost $600."[45] What we are seeing here is the conflict over the resources of the Columbia River. Windsurfers and Native fishers do not coexist peacefully on the actual river, although they do on the virtual river created by the Columbia Gorge Discovery Center.

In the novel *River Song* by non-Native writer Craig Lesley, Willis, an old Native fisherman complains, "when they get us all pushed off the river, maybe they can build more places for the tourists and windsurfers. Maybe they can put up a nice little museum here with statues and pictures, so the gawkers can see what Indians once were like."[46] The museum's lack of connection between windsurfing and Indian fishing rights or the larger issue of who has access to a publicly owned resource is not an accident. The choice to address these issues separately has its roots in a Wasco resident's response to a survey question asked by museum developers in the early stages of design. Museum developers asked, "Do you have any strong personal opinions regarding any topic that should or should not be addressed in the Discovery Center?" That resident responded, "with any controversial subject (e.g., land use, salmon runs, timber) stay positive. Avoid any sense of criticism."[47] The problem with avoiding any sense of criticism is that the museum risks sacrificing history by dodging its contentiousness and complexity. As an official narrative, the Discovery Center could make connections and, at its best, revise stereotypes that plague discussion of the river and its history.

The exhibits at the Discovery Center are artful and often skillfully mix the mediums of photography, sound, and moving pictures into narratives about the Columbia River and the people who lived and worked near it. Despite these successes, the decision to avoid historical conflicts regarding the resources of the river prevents the museum from providing much understanding about the contemporary and highly contested space of this important waterway. Even as the center is multicultural in its portrayal of history—telling the (always partial) stories of Indian fishing and Chinese cannery labor, for example—it is not multicultural or even multidimensional in its perspective. It addresses the various uses of the river, but without revealing that they are in competition with one another; that systems of value are attached to these competing uses; or that race, ethnicity, and class intersect with resource use and development. Instead, the center (the historical museum, in particular) focuses on the transformation of Wasco County along traditional narrative lines despite the initial exhibit on mid-twentieth-century Native fishing from the falls: beginning with Native inhabitants, moving to missionaries, white settlers, the advent of farming and early industries like canneries, and finally proceeding to dam building and other modern uses of the river. This is a covertly political thematic construction that denies the contested nature of the river environment.

The Yakama Nation Cultural Heritage Center

Generations of our ancestors, unnumbered,
Are buried here beneath this ground.
So surely there can be no wonder
That this land of ours is sacred,
To be protected, and handed on
To generations yet unborn.

POEM ON A PLAQUE JUST INSIDE THE ENTRANCE OF THE
YAKAMA NATION CULTURAL HERITAGE CENTER

Harvest of nature
The Salmon returned to the spawning
Grounds and at a falls they could be speared
And netted. Nature must not be
Violated by our actions. Our actions
When timed to nature, give abundant harvest.

POEM NEAR A DIORAMA OF CELILO FALLS AT THE
YAKAMA NATION CULTURAL HERITAGE CENTER

James Clifford, a historian of anthropology and cultural critic, describes the differences between majority museums and tribal museums in the following way: "majority museums articulate cosmopolitan culture, science, art and humanism—often with a national slant. Tribal museums express local culture, oppositional politics, kinship, ethnicity, and tradition."[48] Although it is difficult to imagine the history of The Dalles, Oregon as cosmopolitan, the distinctions between majority and tribal museums described by Clifford generally hold true for the two museums examined in this chapter. Whereas the Columbia Gorge Discovery Center concentrates on themes of river use and a shared environment without revealing the contentious nature of these themes, the Yakama Nation Cultural Heritage Center focuses on themes of oppositional politics, ethnicity, sovereignty, and obligation to and reciprocity with the natural world.[49]

The exhibits in the 12,000-square-foot Heritage Center are arranged to form a large circle that surrounds a replica of an earth lodge, the traditional housing of the tribes who formed the Yakama Nation.[50] A museum employee directs visitors to follow the outer circle of the museum, where they can view dioramas, cases filled with artifacts and war memorabilia, several paintings, and two temporary photography exhibits. The lighting is low and there are sounds of water flowing into an artificial pond, a recording of birds chirping, and pop music from a radio somewhere in the building. Several benches allow visitors to sit and view a number of the exhibits at once. At this museum, non-Indian visitors are educated about the treaty of 1855 that reserved thousands of acres of land for the tribes living on the Yakama Reservation. Most importantly, non-Indians are taught that the Yakama Nation is a sovereign body that preceded the founding of the state of Washington by thirty-four years and whose treaty "takes precedence over the state."[51]

Unlike the Discovery Center, which changes little in style from exhibit to exhibit, the Heritage Center is an amalgam of several exhibit styles. Many were clearly installed in the 1980s and have become examples of museum history themselves. Others, like an exhibit on great Indian leaders throughout what is now the United States, were not specifically designed for the museum space. Toward the back of the museum, there is an exhibit highlighting the Indian Club at the Wapato Middle School, a group that traveled to several Pacific Northwest powwows to dance and drum. Pictures of those trips, along with clippings about them from the *Yakama Nation Review* ("Red from cover to cover") are hung in the least professional (but one of the most interesting) exhibits. Instead of using enlarged, professional photographs, the exhibit used snapshots that were framed by strips of construction paper. Two quite different exhibits focus on Celilo Falls and Indian fishing issues.

Midway into the museum space is a diorama of an Indian man helping his son prepare a dipnet for fishing at the falls. Both mannequins are in traditional dress and the setting appears to be precontact. A recording of a falls can be heard, but it is soft and does not prevent visitors from talking to one another as would the actual sound of Celilo Falls. Because it does not incorporate evidence of intertribal or postcontact trade, the diorama attempts to evoke an "authentic" river Indian culture devoid of the cultural politics of contemporary or even historic Indian fishing. This effect is mitigated by a preceding diorama that consists of a small photo display of Indians fishing at Celilo Falls. In one photograph, Chief Tommy Thompson is pictured with his son, Henry Thompson, in the background.[52] It is a large, beautiful photograph, although neither man is directly identified. The display is accompanied by a poem that might allow a viewer to identify the older man:

> *Chief Tommy Thompson of the Yakima Nation makes his ceremonial*
> *   appearance.*
> *He is in a crowd of brown people who are all related.*
> *He is old.*
> *The Yakima Valley could be his daughter.*

The poem echoes two related themes that shape the museum's narrative: (1) Yakama Indians are an integral part of the landscape they inhabit; the narrative depicts white settlers and their descendants as newcomers, only the most recent residents of the Pacific Northwest; and (2) the lives of the land and of the Yakama people are intertwined, one the child of the other. Not only are the Indian people of the Northwest all related, but the region's valleys, mountains, and rivers are related to its first occupants as well. These are clearly political themes that indirectly speak to issues of sovereignty such as the Yakama claim to nonreservation places like Celilo Falls.

The second exhibit that addresses Celilo, "Respecting this Earth: Native Americans of the Mid-Columbia River," focuses on contemporary fishing rights. It is a moveable triptych upon which photographs and several lengthy sections of text are displayed. It is the only exhibit in which informational prose is featured rather than the poetry that dominates the other exhibits at the Heritage Center. Funded by the Washington Committee for the Humanities and sponsored by the Yakama Nation Museum, the exhibit includes photographs by Jacqueline Moreau and a section written by novelist Craig Lesley. It addresses issues surrounding in-lieu sites on the mid-Columbia, river access, the continued practice of fishing in traditional ways, and the passage of environmental knowledge from one generation to the next. The text claims that, by 1993, fishing on the river using traditional methods was an act of resistance and cultural survival.

This exhibit, with its reliance on text, as well as images, to tell the story of a contemporary and contentious issue, is a marked departure from some of the older exhibits in the museum. The fishing exhibit examines not only past but continued injustice a few miles away from the museum itself. By doing so, it connects historic themes to contemporary ones and makes explicit threads that tie current struggles to seemingly bygone events. Moreover, it introduces the visitor to the participants in the struggle to preserve fishing rights; rather than the nameless mannequins of the Celilo exhibit, the photographs in this one are accompanied by captions that identify who is being pictured. Finally, it is the only exhibit in either museum that connects Indian fishing rights to dam building, one of the most significant events to affect Native fishing during the last century. By employing these strategies, this exhibit models how museums might approach contemporary struggles over river resources by linking what occurred on the river in the past to the kind of river we live with today.

Because it seems to have updated exhibits piece by piece, the Yakama Nation Cultural Heritage Center is inconsistent in its history of the people of the Columbia River. Nonetheless, it does weave some essential themes throughout the collective narratives. The center portrays the Yakama as the rightful caretakers of a place that has been nearly destroyed in a little over a century of white occupation. Furthermore, the histories of Celilo Falls and other traditional fishing sites on the river become examples of native resistance to and tolerance of a dominant culture that values neither Indians nor the environment that sustains them. As a final point to this claim, visitors are asked to mark with a pin their own "homeland" on a laminated map of the United States on their way out of the museum.

The Columbia River and Other Cultural Resources

The development of our narratives about place and identity today mirror conflicts over more tangible resources like salmon, riverfront access, and hydroelectricity. The stories themselves are a kind of resource for regional development that parallel the unequal distribution and the struggle to allocate and use the resources of the Columbia River. Those who write the history/mythology of the region influence how residents and nonresidents alike perceive past and present allocations of material resources and can secure the status quo or effect change.

When the Discovery Center was being developed, Marilyn Malatare, one of the curators of the Yakama Nation Cultural Heritage Center, reminded Columbia Gorge Discovery Center organizers about the importance of keeping other museum coordinators informed: "The first time I saw anything on the . . . Discovery Center was yesterday when one of our culture research specialists gave me a handout on the meeting tonight. I talked with several people in our tribal council and not one of them knew anything about this, [in] our area we weren't notified. We would like to say we . . . would like to be part of this and work cooperatively and hope you will keep us informed."[53]

Documents regarding the development phase of the Discovery Center confirm that there was little contribution solicited from the Yakama, although photographs of two consultants from Warm Springs greet visitors of the center.[54] In fact, one presumably non-Native participant at the meeting suggested that (in the shorthand of notes) "it is doubtful [if] the present-day Indians [can] account [for] their old culture. Should take from Smithsonian reports." This casts doubts on the ability of contemporary Indians to participate in cowriting a regional narrative at all.[55]

One needs only to look at the battles over new western history during the past decade to conclude that narratives about any region are highly contested. We wage battles to determine dominant narratives because it is through stories that we build an understanding of place and of ourselves in connection to that place. The histories we produce tell us who and what is important and why, they explain the relationships between subjects, and, most importantly, they provide context for the present. Attempting to define and reflect that dominant narrative is the mistake that museums make; the designers of the Columbia Gorge Discovery Center are a good example. Although the multiple perspectives present at the Yakama Nation Cultural Heritage Center may be an inadvertent by-product of funding and the age of the museum, its fractured narrative is a refreshing departure from the dominant story of place and people told at the Discovery Center. The Discovery Center's treatment of Pacific Northwest history is multicultural, but not multidimensional. The Yakama Nation Cultural Heritage Center is neither multicultural nor multidimensional (it presents history from an ethnocentrically Yakama perspective), but it does succeed in dismantling the dominant narratives to which it is a necessary response.[56] It is only by visiting both the Heritage Center and the Discovery Center that the disjunctures between Indian-centered and white-centered history are revealed. It may be too much to ask that a single site encapsulate the cacophony of voices of this region's history, but it is crucial that our museums move toward a model of multivocality and conversation if they are to reflect who we are. Without that transformation, museums miss an opportunity to tell a compelling story about how resources bring communities together and divide them; how resources and access to them define insiders and outsiders; and how we legitimize the monopoly of resources, the taking of resources, and their transformation for the benefit of particular constituencies. These are the very issues that shape the

Columbia River today, literally with dams, figuratively in the way we think about our relationships to the river and to each other.

Notes

Research for this chapter was supported by the Summer Graduate Assistantship from the Graduate School at Washington State University and the Johnson Fellowship from the History Department at Washington State University. I am indebted to the Center for Columbia River History and its director and associate director, William Lang and Laurie Mercier. Thanks also to Noël Sturgeon, Susan Armitage, William Robbins, William Lang, and Paul Hirt for reading previous versions of this essay. Special thanks to Don Croker.

[1] Mary Dodds Schlick, Carol Mortlnad, Elizabeth Woody, and Frederick Cramer, *Celilo Falls: Remembering Thunder, Photos from the Collection of Wilma Roberts* (The Dalles, Oregon: Wasco County Historical Museum Press, 1997), 32. Roberts's photographs are not dated, but, according to Schlick's introduction, they were taken between the end of World War II and 1957, the year The Dalles Dam engulfed Celilo Falls.

[2] Ibid., 19.

[3] William Cronon, "A Place for Stories: Nature, History, and Narrative," *The Journal of American History* 78 (March 1992): 1375. See also, William Robbins, "Narrative Forms and Great River Myths: The Power of Columbia River Stories," *Environmental History Review* 17 (Summer 1993): 1-22.

[4] Mike Wallace, *Mickey Mouse History and Other Essays on American Memory* (Philadelphia: Temple University Press, 1996), 25.

[5] Ivan Karp and Steven D. Lavine, "Introduction: Museums and Multiculturalism," in *Exhibiting Cultures: The Poetics and Politics of Museum Display*, ed. Steven D. Lavine and Ivan Karp (Washington, D.C.: Smithsonian Institute Press, 1991), 2.

[6] Given more space and time, additional museums that have Celilo-related exhibits, such as the Columbia Gorge Interpretive Center and the Museum at Warm Springs, could have been explored in this essay. Instead, I have chosen to focus on two museums that I believe represent larger currents in historical narrative in the Pacific Northwest.

[7] USDA Forest Service, "Crate's Point Interpretive Complex, Project Prospective," September 1994, 1. Linda Porter made this, along with public meeting records and architectural reports, available to me when I visited the museum's offices in July 1996.

[8] Marilyn Malatare, museum director at the Yakama Nation Cultural Heritage Center, to author, 21 July 1997.

[9] These 1990 figures come from the U.S. Census Bureau web site, census.gov/population/www/censusdata/density/html, date of access 23 February 1999.

[10] Both museums face real-world constraints of time, space, and money as well as the need to appeal to diverse audiences. It is not my aim to obscure these limitations, but to challenge institutions to address difficult issues with the necessary complexity.

[11] Robin Cody, *Ricochet River* (Hillsboro, Oregon: Blue Heron Publishing, 1992), 34.

[12] B. Robert Butler, "The Physical Stratigraphy of Wakemap Mound: A New Interpretation" (master's thesis, University of Washington, 1960), citing Luther S. Cressman, "Cultural Sequences at The Dalles, Oregon," 1958, unpublished report for the National Park Service.

13 For more information on Celilo Falls as part of a traditional trade network, see Robert Boyd, *People of The Dalles, The Indians of Wascopam Mission: A Historical Ethnography Based on the Papers of Methodist Missionaries* (Lincoln: University of Nebraska Press, 1996), 63–71; Angelo Anastsio, "The Southern Plateau: An Ecological Analysis of Intergroup Relations," *Northwest Anthropological Research Notes* 6(2): 109–229; Eugene Hunn, *Nch'i-Wána, "The Big River": Mid-Columbia Indians and Their Land* (Seattle: University of Washington Press, 1990), 224.

14 This becomes particularly evident in the First Salmon Ceremony, a ritual meal shared from Alaska to California in which the return of seasonal salmon runs are celebrated. The First Salmon Ceremony is still celebrated at Celilo Village in Oregon. For more information, see Erna Gunther, "An Analysis of the First Salmon Ceremony," *American Anthropologist* 28 (1926): 605–17 and "A Further Analysis of the First Salmon Ceremony," *University of Washington Publications in Anthropology* 2 (1928): 129–73. For a more recent treatment of the First Salmon Ceremony, see Pamela T. Amoss, "The Fish God Gave Us: The First Salmon Ceremony Revived," *Arctic Anthropology* 24 (1987): 56–66.

15 See Gunther, "An Analysis of the First Salmon Ceremony" and "A Further Analysis of the First Salmon Ceremony."

16 Gunther, "An Analysis of the First Salmon Ceremony," 614.

17 "Special Report on the Indian Fishery Problem, The Dalles Dam, Columbia River, Washington-Oregon," U.S. Army Corps of Engineers, 10 March 1952, 11.

18 Charles Wilkinson, *Crossing the Next Meridian: Land, Water, and the Future of the West* (Washington, D.C.: Island Press, 1992), 179.

19 Alexander Ross, *Adventures of the First Settlers on the Oregon or Columbia River, 1810-1813* (Lincoln: University of Nebraska Press, 1986. Reprinted by Oregon StateUniversity Press, 2000), 130.

20 Ibid.

21 Kathryn Anne Toepel indicates that most of the actual trading activity occurred from about August through October after fishing slowed. Stephen Dow Beckham, Rick Minor, Kathryn Anne Toepel, and Jo Reese, "Prehistory and History of the Columbia River Gorge National Scenic Area, Oregon and Washington," USDA Forest Service, 15 July 1988, 124.

22 Anastasio, "The Southern Plateau."

23 Lewis and Clark estimated that approximately 600 Indians lived near Celilo Falls when they passed through in October 1805. Boyd, *People of The Dalles,* 50.

24 Ross, *Adventures of the First Settlers,* 129.

25 Lowell Stockman, U.S. House of Representatives, Oregon, Civil Functions, Department of the Army, Appropriations for 1952 Hearings, Part II, 802.

26 Watson Totus, Yakama Tribal Member, 7 May 1951, Civil Functions, Department of the Army, Appropriations for 1952 Hearings, Part I, 321.

27 Schlick et al., *Celilo Falls,* 3.

28 Ibid.

29 "Celilo Falls Memories Still Alive," *Oregonian,* 18 July 1997.

30 USDA Forest Service, "Crates Point Interpretive Complex," 9.

31 Wallace, *Mickey Mouse History,* 110.

32 Randy Gragg, "Museums with a Brand-New Mission," *Oregonian,* 22 May 1997.

33 For more information about this conflict, see Katrine Barber, "After Celilo Falls: The Dalles Dam, Indian Fishing Rights, and Federal Energy Policy on the Mid-Columbia River," (Ph.D. diss., Washington State University, 1999), ch. 2. This conflict was finally resolved when Judge Alger Fee ruled that Indians had a superior right to fish the falls over the Cramers, *United States v. Earnest Cramer and E. R. Cramer,* Civil and Criminal Case Files, 1922-1943, no. 3557, District

Court of Oregon at Portland, Box 928, Record Group 21, National Archives, Pacific Northwest Region, Seattle, Washington.

34 Ibid.

35 James H. McCool, "Tribes Defy Joint Pact on Fishing; Redskins, White Swap Punches in Celilo Falls Scuffle," *Oregonian,* 27 August 1946.

36 Francis Seufert, *Wheels of Fortune* (Portland: Oregon Historical Society, 1980).

37 Seufert, *Wheels of Fortune,* 102.

38 Richard White, *"It's Your Misfortune and None of My Own": A New History of the American West* (Norman: University of Oklahoma Press, 1991), 282.

39 Quoted in Courtland Smith, *Salmon Fishers of the Columbia* (Corvallis: Oregon State University Press, 1979), 23.

40 Seufert, *Wheels of Fortune,* 103. For more information on the use of Chinese laborers at salmon canneries in the Northwest, see Chris Friday, *Organizing Asian American Labor: The Pacific Coast Canned-Salmon Industry, 1870-1942* (Philadelphia: Temple University Press, 1994).

41 H. U. Sanders, "Report on the Sanitary Conditions at Celilo, Oregon," 10 October 1940, Property and Plant Management, Celilo Relocation Records, 1947-1957, Portland Area Office, Box 1934, Bureau of Indian Affairs, Record Group 75, National Archives, Pacific Northwest Region, Seattle, Washington.

42 U.S. Bureau of Indian Affairs, "Program: Celilo, Oregon, 1946-1955," March 1944, Yakima Agency, Washington, 20.

43 Robin Cody, *Voyage of a Summer Sun: Canoeing the Columbia River* (Seattle: Sasquatch Books, 1995), 252.

44 William Robbins, "The Indian Question in Western Oregon: The Making of a Colonial People," *Experiences in a Promised Land: Essays in Pacific Northwest History,* ed. G. Thomas Edwards and Carlos A. Schwantes (Seattle: University of Washington Press, 1986), 53.

45 Cody, *Voyage of a Summer Sun,* 251.

46 Craig Lesley, *River Song* (Boston: Houghton Mifflin, 1989), 175.

47 Thomas Hacker and Associates, "Public Meeting and Other Public Comments," 30 November 1994. Linda Porter made this available to me when I visited the museum's offices in July 1996.

48 James Clifford, "Four Northwest Coast Museums: Travel Reflections," *Exhibiting Cultures: The Poetics and Politics of Museum Display,* ed. Ivan Karp and Steven D. Lavine (Washington, D.C.: Smithsonian Institution Press 1991), 225.

49 It should be noted that within the reservation world of the Heritage Center, its politics are hardly oppositional. It is only in comparison with mainstream museums that the center's politics should be considered as in opposition.

50 A fact sheet about the center and the Yakama Nation explains that earth lodges were used "thousands of years ago" and were replaced by tule-mat homes.

51 Quoted from exhibit signs at Yakama Nation Cultural Heritage Center, July 1998.

52 Tommy Thompson was chief of the unenrolled Indians at Celilo Village from the time he was 20 years old to his death at about 104 years in 1959. Although he applied for enrollment on the Warm Springs Reservation in 1943 (stating that "I have always felt that I am closely related to the Warm Springs—closer than to any other tribe"), he remained unenrolled. Letter from Tommy Thompson to Warm Springs Agency, 5 July 1943, Box 1939, "Thompson, Tommy; Otis and Ellen Andrews—Wilbur Kunehi," Field Agent—The Dalles, Oregon; General Subject Correspondence; 006 Star—Yallup .030 Umatilla, Record Group 75, Portland Area Office, Bureau of Indian Affairs, National Archives, Pacific Northwest Region, Seattle, Washington. His son, Henry Thompson, was enrolled

at the Yakama Reservation. Tommy Thompson died shortly after The Dalles Dam was completed. Henry Thompson succeeded Tommy Thompson. "Death Ends the Vain Fight of Tommy Thompson," *Oregonian,* 14 April 1959.

[53] Thomas Hacker and Associates, "Transcript of Public Meeting and Other Public Comments," 3.

[54] Celilo Falls was located within the territorial expanse of the Wyam, one of the three tribes of the Warm Springs Reservation. Although the falls drew Indians from as far away as western Washington, California, and Montana by the 1940s, there is some dispute regarding who had fishing rights at the mid-Columbia sites. Some Wyams claimed that only they had fishing rights at the falls. By the mid-1950s, however, enrolled members of the Yakama Nation comprised two-thirds of the fishers in the area.

[55] Thomas Hacker and Associates, "Transcript of Public Meeting and Other Public Comments," 5.

[56] "Yakama perspective" is a bit of a misnomer because there is, of course, no single perspective. Both museums tend to flatten the many fractures in identity within even small groups of people to create a single narrative voice.

Failed Federalism:
The Columbia Valley Authority and Regionalism

William L. Lang

✥

*R*egionalism* and *regional identity* are frustratingly slippery terms: Pacific Northwest, Northwest Coast, Inland Empire, Old West, New West, Ecotopia. What do these appellations actually describe? What do they mean? The answers are usually vague appropriations of iconographic stand-ins: Seattle's Spaceneedle, Idaho's potatoes, Oregon's firs or salmon. But these symbols are reductionist to a fault. They just replace slipperiness with hopelessly constrictive and limited representations. The frustration remains. It is also true, as cultural geographers remind us, that where we stand (that is, from what point we view the place) probably shapes identity more than any other factor. Our identity is a mixture of who we say we are to ourselves and what others perceive us to be, plus this equation's feedback—who we say we are not. Unlike Californians, Northwesterners are iconoclastic and environmental: Tom McCall versus Ronald Reagan.[1]

One obvious candidate as a representation of the Pacific Northwest is the Columbia River. Its 259,000-square-mile drainage basin incorporates portions of seven states and one Canadian province. There is little in the region, especially in the twenty-first century, that remains untouched by the river's influence, from electrical power to agriculture to high-technology industries. A second reason for focusing on the Columbia relates to another characteristic of identity making. Instances of political urgency and pressurized policy-making can stimulate representations and reflections on place, including regions. In other words, important regional decisions often beg the question of regional identity. During the twentieth century, political urgency twice roiled the waters of the Columbia, once in the early years of dam building, during the 1930s and 1940s, and as environmental problems threatened the dam-driven river system, during the 1990s. In both cases, political urgency generated broad-ranging discussions about the Columbia's role in the lives of Pacific Northwesterners.

These two sets of events share a lot, and it is intriguing that among the similarities is a focus on regionalism and regional identity. We are familiar with the crisis atmosphere that the region breathes nearly daily about the fate of salmon in the Columbia River Basin. Triggered by Endangered

Species Act listings of specific Columbia River Basin salmon runs in 1992, the political urgency for solution to the decline in fish populations has pitted local and regional ingenuity against the certainty of stern and restrictive measures from the federal government. Facing this challenge has increasingly engaged people of the region in prolonged discussion. It has spared no forum, no political persuasion. The questions are urgently asked and endemically felt. Will Northwesterners peg the region's future to the future of salmon? Will they pay for the lives of fish? Is there political will to change Columbia River management? How expensive is regional autonomy in a federal system? The questions equate to a regional conundrum: What are the content and value of our regional lives?

This condition has an analog in the first of two politically urgent crises that centered on the Columbia River. The urgency began with the federal decision in 1933 to establish huge public works projects on the river, the Bonneville and Grand Coulee Dams. By all accounts, Northwesterners eagerly embraced these massive endeavors. In fact, residents of localities in the basin had vigorously lobbied private, state, and federal groups for support of similar projects since the early 1920s. Promised benefits of the big dams swelled expectations. As *Oregon Journal* editor Marshall Dana put it in 1934: "The Columbia is the miracle of power streams, the divider of mountain ranges . . . the reclaimer and energizer of an empire. Population follows power. Develop power and other growth will come."[2] An empire might have been on the horizon, but what kind of empire, under whose direction, and how would it be organized? These questions were left unanswered in the open acceptance of federal largesse.

Nonetheless, there was urgency in answering these questions. Completion of Bonneville and Grand Coulee Dams meant that an enormous stream of electrical power would soon be available, but there was no plan for control or distribution. With that challenge in mind, in January 1935, Washington Congressman Knute Hill and Idaho Senator James Pope introduced companion bills to create a Columbia Valley Authority (CVA). The bills designated a corporation to craft a comprehensive and integrated development of the Columbia River Basin. A three-person appointed board would generate policy and report to the president. The idea inherent in this legislation, and in all subsequent CVA bills, assumed some kind of regional identity, but its shape remained unclear and included contradictions. For example, part of the regional identification came from lobbying groups in Wenatchee, Walla Walla, The Dalles, Spokane, and other interested localities who hoped for direct benefits, but only a broad and equitable distribution of hydroelectric power would bring the desired regional results, and that seemed to argue for a regional authority. In 1934, members of state planning boards in Oregon, Washington, Idaho, and Montana raised no objections when one member characterized the region as "a highly homogeneous area" which shared "a community of cultural and economic interests, [and] common problems of regional drainage." Their consultant, Roy F. Bessey, underscored the appropriateness of a comprehensive regional agency, when he recommended "an authority with rather broad powers, patterned generally on the Tennessee Valley Authority."[3]

The Tennessee Valley Authority (TVA) had been in existence only two years in 1935, but it had already become the existing model for river authorities and one of the New Deal's stellar achievements. President Franklin D. Roosevelt described it as "a corporation clothed with the power of government but possessed of the flexibility and initiative of a private enterprise." TVA's operating principle and the basis for other "basin authority proposals" was "integrated development . . . through planning." The expectations were grand. As one of the first managers at TVA put it: "the [Tennessee] Valley will become an example to the rest of the United States, possibly to the world, as the best way man can live in an industrial society."[4]

Northwesterners' desire for rapid and full development seemed to argue in favor of the TVA model, but the two regions differed in physical, economic, and social components sufficiently to raise questions. In addition, TVA had drawn critics from its inception, some complaining "that Washington [D.C.] . . . regarded the [Tennessee] valley as a colony."[5] The Pacific Northwest Planning Commission, which represented planning boards in the four states, wrestled with these questions in 1935 and 1936, recommending against a TVA-type agency but supporting comprehensive planning and integrated development of the basin. By 1936, two additional bills proposing a regional plan came from Washington's two Democratic senators, Homer Bone and Lewis Schwellenbach, and Oregon's two Republican senators, Charles McNary and Frederick Steiwer. In Senate hearings on the competing bills in 1936, proponents and opponents of the legislation staked out fundamental positions that would remain relatively constant throughout the debates on CVA legislation. In total, Congress deliberated on more than a dozen bills between 1935 and 1952.[6]

Nearly every historian who has surveyed the history of CVA proposals agrees on the dividing points among the supporters and critics. CVA supporters tended to represent liberal political beliefs, organized labor, small farmers, and social activists. Opponents represented political conservatives, the private power industry, manufacturers and most big industry, and some large agriculturalists. Oregon's politicians tended to resist the idea of the CVA, while Washington's supported the idea and Idaho's and Montana's lined up as ambivalent or on the negative side. These positions can be reduced to several economic and political binaries: unfettered private enterprise versus government-controlled or regulated enterprise; agricultural versus nonagricultural users of the river; and state and local rights versus federal control. The issue was and is more complex than these constructed dualities. Anomalies and political contradictions arose during two decades of discussions over CVA. Much of it bears on regionalism.[7]

The CVA debates asked a fundamental question: should the Northwest band together in developing the Columbia River Basin? The answer depended on politics, but it also depended on the legitimacy and practicality of considering the basin as a region. In testimony before the Senate in 1936, for example, the chair of the Pacific Northwest Planning Commission observed: "Considering all of the factors—political administrative, functional, physiographic, economic, metropolitan, cultural, and traditional—that tend to define regions, it is concluded that the Pacific Northwest constitutes an unusually well-defined and coherent interstate, sub-national region. . . . If all the relevant social and economic factors, and not merely physical drainage, were considered, the Columbia Basin region would include [Washington, Oregon, Idaho, and western Montana]."[8]

Senator Schwellenbach, who had proposed CVA legislation, took the occasion to embrace a broad, practical regional agenda and to distance himself from those he considered parochial:

> *Personally, I have no provincial attitude toward the dams out there [in the basin]. I take the peculiar position as a resident of the city of Seattle that the building up and the prosperity of the city of Portland is just as important to the city of Seattle as to anyone else. I do not take the position that we are going to fight between Oregon and Washington about these dams. We have got to get population out into the Pacific Northwest, and if they have a million people in Portland we are going to benefit from it in the State of Washington. . . . I think the more people we get in Portland the better off we will be in the State of Washington.*[9]

The advocates of a TVA-like agency failed in 1936 and, accepted the temporary Bonneville Power Administration Act in 1937 as a necessary solution to the problem of electrical distribution. The CVA idea, however, did not subside. Between 1940 and 1942, Congress debated four CVA proposals, each directed at broad regional development of water resources. They cited planner Lewis Mumford's widely circulated "Memorandum" to the Northwest Regional Council in 1939, the result of his on-site survey of Columbia River Basin planning efforts. In Mumford's view, "the problem in the present state of American society, has nothing whatever to do with population: it is a matter of complicated economic readjustment, involving among other things the socialization of natural monopolies, the collective

control of quasi-monopolies, the wiping out of inflexible price structures
. . . the raising of real wages through trade union pressure on one hand
and through the expansion of vital public works, financed by current
taxation, on the other."[10]

Mumford enthusiastically supported TVA-type authorities and criticized
less ambitious planning regimes. Mumford emphasized the importance of
timely action, arguing that a "new kind of regional authority" could stave
off problems that more developed regions of the country had experienced.
In the Northwest, Mumford urged that a new arrangement could be "put
immediately to work if the best development of the Columbia River Valley
can take place; and since this is a spinal development, [it is] of critical
importance to every other part of the region—including, of course, the
whole Inland Empire—[and] a failure to organize resolutely here will
undermine other efforts at regional rehabilitation or improvement."[11] CVA
proponents avidly took up Mumford's suggestions and sought to redefine
the idea of region and regional development. First, they used his
identification of "natural monopolies" and the "collective control of quasi-
monopolies" to battle against the older and entrenched views of region
and regional development. Second, they highlighted his description of the
region as a potentially integrated place, with the Columbia as its spine and
the interior sections connected to coastal areas. The CVA, they argued,
would be an enlightened, progressive, and equitable regional administration.

Unfortunately for CVA advocates, the bills submitted to Congress from
1940 through 1942 became mired in controversy over the demand by
Secretary of the Interior Harold Ickes that the regional agency have one
administrator who answered to him. This top-down, single-administrator
plan drew immediate criticism from Senator George Norris, the father of
TVA, and even forced friends of CVA, such as Oregon's Walter M. Pierce,
to abandon the effort. "I would rather have no legislation at all," Norris
wrote a colleague, "than to surrender this great project in Washington and
Oregon to a Bureau in Washington." In addition, Ickes's advocacy of public
power highlighted the already divisive issue of who should develop
hydroelectric sites in the basin, private industry or the government.[12]

World War II delayed discussion, but the growth of industry and the
operations of wartime government management brought the idea back in
1945 with even more urgency and commitment. The chief CVA proponent
at the war's end was Washington Senator Hugh B. Mitchell, who introduced
bills in February and December 1945 with Washington Congressman
Henry M. Jackson and spurred the organization of the Columbia Valley
Authority Information League to aid the first bill and the League for CVA
to aid the second. Mitchell's second bill called for a corporation that would
take over planning and integrated management, including budget, for

existing principal federal agencies with water resources responsibilities in the basin. Mitchell proposed that the corporate board report directly to the president and "establish procedures for regular consultation and interchange of views on matters of policy" with the basin states and representative regional interest groups. "I am recommending," Mitchell told Senate colleagues, "that the fundamentals of the TVA pattern should be adhered to in the Columbia Valley . . . give us the tools to do the work."[13]

Opponents to CVA mustered support from chambers of commerce, private electrical companies, and the National Reclamation Association, an organization of irrigation project beneficiaries that feared losing access to water if any basin authorities became reality. The opposition used the region's newspapers, periodicals, and trade publications to mount an attack against the CVA idea. "The 'Authority' principle," one critic wrote, "is decidedly undemocratic, since all development is in the hands of a small group appointed by the President, with no direct responsibility to the people of the basin." Publicity from the industry-sponsored Pacific Northwest Development Association, formed in May 1945 to defeat CVA, charged that "all authority legislation has been socialistic, even communistic."[14]

CVA advocates countered with the League for CVA, a loose organization of farmer and labor groups in the Columbia River Basin. Girard C. "Jebby" Davidson, a former chief counsel of the Bonneville Power Administration and proponent of CVA, had advised Hugh Mitchell in May 1945 "that the opposition is pretty well organized in its program and that the main thing that is needed by the supporters and proponents is some overall direction . . . it is about time to start welding together the proponents of the Authority."[15] Mitchell organized the league with Davidson's ideas in mind and the goal of forging a truly regional alliance of leaders. By early 1946, they included heads of the Washington State Grange, the Idaho State Farmer's Union, former Washington Senator C. C. Dill, and the regional director of the Congress of Industrial Organizations.

The League for CVA organized meetings in each state, using existing county Grange, irrigation district, and labor groups to draw audiences. In Idaho and eastern sections of Oregon and Washington, league representatives had to argue strenuously that CVA would not grab irrigation water for "use in the lower country," a reference to westside industrial interests, especially the Pacific Northwest Development Association.[16] CVA advocates found themselves arguing against the fear-mongering claims of two groups, organized irrigationists and organized private power, who saw each other as competitors for Columbia River Basin water. Both groups worried that CVA would be a daunting weapon in the hands of their competition. CVA supporters relied on community meetings and plain-speaking counterattacks published in the labor press. An editorial in the International Woodworkers of America publication, *The Woodworker,* laid out the choice: "Rivers are the people's property. . . . To get the most out of a river . . . you have to make a master blueprint. Not a power-trust blueprint, not an irrigation engineer's blueprint, not a navigator's blueprint. It means a blueprint . . . made by a team."[17]

The Truman administration stepped into the discussion by sending Secretary of the Interior Julius Krug on a regionwide tour with Jebby Davidson, newly designated point man on CVA in the Interior Department. Davidson had lined up key opinion leaders in the Northwest, including E. B. McNaughton of the Portland *Oregonian* and arranged for small, focused meetings with local business and community leaders. In July, McNaughton gathered a group of Portland businessmen for a session with Krug. By McNaughton's account, the meeting was "helpful and worthwhile" and he was "pleased with the way it went off and with the willingness of the men I invited to cooperate in a workable solution of the [CVA] idea."[18] Despite this and other successes from Krug's Northwest tour, Congress would not act. Additional support from national liberal publications, *The Nation* and *The New Republic,* did not make a noticeable difference, and such agitation in the national press may have actually stiffened conservative fears. Mitchell's bill died in 1946 and, to add personal insult, conservatives won Congress in the fall and turned out Mitchell himself.[19]

The CVA had more lives than its opponents realized, but it took an unexpected event to resuscitate it and give it additional strength. In May and June 1948, a rapid spring thaw quickly released a torrent down creeks and tributary streams in the Columbia River Basin from the heavy snow pack that had built up during the 1947-1948 winter in the Cascade and Rocky Mountains. Not since 1894 had the river run so high and done so much damage, including the dramatic inundation of Oregon's second largest city, Vanport. The flood coincided with congressional discussions about the Columbia's future that had been stimulated by the Interior Department's massive new study, *The Columbia River: A Comprehensive Report on the Development of the Water Resources of the Columbia River Basin.* President Truman personally surveyed the flood damage, vowing to organize the forces of government for flood prevention and river basin improvements. Truman's unexpected reelection in 1948, along with a phalanx of liberals in Congress, made a new CVA bill politically opportune and potentially an answer to a flood-created urgency.[20]

Happily for CVA supporters, Hugh Mitchell won election to the House of Representatives in 1948. He returned to Washington, D.C. armed with a new bill. Mitchell had spent the preceding two years heading up the

League for CVA, spreading the message throughout the basin, and fashioning a new CVA strategy. Mitchell had full support from the Truman administration, which put the CVA issue on the highest executive agenda, including the Department of Commerce, Bureau of the Budget, and Council of Economic Advisors.[21] Mitchell introduced H.R. 4286 in January 1949, with a subtle but meaningful change in the title. The bill called for creation of a Columbia Valley Administration, not an "authority." The drumbeat of opposition to the idea of valley authorities, coming from postwar conservatives like Raymond Moley, convinced Mitchell to use a more acceptable label.

Northwest politicians split on the new bill, which featured a three-person executive board that guaranteed two regional members and a headquarters in the Northwest. The Republican governors of the four Northwest states reacted, as one commentator put it, "with the alacrity of fire horses answering a four-bell blaze," decrying the bill as a serious threat to state sovereignty. Among Washington State politicians, support came from Congressman Henry Jackson, Senator Warren Magnuson, and Republican Senator Harry Cain, the man who had beaten Hugh Mitchell in 1946. In Oregon, Senator Wayne Morse said no to Mitchell's legislation, as did Senator Guy Cordon, but Idaho's Republican Senator Glen Taylor signed on to the new CVA bill. Magnuson introduced a revision of Mitchell's bill in the Senate, S. 1645, with slight modifications in mid-1950.[22]

The split among politicians mirrored sentiment in the region. Richard Neuberger reported in May 1949: "Sentiment among the rank and file of people on CVA is still difficult to assay." It appeared more settled to C. Girard Davidson, Assistant Secretary of the Interior, who remarked when asked in July about the bill's chances: "So far the Republicans and power companies are against it, and the Democrats, labor and farmers are for it. What more could we ask?"[23]

The ambivalence Neuberger sensed prevailed, with the League for CVA again battling it out against the irrigation and private power interests in newspapers, local meetings and rallies, and their own propaganda sheets. As a public utility newsletter foretold just after the bill's introduction: "The farm cooperative future . . . is linked with the outcome of the 'Battle of the Giants' over control of generation and transmission of electrical power." Chambers of commerce and state reclamation interests organized the Western States Council to oppose any CVA or TVA-type legislation. The council harangued against the establishment of any additional federal bureaucracies in the region, claiming that all development would grind to a snail's pace. The League for CVA countered against the newly formed council and the Pacific Northwest Development Association by distributing a promotional pamphlet, "What CVA Means to You." The Pacific Northwest

Development Association replied with their own pamphlet, "Read for Yourself: What CVA Means." Regional newspaper editors liberally excerpted from both publications throughout 1950. The opposition argument focused on loss of local control, imagined threats to water rights, and fearsome predictions about government intentions. Operatives circulated reports that Bonneville Power Administration head Paul Raver had socialistic plans, had perhaps been friends of communists, and illogically had struck a deal with Wall Street bankers to "funnel profits of public power sales" to private groups who planned to bring socialism to the United States. The League for CVA continued to stress that CVA's commitment to a regional headquarters and regional directors, open processes, coordination with federal and state agencies, plus guarantees of state water rights made it safe and efficient for regional interests. Its slogan directly addressed regional development: "A Columbia Valley authority means a united, integrated program for the development of the Northwest." The emphasis, as Henry Jackson remarked on the floor of the House and in regional speeches, was development, development, development—and efficiently done. "CVA will be the stern father," Jackson promised. In reference to the ongoing battles between the U.S. Army Corps of Engineers and the Bureau of Reclamation, he added: "It will put an end to the Federal family squabbles."[24]

The "Battle of the Giants" in 1949–1950 over the Truman administration's CVA bill revealed a fundamental truth in the Columbia River Basin: political water fights defeated regional unity. "The chief hope in turning the tide from depletion of our resources to better use," Bernard Frank and Anthony Netboy wrote in 1950, "is that land use must be socially controlled." The CVA proposal offered a method to achieve that end, but the attacks by private power interests kept communities divided on the issue. The fall elections in 1950 brought back conservatives to Congress and more bad news for CVA advocates. President Truman continued to believe in valley authorities, but his ardency flagged, as war on the Korean Peninsula flared and he struggled to hold together political allies to defend a weakened, but remaining liberal agenda. The election of Dwight Eisenhower and selection of the anti-CVA Douglas McKay as Secretary of the Interior finally killed off the last CVA proposals in 1953.[25]

There is no clear and consistent explanation for CVA's failure. Contradictory arguments by opponents and sometimes-tepid support from federal resource agencies compromised public debate. The economic interests that had argued strenuously against the Bonneville Power Administration in the late 1930s and against the policies and plans of the U.S. Army Corps of Engineers and the Bureau of Reclamation in the early 1940s suddenly became ardent defenders of these agencies after 1945, when the CVA proposal gained added support from the president. Public power advocates, eager to embrace CVA proposals before World War II, put less muscle behind the effort after the war. The urgency created by the great 1948 flood begged for water projects, but the desire in the region and Congress did not produce a CVA. In fact, the postflood urgency might have dimmed CVA's chances and given opponents opportunity to argue against additional federal involvement in the region. Part of the explanation for CVA's failure is in the hyperbole embraced by both sides in the regional discussion. Without CVA, the advocates predicted, economic ruin for the region lay just around the corner. With CVA, the opponents warned, socialism or even communism certainly came next.

We can ask two major questions about the CVA's history. What does this say about regionalism and regional identity? And, is the idea truly dead? For one thing, the CVA experience suggests that regional unity is not a requisite for regional identity. Both proponents of and opponents to the CVA vehemently disagreed, but both coveted the Columbia's waters. The difference lay in the political instruments and arenas they preferred. For another, interests from outside of the region had less impact and influence than we might think. Both groups bashed the federal government, for example, and federal authorities seemed unable to impose political solutions on the region. Finally, both the proponents and the opponents wrapped themselves in regional clothing, arguing that their pathway gave the people what they wanted most—home rule.

On the second question, we need look no further than the Columbia River conundrum of this generation: Will it be salmon restoration or "business as usual" on the river? The 1980 Pacific Northwest Electric Power Planning and Conservation Act created the Northwest Power Planning Council, a forum for regional planning and dispute resolution to provide equity between the demands of hydroelectric producers and salmon advocates for Columbia River water. But after more than a decade of work, the results satisfied no one. By 1996, proposals by the Columbia River Intertribal Fish Commission and the Independent Science Group had urged an abandonment or root revision of technological mitigations on the Columbia. The science group proposed extensive reservoir drawdowns and even breaching the four dams on the lower Snake River to "restore more normative conditions" to reverse "declines in salmonid productivity." Interest groups took sides, much as they had in the CVA discussions, and what regional harmony remained screeched into discord. The public appeared less divided. In Oregon, a statewide poll in late 1997 revealed that an impressive 60 percent of respondents put the interests of salmon above industrial and agricultural uses of the river; 40 percent advocated taking out some dams; 91 percent support salmon-saving policies. Most wanted a regional solution rather than federally designated regulations.[26]

General public support for salmon-saving programs did not guarantee regional acceptance of the "Return to the River" proposals or any other reevaluative scheme. By early 1998, for example, Idaho and Montana had gone on record resisting drawdowns and dam removal. Still, the portent of federal action prompted the design of a new, regional policy-making regime for the Columbia River Basin. Announced in February 1998 as a "high-level political commitment," negotiators from the major policy-makers on the river crafted a new protocol: "The Three Sovereigns Forum." The proposal identified three political aggregations, "sovereigns," to resolve controversies over salmon recovery measures and determine policy in the basin through consensus agreement. Indian tribes with Columbia River treaty standing constituted one sovereign; a second sovereign included federal agencies involved in river management with direct representation from the White House; the four principal basin states, Oregon, Washington, Idaho, and Montana, made up the third sovereign. No sooner had this proposal entered the debate than state legislators objected, complaining that they had been marginalized, that the representatives of the populace could not weigh in with their concerns. In December 1998, Montana and Idaho governors refused to sign on to the Three Sovereigns Forum (recast as the Columbia River Forum), fearing the process would threaten state sovereignty and control of water—an echo of the states' fears from the 1940s. By January 1999, the whole idea seemed destined for the scrap heap of failed regional alloys.[27]

The most recent developments suggest that the region is replaying some of the CVA drama. President Clinton has announced support for direct federal aid in salmon recovery efforts, an action that diminishes a regional solution. Meanwhile, the region's four governors have proposed creating a Pacific Northwest "salmon czar" to centralize policy decisions in the region. The likelihood of Endangered Species Act listings of more than a dozen salmonid species in the Northwest—ranging from Puget Sound to the interior Willamette River Basin—puts major urban areas at risk of austere, federally mandated regulations. Time is running out for a regionally controlled solution.[28]

The CVA's biography is suggestive. If regional political unity is required for self-protection, it is unlikely that it will be crafted in the crucible of a regionally divisive issue, such as saving salmon runs that invokes the potential for breaching dams on the lower Snake River. The public discussion and the political wrangling about salmon of late demonstrates that there is as much political division today among agencies, states, and tribes in the Columbia River Basin as existed in 1950. It is possible that CVA might have prevented this generation's disunity, especially if Indian tribes had been part of it, because the CVA's promised rationalization at the federal level might well have forced a bureaucratic agreement, thereby limiting a rancorous public discussion. But might-have-beens are poor history and poorer arguments for action. The fact is that conditions have changed dramatically on the Columbia. The river is much different at the beginning of the twenty-first century than it was during the New Deal. The river may well be too divisive to stand as an icon for regional identity. Nonetheless, a successful regionalism requires some measure of unity or shared political responsibilities beyond the component states, and that unity will satisfy only if it includes culturally legitimate images and politically practical instruments. The Columbia River is still powerful enough in the regional imagination to suggest unity, and its future—beyond salmon and beyond energy—is perhaps the best reason for creating a new political understanding of regionalism.

Notes

[1] For a recent challenge to the idea that the Pacific Northwest is a region defined by its residents, see John Findlay, "A Fishy Proposition: Regional Identity in the Pacific Northwest," in *Many Wests: Place, Culture, and Regional Identity,* ed. David Wrobel and Michael Steiner (Lawrence: University of Kansas Press, 1997), 37–50. On the geographical perspective, see Robert David Sack, *Homo Geographicus* (Baltimore: Johns Hopkins University Press, 1997), 156–60.

[2] MS address, Marshall Dana, 12 December 1934, Box 10, Folder 24, Marshall Dana Papers, Oregon Historical Society Archives, Portland (henceforth Dana Papers).

[3] Pacific Northwest Regional Planning Commission, "Progress Report" (1935), p. 29, Box 2, Folder 4; Roy F. Bessey to Marshall N. Dana, 12 November 1934, Box 10, Folder 12, Dana Papers.

[4] National Planning Board, "Final Report, 1933-34" (Washington, D.C.: Government Printing Office, 1934), 93; Roland Wank, quoted in Walter L. Creese, *TVA's Public Planning: The Vision, The Reality* (Knoxville: University of Tennessee Press, 1990), 6. On the place of TVA and other "authorities" in the history of river basin planning, see S. K. Saha, "River Basin Planning as a Field of Study: Design of a Course Structure for Practitioners," in *River Basin Planning: Theory and Practice,* ed. S. K. Saha and Christopher J. Barrow (New York: John Wiley and Sons, 1981), 9–40.

[5] James R. McCarthy, "The New Deal in Tennessee," *Sewanee Review* (1934), quoted in Creese, *TVA's Public Planning,* 92.

[6] For an extended discussion of TVA and its relevance to Columbia River Basin planning, see Charles McKinley, *Uncle Sam in the Pacific Northwest: Federal Management of Natural Resources in the Columbia River Valley* (Berkeley: University of California Press, 1952), 63–64, 480–542; Herman Pritchett, "The Transplantability of TVA," *Iowa Law Review* 32 (January 1947), 332–36.

[7] The best summaries and analyses of CVA are: McKinley, *Uncle Sam in the Northwest;* Elmo Richardson, *Dams, Parks, and Politics: Resource Development and Preservation in the Truman-Eisenhower Era* (Lexington: University of Kentucky Press, 1973); Herman C. Voeltz, "Genesis and Development of a Regional Power Agency in the Pacific Northwest, 1933–43," *Pacific Northwest Quarterly* 53 (April 1962): 65–76.

[8] Testimony, Marshall Dana, National Resources Committee, Interior Department, *Hearings Before a Subcommittee on Agriculture and Forestry,* U.S. Senate, 74th Cong., 2d sess. S. 869, S. 3330, S. 4178, S. 4566, 7, 8, 9, and 13 May 1936 (Washington, D.C.: Government Printing Office, 1936), 81-82.

[9] Statement, Senator Lewis Schwellenbach, Ibid., 87.

[10] Lewis Mumford, *Regional Planning in the Pacific Northwest: A Memorandum* (Portland: Northwest Regional Council), 6.

[11] Ibid., 15. For another interpretation on Mumford's advice, see Richard White, *The Organic Machine: The Remaking of the Columbia River* (New York: Hill and Wang, 1995), 64-69.

[12] Norris quoted in Richard Lowitt, *George W. Norris: The Triumph of a Progressive, 1933-1944* (Urbana: University of Illinois Press, 1978), 401; Voeltz, "Genesis and Development," 69-71.

[13] Text, S. 1716, 79th Cong., 1st sess., 20 December 1945; Draft Address–CVA, December 1945, Box 8, Folder 21, Hugh B. Mitchell Papers, University of Washington Archives, Seattle (hereafter Mitchell Papers); McKinley, *Uncle Sam in the Northwest,* 553-56.

[14] Marshall Dana, "Proposed Substitute for River Valley Authorities," *Civil Engineering* 15 (April 1945): 182; clipping, Pacific Northwest Development Association circular (February 1946), Box 8, Folder 21, Mitchell Papers.

[15] C. Girard Davidson to Hugh B. Mitchell, 15 May 1945, C. Girard Davidson Papers, Box 8, Folder Columbia Valley Authority, memoranda 1944-50, Harry S. Truman Library, Independence, Missouri (hereafter Davidson Papers).

[16] Herbert Peet to Roy W. Atkinson, 3 May 1946, Box 8, Folder 20, Mitchell Papers.

[17] Editorial, *Woodworker* (1946), Box 8, Folder 21, Mitchell Papers.

[18] E. B. McNaughton to C. Girard Davidson, 17 July 1946, Box 4, Folder Correspondence File, Mc–general, Davidson Papers.

[19] Catherine Bauer, "Columbia Basin: Test for Planning," *The New Republic* 107 (7 September 1942): 279-81; Carey McWilliams, "The Northwest Needs CVA," *The Nation* 160 (2 June 1945): 622-24, "Power is the Banker," *The Nation* 160 (9 June 1945): 645-47, "Columbia River Bureaucrats," *The Nation* 160 (23 June 1945): 693-94.

[20] J. A. Krug, *The Columbia River: A Comprehensive Departmental Report on the Development of the Water Resources of the Columbia River Basin . . .* (Washington, D.C.: U.S. Department of Interior, 1947).

[21] *New York Times,* 25 January 1949; Hugh B. Mitchell to Harry S. Truman, 24 January 1949, Box 1051, Folder 360-A miscellaneous, Harry S. Truman Library, Independence, Missouri.

[22] Raymond Moley, *Valley Authorities* (Washington, D.C.: American Enterprise Association, 1950); Ancil Payne, "Who Is Fighting CVA?" *Oregon Democrat* 17 (July 1949): 8-9; Richard L. Neuberger, "Morse vs. Morse," *The Nation* 165 (14 January 1950): 29-32.

[23] Richard L. Neuberger, "River Authority for the Northwest," *St. Louis Post-Dispatch,* 15 May 1949; C. Girard Davidson to Charles Murphy, 28 January 1949, Box 21, CVA, Charles Murphy Files, Harry S. Truman Library, Independence, Missouri.

[24] *New York Times,* 30 March 1949; "The NW Chills as Giants Battle over Power, CVA," *Pacific Northwest Cooperator* (February 1949); "Democratic Committee Takes Issue with Power Suggestion, *Walla Walla Union-Bulletin,* 31 July 1949; Charles Van Devander, "Digest's Article on Public Power Blasted in House," *New York Post,* 30 July 1950; "The Public and You," electric companies' advertising

pamphlet, January 1950, Box 8, Folder Columbia Valley Authority, memoranda 1944–50, Davidson Papers; "League for CVA," pamphlet, 1950, Box 44, Folder 3, Henry M. Jackson Papers, University of Washington Archives (hereafter Jackson Papers); Jefferson-Jackson Day Speech, Vancouver, Washington, 17 June 1949, MS, Floor Address, Henry M. Jackson, 24 July 1950, Box 51, Folder 25, Jackson Papers.

25 Bernard Frank and Anthony Netboy, *Water, Land, and People* (New York: Alfred A. Knopf, 1950), 286–87; Richardson, *Dams, Parks, and Politics,* 35–37.

26 Columbia River Intertribal Fish Commission, *Wy-Kan-Ush-Mi-Wa-Kush-Wit: The Spirit of the River* (Portland, CRITFC, 1995); Independent Science Group, *Return to the River: Restoration of Salmonid Fisheries in the Columbia River Ecosystem* (Portland: Northwest Power Planning Council, 1996), 506; Oregonian poll, *Oregonian,* 7 December 1997. For the changes in policy and relevant documents, see Joseph Cone and Sandy Ridlington, eds., *The Northwest Salmon Crisis: A Documentary History* (Corvallis: Oregon State University Press, 1996), especially Section V, 240–347.

27 *Oregonian,* 8 December 1997; 2, 25 February 1998; 16 October 1998; 15 December 1998.

28 "Fish Listing Certain to Jolt Region," *Oregonian,* 31 January 1999.

Stories about Livelihoods:
Cultural Inertia and Conceptual Confusion in a Transitional Economy

Thomas Michael Power

⌁

An Introduction to Popular Economic Stories: Pacific Northwest Folk Economics

THIS CHAPTER EXPLORES the ways in which we think about the regional and local economies of the Pacific Northwest. Our understanding of the local economy is largely based on several economic metaphors, or stories, about how we provide ourselves with livelihoods in the region. Those economic stories are so embedded in our collective thinking that they have become cultural beliefs unrelated to current economic reality. These stories have two sources: they are loosely tied to the history of the region's original European settlement and they reflect even older economic theories that stretch back into the eighteenth century. They cannot be viewed simply as quaint regional folk tales or innocent cultural oddities because they have a profound impact on public economic dialogue and the economic policies that flow from that dialogue. In particular, the stories guide our economic vision away from current reality and emerging trends toward the "view through the rear-view mirror." Thus, they distort our view of the present and distract us from focusing on some of the most important determinants of current and future economic well-being. If we are going to develop productive public economic policy for the future, we need to modify or abandon those old stories and develop a new popular economic story about our region.

In the mid-1930s, John Maynard Keynes warned about the damage that a hypnotic gaze in the economic rear-view mirror could have: "the ideas of economists and political philosophers, both when they are right and when they are wrong, are more powerful than is commonly understood. Indeed the world is ruled by little else. Practical men, who believe themselves to be quite exempt from any intellectual influences, are usually the slaves of some defunct economist. Madmen in authority, who hear voices in the air, are distilling their frenzy from some academic scribbler of a few years back."[1]

In this chapter, I critique and argue the need to modify, supplement, and/or discard the following popular economic stories: (1) all economic wealth springs ultimately from the earth and the natural resource industries that work the earth; (2) manufacturing activities are superior to the provision of services; (3) only exports energize the local economy and locally oriented economic activity is parasitic on those exports; and (4) only monetary income matters in determining economic well-being.

In the Pacific Northwest, these stories overemphasize the importance of natural resource industries such as forest products, agriculture, and mining. In our large metropolitan areas, where it is no longer plausible to solely emphasize these natural resource sectors, manufacturing activities such as computer component and aerospace production are seen as the dominant economic base. In nonmetropolitan areas, where neither old nor new manufacturing can explain local economic vitality, tourism is seized upon, almost by default, as the industry driving the ongoing economic transformation of the region. None of these assertions about the region's economic base are complete or accurate.

Does All Real Wealth Spring from the Earth?
The Material Requirements Approach to the Economy

When I describe the centuries-long shift in production from natural resource to manufacturing to service activities, I am criticized regularly by political leaders and natural resource interests for ignoring the "fact" that natural resource industries hold a special position within the economy. Natural resource industries are often labeled as *primary* economic activity because they provide the raw materials on which all other economic activity depends. Without food, we would have no labor force. Without minerals and fiber, we would not have the materials that our manufacturing industries transform into useful goods or the energy that drives an industrial economy. In that fundamental sense, natural resource activities are the prerequisite for all other economic activities.[2] There is no disputing the materials flow concept that is the basis of this particular economic story. What is at issue is the economic importance of these material connections.

The first efforts at economic modeling put natural resources at the center of the economy as the ultimate source of all economic value. During the mid–eighteenth century, a group of French intellectuals in the royal court applied the newly discovered circulatory model of the human body and its health to the national economy. These "physiocrats" modeled the economy in terms of the value created by natural resources, especially agricultural output, flowing through and enabling economic activity at every level beyond basic natural resource production. From the grain grower to the miller to the bakery flowed the food to support the labor effort that was then exerted in all other industries. This crude depiction of the interconnections among economic activities was one of the fundamental insights in economics and was the basis for economic analysis as diverse as that of nineteenth- and twentieth-century Marxists as well as modern mathematical input-output analysis. One insight of the physiocrats also has endured—the unique position of natural resources in the economy. All economic activity after natural resource production simply processes and transforms the initial value created. The physiocrats argued emphatically that this processing and transformation in manufacturing, finance, and retail trade did not add economic value. It merely passed the value originally created in primary production to other parts of the economy, much the way the body distributes food energy to the various muscles that allow us to engage in a variety of different types of activities.[3]

This concept of an economic circular flow was a significant insight that remains central to many modern economic models. But the implication that natural resources hold a special, central place in the economy is not a useful insight. Knowing that something is required in an economic process does not establish its economic value. In most economic processes, many different resources have to be combined to produce the final product. Knowing that each of these resources is required does not tell us anything about the relative contribution each makes to the value of the final product. Crops and livestock forage require the presence of certain trace minerals. Without those trace elements, healthy crops and profitable grazing operations would not be possible; however, that does not mean that the dominant economic resources are the trace elements. Knowing that there is a necessary physical relationship in a production process does not tell us much about the relative economic values involved.

It is not clear why the advocates of natural resources' special place begin with the human need for food, fiber, and other raw materials. Humans also need air, water, climates within a certain range of physical tolerances, and particular vitamins and minerals. For instance, we all need vitamin C. Without it our health and productivity will deteriorate and we will die. The same can be said for table salt. Knowing these physical or biological relationships does not provide us with much economic information. It is not possible to go from this knowledge to a conclusion about the relative economic value of vitamin C or table salt or the economic importance of those who produce and distribute these materials to us. Economic analysis and valuation are not tied directly to such physical relationships, even when those physical relationships undeniably are prerequisites for economic activity. Vitamin C purveyors are not a dominant source of economic value.

The relative economic importance of natural resources is established by the interaction of supply and demand. If agricultural or other commodity supplies were to shrink relative to demands, that could undoubtedly have a profound impact on the rest of the economy. Just as interruptions in energy supplies in the 1970s and early 1980s had a disruptive impact on the economy, so too could falling agricultural production have a cascading impact on the overall economy.

Of course, natural resource shortages and rising commodity prices are not what we have been experiencing for the past century. Commodity supplies have risen faster than demand and commodity prices have been depressed, often to record low levels. Technological innovation has allowed farms and natural resource firms to survive and expand production despite the falling commodity prices, but the size of the workforce needed for this expanding production has steadily shrunk while the aggregate value of the natural resource output has not kept up with the expanding economy. As a result, the relative economic importance of natural resource activities has steadily declined.

This decline in the relative importance of natural resource industries has been especially dramatic in the Pacific Northwest, where timber harvest and processing has historically been very important. Between 1978 and 1996, 53,000 wood-products jobs were lost in the region. During that same period, rather than the regional economy declining in response to these dramatic job losses, it added more than *2 million* new jobs. As a result of these divergent trends, the relative importance of wood products as a source of employment in the region declined by almost 60 percent. There were employment and population gains even in those counties within the Pacific Northwest that especially relied on timber harvest for employment and income.[4]

By linking almost all economic activity to natural resource sectors, the material flows view of the economy diverts our attention to the primary sources of high economic productivity. The nations with the largest populations or the largest stores of natural resources have not been the most economically productive. Rather, nations that have improved the *quality* of their workforce; improved the state of knowledge; harnessed new technologies; and developed supportive social, political, and economic institutions have prospered.[5] It is important to note that these actions are largely nonmaterial. That is not to say that we can safely ignore the material basis of all economic activity. We cannot, especially if we are concerned about environmental degradation and sustainability. It remains crucial, however, to look beyond just the material flows and study the entire process by which economic value is created and economic well-being improved.

The Goodness of Goods Production

In our public dialogue, manufacturing is assumed to be the preferred type of economic activity. Along with the natural resource sectors and construction, this type of economic activity produces material products that are storable as wealth and tradable. Services seem to lack such a palpable economic reality and therefore are treated as inferior, if not parasitic (for example, "middleman"), activities. The service-producing sector is often accused of not really producing anything.

Although this view is common, its economic logic is difficult to discern. From the point of view of economics, well-being is enhanced by stretching the productivity of the scarce resources available to us so that more and more of our needs and desires can be satisfied. If what we most deeply desire is a continuously expanding flow of material goods, then that has to be one focus of our economic efforts. The other focus has to be on boosting the productivity of our scarce resources. However, it is certainly possible that some of the things that we most deeply desire are not material goods, but higher-quality services. It's possible that rather than more cars, we want better cars; rather than larger homes, we want more attractive, convenient, and pleasing living environments; rather than more calories of food energy, we want more tastefully prepared, more convenient, or healthier foods; rather than more things to stuff into our houses, we want better child care, better health care, more inspiring entertainment, or greater understanding of ourselves and life's mysteries. It seems unlikely that one can categorically reject these possibilities and convincingly argue that now and forever only more material goods will serve our needs and desires.

Also, we must consider the other determinant of economic well-being: improving the productivity with which we use scarce resources. Such improvements in resource productivity have been identified as the source of the "wealth of nations" since at least Adam Smith's time. Designing better ways to produce the things we desire has been the primary source of economic progress. This has involved science, applied technology, management, knowledge, and improved labor skills. Importantly, all of these flow out of the services sector.

Increasingly, both what we want most from our economy and the inputs most capable of boosting the productivity of our economy originate in the services sector. It simply is not true that producing more bushels of wheat will contribute to our well-being more than improved health care. Nor is it true that the best way to produce more wheat is to commit more land, people, tractors, and gasoline to it. Agronomists, biologists, and management specialists are far more likely to make a contribution. It also is not true that mining and smelting more copper will contribute more to our economic well-being than a computer designer or a software engineer. Clear-cutting more trees will not contribute more to our well-being than the design of houses that are more efficient in their use of raw materials or a recycling program that keeps us from wasting most of the wood fiber we produce. There is nothing insubstantial or unproductive about services. They are what energize the productive side of our economy. Services are also what we increasingly want from the economy to make our lives more stimulating and satisfying.[6]

Data on the characteristics of service-producing jobs do not support the popular perception that service jobs are an inferior type of employment. Some of these jobs are undoubtedly "lousy," but that is also true of some goods-producing jobs. There are, of course, minimum-wage manufacturing and construction jobs as well as minimum-wage service jobs. Telling stories about particular jobs, such as the often-repeated reference to "burger flippers" does not get us very far, however. If we take a statistical look at goods and broad services or at manufacturing and narrow services, evidence supports the following characterizations of services jobs: (1) When we take into account the lower wages paid to women in both goods and services jobs and the predominance of women in service sectors, pay per hour in services-producing jobs is as high or higher than in goods production. (2) Whereas wages in services tend to match those in goods production, nonwage benefits, especially health insurance and retirement benefits, do not. In that sense, service jobs tend to be inferior. (3) Narrow-services jobs are much more likely to be found in the more skilled occupations (managerial, professional, technical) than are manufacturing jobs. (4) Narrow-services jobs are held by people with higher levels of education and that education is rewarded more than in manufacturing. (5) The rate of economic improvement with age for workers in narrow services is faster than it is in manufacturing. Services wages start lower, but then rise to or surpass the wages paid in manufacturing. (6) Job security is significantly greater in services-producing jobs. (7) Over the last two decades, while the real wages in goods production has been declining, real wages in narrow services have been increasing. (8) Services-producing jobs are more likely to be part-time jobs. For those seeking full-time work, services may involve underemployment. However, most part-time employment is voluntary, and these jobs help workers combine other goals with earning income.[7]

Overall, there is nothing inferior about services jobs when they are compared to goods production. For some specific characteristics, services jobs *are* inferior, but for other characteristics they are decidedly superior. It is important to realize that many manufacturing jobs now are minimum-wage jobs located in rural areas or, increasingly, jobs that are being shifted to Third World countries to be carried out in sweatshops or by child labor. Meanwhile, the range of service jobs paying relatively high incomes in medical, business, computer, and entertainment services continues to expand. The Microsoft empire that has contributed so much to the Puget Sound economy is, after all, an empire built around computer services.

The source of the popular suspicion that service production is inferior to goods production lies, I think, not in the actual economic characteristics of the two types of jobs, but in cultural prejudice. Our culture has always demeaned "women's work," while lending heroic dimensions to the jobs that men tend to do. Women's entry into what was historically the males' realm has not softened the suspicion that there is something insubstantial and demeaning about service jobs. Work with muscle and sweat that produces things is seen as superior to work based on the heart and mind that cares for people, which is what services are all about. As a result, relatively unskilled steel workers have always been paid more than well-educated teachers and nurses. It is not a technical economic relationship that explains this; it is cultural values. The economic stories we tell are important. They have real impacts.

Only Exports Matter:
Modern-Day Mercantilism and the Economic Base

One of our most widely shared economic stories has been taught to us since our first introduction to economic geography in elementary school. Most of us remember the maps in our social science books that associated regions with particular types of economic activity. On a map of the United States there would be an icon in the Pacific Northwest of Paul Bunyan and his blue ox; in Idaho and western Montana, a miner with a pickax over his shoulder; in Pittsburgh, a blast furnace; in Detroit, an automobile; in Iowa, corn; in Milwaukee, beer; in the Deep South, cotton. The economic lesson being taught by such maps (and the National Geographic Society still produces them) was that one could explain the geographic pattern of settlement by looking at the site-specific economic activities that drew people to certain areas and supported them there. That is, it was the geographically specialized economic activities that explained why people lived were they did.

The economic theory behind this view has come to be labeled the *economic base model*.[8] It argues that for people to inhabit any area, they need to have the money that allows them to purchase from the larger, external economy those things that they cannot easily produce themselves. To earn that income, they in turn must successfully market some exportable product. It is the income from their exports that allows them to pay for the imports that make life in that particular location viable.

In that sense, all economic activity is not of equal importance. Spending on locally oriented economic activities (for example, child care, restaurant services, grocery stores) depends on income that is earned in the export sectors. That export-oriented economic activity is the basic driving force in the local economy, it is primary economic activity, whereas the locally oriented activity is derivative or secondary. Export activity drives the rest of the economy in this model.

This familiar view of the local economy also has a not-very-subtle political message in it: Some economic actors are significantly more important than others. A particular subset of all economic activities either directly or indirectly "butters all of our bread." Those primary, usually export-oriented, economic activities need to be nurtured and supported because, without them, our communities would cease to be viable and would begin the downward drift toward being ghost towns.

A standard interpretation of the economic base model is that exports and the income they inject into the local economy are all that really matter. Those income injections enable all other economic activities, and the impact of those injections is amplified by a "multiplier" impact. But this is *not* the only or most appropriate interpretation of the economic base model. This interpretation ignores what it is that determines the multiplier impact. The multiplier is determined by the character and structure of the local economy. The more quickly the injected income leaks out of the local economy, the smaller the multiplier. The multiplier is inversely related to the fraction of local spending that goes to importing goods. The more self-sufficient a local economy is, the more often the injected income circulates within the local economy and the larger is the overall multiplier impact.

In that sense, the impact of any particular level of export earnings on the local economy is determined by the structure of the local economy and the range of locally produced goods and services available. It is not just export earnings that matter. The character of the local economy is crucially important too. The standard interpretation of the economic base model would dismiss a restaurant or recreational facility as derivative, or secondary, because it passively relies on export earnings to survive. The alternative interpretation is that such local economic activities absorb and hold dollars longer in the local economy, thus increasing the jobs and income that result. Locally oriented economic activity directly generates jobs too. In fact, it is the richness and diversity of those locally oriented sectors that determine the size of the multiplier.

An expansion in an already specialized export industry rarely can be labeled *economic development*. True economic development consists of spinning a complex web of locally oriented economic activities that make an area increasingly less dependent on imports and, as a result, less dependent on export earnings. In addition, successful import substitution activities often lead to new exports and the diversification of the economy.

Economic development does not consist of increased specialization in a few exports. That is a prescription for dependence and instability. Fluctuations in the national and international markets are imported into the local economy through the export industries. Commodity price cycles, general business cycles, and long-term declines tied to technological change all threaten an economy that specializes in the export of a few products. The instability that goes with such specialization explains the lack of prosperity in most of our mining, mill, or agricultural towns. Many of these specialized export centers have a run–down, decaying look to them. Because of the instability and uncertainly associated with the export markets, both individuals and business are hesitant to reinvest in these towns. As a result, despite high wage levels, these areas are anything but prosperous.

Only Money Matters?
Contrary Evidence from People Voting with Their Feet

The average level of local economic well-being is typically measured by looking at the average money income that residents receive. Because that income can be used to purchase those things that households need and want, average income might seem to be a reasonable approximation for economic welfare that has the advantage of being easily measured.

Between 1978 and 1988 *all* of the Pacific Northwest states (actually all of the western states) saw their average incomes decline relative to the national average. In Montana, Idaho, and Oregon, there were double–digit losses relative to the nation, and Washington almost made it into this category. One interesting aspect of these declining relative incomes is that the decline took place while the West was the fastest growing region in the nation in terms of population. In both the 1978--1988 and 1978--1996 periods, Montana, Idaho, Oregon, and Washington saw population growth rates that were more than twice the national average. Clearly, the type of rapid economic growth experienced by the region does not assure average income gains relative to the nation. Because average income is total income divided by population, high population growth that is not matched by income growth as high or higher can lead to declines in average income.

It is important to note that low relative incomes in states like Montana, Idaho, Utah, New Mexico, and Arizona did not discourage new residents from moving into these states during the 1990s. These states gained population at a rate almost three times the national average. Since 1978, their population has grown by 50 percent. States like Idaho, Montana, New Mexico, and Utah, whose average incomes were about 20 percent below the national average, had significant net immigration nonetheless. The ongoing attractiveness of these states despite low average incomes indicates that average income may not be a good measure of overall well-being in a particular location as judged by the residents themselves.

The coincidence of low and falling relative incomes and significant net immigration to the western states unavoidably raises the question of whether average income is a reliable measure of relative economic well-being. There has not been a positive correlation between states' relative average incomes and net immigration since at least the 1960s. That is, people "voting with their feet" have not indicated that the higher-income states offered higher levels of economic well-being. During the 1990-1998 period, there was a statistically significant negative relationship between a state's 1990 average income and net domestic immigration to the state.[9] Most of the states with above-average incomes in 1990 experienced a net loss of population during the 1990s, whereas most of the states with below-average incomes experienced net immigration. In fact, the top six states in average income and ten of the top twelve states experienced a net loss. In contrast, ten of the twelve lowest-income states experienced net immigration.

Many explanations can be offered for this phenomenon of people moving away from high-income states and into low-income states. The most plausible is that the differences in average incomes do not necessarily reflect differences in average well-being. It is possible that the differences in average incomes are compensating for differences in cost of living and quality of life among the states. Regional differences in birth, labor force participation, and leisure rates could also add considerable variation in average incomes.

These anomalies can be explained if one simply recognizes a basic fact about human preferences: People care where they live and act on their preferences for higher-quality living environments. People know that their well-being is determined by more than just their monetary incomes and the range of commercial opportunities available to them in a particular location. People are aware of the positive and negative, nonmarket characteristics associated with living in various locations. They know when the crime rate is high, air pollution is discomfiting or dangerous, a sense of community is nonexistent, congestion immobilizes them or consumes their time, and they cannot escape from the dense human-built urban environment for solitude, renewal, and recreation.

Because these things matter to people and because these qualities are not uniformly distributed across the nation, the character and quality of the living environment at various locations has a very real impact on the location of people and economic activity. The impact of these location preferences has been anything but trivial on our national and local economies. The pursuit of improved living environments has transformed the economic landscape of the nation during the last half century. Those amenity-driven changes include the shift from center city to suburb; the shift from the Frost Belt to the Sun Belt, including the rapid growth of California and the desert Southwest as economic centers; and the resettlement of many of our nonmetropolitan areas by refugees from our large urban areas.[10]

Given the clear residential preferences of the population and the tendency of economic activity to follow peoples' residential choices, environmental quality is no longer just an aesthetic concern to be pursued *if* a community feels prosperous enough to be able to afford it. Environmental quality instead becomes a central element of the area's economic base and a central determinant of local economic vitality. A community is unlikely to show very much vitality, economic or social, if no one really wants to live there. If the population in a particular area is just "putting in time" until they can afford to move away, investment will be depressed and economic infrastructure, both private and public, will be underdeveloped. The economy will be unstable. It will follow slavishly the fluctuations in some distant commodity markets and will import that volatility into the local community. The community will also be socially and culturally underdeveloped because it will tend to be populated by people who are hesitant to make a commitment to place. The community is also likely to contain a disproportionate number of transients or commuters. This combination of characteristics is unlikely to lay the basis for economic development. There may be waves of booms and busts with accompanying wide fluctuations in resident population, but a rooted community committed to place and steadily developing the increasingly sophisticated web of economic interdependencies that we call economic development is unlikely to evolve. What is missing is a reason, other than short-term income, for the population to commit to that location.

Commitment to place is important to economic development and, because of that, the qualities that lead to such commitments have economic importance in addition to whatever social, biological, or cultural importance they have. One important determinant of such a "sense of place" has always been the natural landscape. Another has been the quality of the social environment. Efforts to protect that landscape and enhance the social environment have to be looked at as integral to any economic development strategy. These are not simply social or aesthetic concerns. As communities organize themselves to assure continued economic vitality, concerns with the qualities that make an area an attractive place to live, work, and do business are not only legitimate, they are central.

The Environmental Model of the Local Economy: One Element of a New Story

If we step away from the economic stories discussed above, a very different picture of the source of economic vitality emerges. The story does not assume that the natural resource sectors or export-oriented goods production are the primary economic engines of the region. It does not assume that the region's commercial business are the only source of economic well-being. Other powerful economic forces can be seen. It is largely these alternative economic forces that have been transforming the region, while the historical economic base shrinks in absolute and relative importance.

If one begins with the fact that people care where they live and act on those preferences for higher-quality living environments, what I have labeled an *environmental* view of the economy emerges.[11] That label was chosen because it emphasizes that the location decisions of population can have a major impact on the location of economic activity. Changes in communication and transportation technologies and changes in the value-to-weight ratio of what we produce has made both the population and our businesses more footloose. The economic cost of acting on one's preferences for higher-quality living environments has been systematically declining. As a result, locally specific amenities have grown more important in determining the location of economic activity. This emphasis on peoples' location decisions contrasts with the more primitive versions of the economic base view, which claims it is the site-specific natural resources that industry can extract and process that directly and indirectly are responsible for almost all jobs and, therefore, the ongoing survival of the local economy.

The environmental view recognizes that people prefer high-quality living environments and satisfy those preferences by moving to different social and natural environments. This creates an available supply of labor at relatively low cost because of the relative excess supply of people trying to live in those particular areas. That labor supply attracts economic activity. In addition, those residential location decisions inject income into the local economy as individuals expend savings and make investments as they seek to make a living in those particular areas. Retirement incomes also follow the residential location decisions made by retirees. The net effect is an expansion of the local economy. Entrepreneurs seeking to remain in these areas will explore every opportunity to replace imported goods or to capture dollars that would otherwise flow out of the area by developing a more sophisticated array of locally available goods and services. Those businesses that are most successful at displacing imports and serving local needs may build on that success and begin exporting to the larger economy.

All of this allows the number of residents that the local economy can support to expand. This increases the "critical mass" of the economy and expands the range of goods and services that can be produced and marketed locally. The more sophisticated local economy reduces the isolation and the cost of inputs that might otherwise be barriers to the relocation of economic activity to the area. This allows ongoing cycles of expansion as long as the area remains a relatively attractive place to live, work, and do business.

Clearly this environmental economic story guides our vision and public policy in a different direction than do previous stories. The environmental view focuses on the economic forces that are actually transforming our economy, rather than focusing on the past. It explains the ongoing economic expansion with which our communities have had to grapple, rather than seeing our economies as declining because the historical economic base is in at least relative decline. In that sense, the environmental view guides our vision to one of the most important economic problems faced by the region: productively coping with rapid growth and change in ways that allows us to protect those things about our communities and landscapes that are most important to us. The fundamental point is that there is a broad range of economic forces afoot that is more than offsetting the jobs losses in extractive and heavy industrial activities. These positive, offsetting changes are largely invisible when the local economy is viewed through the widely shared set of cultural beliefs that make up the economic base perspective. As a result, we cannot see what is actually happening around us. A prerequisites for a more complete and useful view of our communities is that we avert our gaze from the rear-view mirror and abandon other elements of the popular folk economics that are embedded in our cultural beliefs.

Notes

[1] John Maynard Keynes, *The General Theory of Employment, Interest and Money*, (London: Macmillan, 1936), 383. Ironically, many conservatives came to believe that Keynes himself was one of these "academic scribblers" who haunted public economic policy in unproductive ways.

[2] The U.S. mining industry has made this claim directly with a study entitled "Everything Begins with Mining," which, as one might expect, points out that almost all of our lives and economic activities depend on material goods and energy, almost all of which are derived from mineral resources. George F. Leaming, *Mining and the American Economy: Everything Begins with Mining* (Washington, D.C.: National Mining Association, 1997).

[3] For a further discussion of the role of the physiocrats in the development of modern economics, see Mark Blaug, *Economic Theory in Retrospect*, 4th ed. (Cambridge, U.K.: Cambridge University Press, 1985), 24–28.

[4] The data for the preceding statements come from the U.S. Department of Commerce, Bureau of Economic Analysis, Regional Economic Information System, CD-ROM, 1969-1996.

[5] Edward F. Denison spent his career analyzing the empirical basis of the different rates of economic growth in different countries. These assertions about the importance of the "state of knowledge," new technology embodied in capital investment, and the quality of the labor force are based on his work. *Why Growth Rates Differ: Postwar Experiences in Nine Western Countries* (Washington, D.C.: Brookings Institution, 1967); *Trends in American Economic Growth: 1929-- 1982* (Washington, D.C.: Brookings Institution, 1985).

[6] The shift in employment from goods toward services, the creation of the "service economy," is partially a reflection of this.

[7] For the empirical basis of these assertions, see Thomas Michael Power, *Lost Landscapes and Failed Economies: The Search for a Value of Place* (Washington, D.C., Island Press, 1996), 65-78.

[8] The contemporary economic base model was promoted by one of the twentieth century's leading regional economists, Charles Tiebout, *The Community Economic Base Study* (New York: Committee for Economic Development, 1962). For a discussion of the drawbacks of using this popular model, see E. Niemi and T. M. Power, *The Economic Impact of River and Wetland Preservation and Rehabilitation: A Conceptual Manual* (Denver: U.S. Environmental Protection Agency, Region 8, 1998).

[9] Average income data is from the Bureau of Economic Analysis Regional Economic Information System; the immigration data is from the U.S. Bureau of the Census estimates of state populations and the demographic components of population change.

[10] For further development of and support for these assertions, see Thomas Michael Power, *Environmental Protection and Economic Well-Being: The Economic Pursuit of Quality* (Armonk, NY: M. E. Sharpe Publishers, 1996).

[11] For further development of the "environmental model" and contrasts of it with the economic base model, see Powers, *Lost Landscapes and Failed Economies.*

The Maturation of Science in the Pacific Northwest: From Nature Studies to Big Science

Keith R. Benson

❧

T
HIS CHAPTER'S TITLE does not simply refer to historical change over time, but to the dramatically different scientific landscapes that have characterized the legacy of science in Oregon and Washington. An excellent way to frame these differences is to contrast the ever-present, but strikingly different, federal presence supporting science in this part of the American West. In fact, the very first expenditure in support of basic or applied science in the United States was the early-nineteenth-century pursuit of information from the Pacific Northwest, then a part of the contested frontier of the new nation. President Thomas Jefferson's sent Meriwether Lewis and William Clark to the far-western reaches of the continent in a conscious decision to explore and catalogue what the West held. Following this adventure, Congress later appropriated funds to support the U.S. Exploring Expedition. One of its major aims was the exploration of Washington and Oregon, which was carried out during the late fall of 1841 and early winter of 1842. Today, the federal government still funds the pursuit of science in Oregon and Washington at a disproportionately large rate per capita compared to the rest of the country. But the landscape of this federal largesse has certainly changed in a dramatic and profound fashion and reflects the changes in the character of science in this region.

Obviously, federal support of science does not tell the whole story of the emergence, development, and maturation of science in the West. But framing this support between the Lewis and Clark expedition and today's funding from the National Institutes of Health (NIH), the National Science Foundation (NSF), and a host of other federal agencies creates a significant means to evaluate the historical transitions of science in the West. Most of the following observations are based on changes in the life sciences, an area representing my own expertise, but they also occasionally include developments in the physical sciences and technology. Additionally, I do not purport to provide a final assessment of science in the Northwest, rather my aim is to provide an overview the historical investigations that have been directed toward Oregon and Washington. Perhaps even more importantly, my intent is to point to the rich opportunities remaining for scholars to examine.

✦

George Basalla, in his now-classic work on the relationship between science in the American colonies and the scientific establishment in Europe, interpreted the three developmental stages of "colonial science."[1] Because Basalla's generalized notion of "colonial science" resonates so nicely with this region, I will use the same analytical structure, modified slightly by my own liberal interpretation, to examine the developments of science in the Northwest. Basalla claims the first stage to be the exploration phase in which the colonial power, in the case of the Pacific Northwest the U.S. government, sent expeditions to chart, explore, and evaluate the new colonial lands to the west. As part of this endeavor, Easterners traveled westward to collect specimens and to make observations of the natural world, both activities designed by the colonial power for its own use. Examples of this stage are the Lewis and Clark expedition at the beginning of the nineteenth century, the U.S. Exploring Expedition (also known as the Wilkes expedition) of the 1840s, and a host of railroad and boundary surveys in the 1850s. Remarkably, given the pronounced interest within the history of science community for American science, there has been scant historical attention to these expeditions.[2] Although the Lewis and Clark bicentennial is rapidly approaching, there still is no careful study of the scientific accomplishments of these two intrepid explorers. Even the recent best-seller by the American historian Stephen Ambrose hardly mentions the natural history accomplishments of the expedition.[3] Charles Wilkes's investigations in Puget Sound, southwestern Washington, and the Willamette Valley of Oregon are briefly discussed in *Magnificent Voyages* by Herman Viola and Carolyn Margolis, the catalogue prepared for the Smithsonian Institution's 1985 traveling exhibit about the U.S. Exploring Expedition. Also, William Stanton has described, in brief, aspects of the natural history of Wilkes's important voyage.[4] But given the pivotal role that the collections from the U.S. Exploring Expedition played in the formation of the natural history holdings at the new Smithsonian Institution (established in the nation's capitol in 1848), even this exploration deserves much more attention. Finally, the various surveys sponsored by the federal government have barely attracted any historical work, despite the riches held in the many volumes of results from the investigations. Even the 1899 Harriman expedition to Alaska, perhaps the final "colonial" episode to the

West, has scarcely been scrutinized by scholars. William Goetzmann and Kay Sloan have written a descriptive account of the summer voyage aboard E. H. Harriman's private yacht, on which Noachian Harriman took pairs of naturalists (two geologists, two ornithologists, etc.), but the journals of the trip remain largely unmined.[5]

In the second phase of Basalla's schema, the stage of local exploration, the new local residents, often migrants to the new country from the colonial power, collect specimens from or record observations about the natural world for use by professional scientists or scientific organizations situated physically outside the colony. In the case of Oregon and Washington, naturalists began to collect in earnest in the 1870s and 1880s, sending impressive samples of the native fauna and flora, including important paleontological forms, to the museums, scientific societies, and universities in the East, particularly those in Philadelphia, New York, and Boston. Doc Folsom, an alcoholic physician trained at Harvard who escaped his domestic responsibilities in Boston in exchange for the free life in northern Washington, was an early exemplar of Basalla's second stage. Folsom founded the Athenaeum in present-day Monroe, Washington, a natural history museum that collected and exchanged specimens with naturalists in the East. Nancy Rockafellar has completed an unpublished study of Folsom as part of her graduate training at the University of Washington.[6] The Oregon-based natural theologian cum geologist Thomas Condon is another example of a naturalist working during the exploitation phase. He has received a fair amount of historical attention from his biographer, Robert Clark, and from examinations of his geological work by Ellen Drake.[7] But much of his important natural history work, including his tantalizing speculations of the existence of a vast, inland sea covering most of Washington and Oregon (thus creating the isolated populations of flora and fauna in the process); his extensive relationships with eastern naturalists; and his fascinating role as one of the most important propagandists for evolutionary theory in the Northwest until 1900, remains unexplored.[8] The Seattle-based Young Naturalists' Society, an amateur natural history establishment loosely affiliated with the Territorial University of Washington (later the University of Washington), has received some scholarly attention, especially emphasizing its connection to and participation in the natural history exchange network.[9] It is interesting to note, in reference to Basalla's historical thesis, that most of the specimens collected by these naturalists were transported eastward, with very few specimens actually coming back to the Northwest from the more established natural history museums. P. Brooks Randolph, one of the young men who founded the naturalists' society in Seattle, was a local colonialist who literally sent carloads of material to eastern establishments. His manuscript collection is replete with letters asking for more and more of the unusual Northwest slug, a species that generated even more interest in Philadelphia. A colleague of Randolph was Trevor Kincaid, a young naturalist who eventually graduated from the University of Washington and then became the university's first zoologist. Despite Kincaid's central position in establishing a professional cadre of zoologists in Seattle, there is no reputable work done on him, either as a young naturalist (he had an international reputation for collecting insects as a teenager) nor as one of the first professional scientists in the region.[10]

In Basalla's third phase, the internalization stage, professional scientific organizations are formed and, consequently, the scientific work becomes indigenous. In the Pacific Northwest, this type of scientific work was not usually undertaken within educational institutions, but within natural history establishments that eventually merged with local colleges and universities. For example, Thomas Condon and his student Orson Bennet Johnson organized the Oregon School and College Association of Natural History, which was originally located at Forest Grove (Pacific University). When Condon moved to Eugene, this collection became the basis of the natural history museum at the University of Oregon. It also inspired a similar organization at Oregon Agricultural College (later Oregon State University) in Corvallis, which was eventually named the Horner Museum of Natural History.[11] A preliminary, unpublished study of the Horner Museum was completed by Rick Reed, while very little is known about Condon's earlier Oregon natural history organization. In 1882, when Johnson moved to the Territorial University of Washington (which became the University of Washington when statehood was conferred in 1889), he brought with him part of his personal collection from the Oregon museum, reorganized the natural history collection of the Young Naturalists' Society, and eventually helped to transfer the entire collection to the university in 1895. At the beginning of the twentieth century, the large collection served as the foundation of the Washington State Museum on the new Montlake campus, which was named the Thomas Burke Memorial Washington State Museum in 1958.[12]

Given the early development and largely independent status of many of the museums in the Northwest, it is not surprising that other ancillary science laboratories and field stations also emerged outside of colleges and universities. Jay Taylor's provocative study of the development of fisheries management in Oregon underscores the role of the federal and state fish commissions in attempting (and failing) to understand the enigmatic anadromous salmon fishery through the financial support of fish hatcheries and research laboratories.[13] Later, much of the work at these sites was transferred to either Oregon Agricultural College or the University of Washington, when both institutions formed schools or colleges of fisheries in the early twentieth century. But there is little information about the development of fisheries science from governmentally supported laboratories to university-based research centers, save Matt Klingle's study of Lauren Donaldson's Fern Lake project at the University of Washington.[14] The university's fisheries program did produce a historical overview of its first seventy-five years' work in Seattle, but it is mainly hagiographical, with little real historical analysis.[15]

As part of the national Hatch Act (1887), two of the country's original fifty-six agricultural field stations were located in Oregon and Washington, one each at the state's agricultural colleges (in Pullman and Corvallis). Barbara Kimmelman has detailed some of the work at the station in Washington, especially its genetics research on wheat, inspired by the rediscovery of Gregor Mendel's paper on hybridization in 1900.[16] But there has been scant investigation of the role these stations may have played in the development of the horticultural sciences in the Northwest, especially relating to the commercial production of fruit, wheat, grass seed, corn, and sugar beets. A striking example of the importance of this work is a popular poster for sale in the ubiquitous "Oregon shops" illustrating the extensive hybridization lineage of the various commercial berry plants. But what was the science behind this lineage that was pioneered early in the twentieth century and may have been related to Mendel's horticultural notions?

Finally, the history of marine laboratories, a subject of deep personal interest, provides another example of the internalization phase.[17] Friday Harbor Laboratories began as a cooperative summer marine station in the San Juan Islands in 1904 (originally as the Marine Station and then the Puget Sound Biological Station). The main goal of the facility's organizers was to establish an educational center for secondary school teachers and beginning undergraduates, thus providing a new educational opportunity not previously available in Oregon or Washington.[18] Two other stations with close ties to the Northwest were built on the southern tip of Vancouver Island, the University of Oregon established one on the central Oregon coast, and a laboratory was later constructed at Newport. But little is known about these stations, their relationship to one another, and their role in the development of science in Oregon and Washington.

Despite the successful formation of an infrastructure for science in the Northwest by the early twentieth century, sophisticated scientific work represented the exception not the rule until after World War II. And most of this sophisticated work was in some way related to national interests, funded from federal sources or from philanthropic sources vetted through national organizations. The boom and bust cycles of the important salmon fishery along the Northwest coastline received increasing attention by the various fish commissions that were charged with regulating and controlling the fishery. Schools and/or colleges of forestry were also founded in the early twentieth century to address another extractive industry, the forest products industry. Finally, by the late 1930s, the federal government promised massive amounts of funding to tap the potential energy sources of the states' rivers, most importantly the mighty Columbia River. Richard White's wonderful essay, *The Organic Machine,* provides an interpretive framework for the history of how much of the funding created a new river, one controlled, regulated, and defined by the ingenuity of engineers working for the U.S. Army Corps of Engineers and the Bonneville Power Administration.[19] But the new power sources were not tapped just to provide local residents and new industries with large supplies of inexpensive energy. As is clear from several essays in Bruce Hevly's and John Findlay's recent book, *The Atomic West,* the new source of power was also needed to produce the powerful atomic bombs that were being prepared at the Hanford Site as part of the Manhattan Project.[20] Obviously, much of this work can be described as narrowly applied research and most of it did not directly involve the academic community (for example, most early fish managers and foresters had backgrounds in those industries, not academic backgrounds). But despite its actual focus or character, the role of the federal government in the development of science between World War I and World War II was extremely important and it has not received the share of historical attention it deserves.[21]

Just before the outbreak of World War II, colleges and universities in the Northwest tried to emulate and duplicate the reforms in higher education that had swept through similar institutions along the eastern seaboard and in the Midwest. The changes called for full incorporation of the sciences within the college curricula to balance the course offerings in the humanities. As a classic example of these reforms, the natural history curriculum centered originally around a museum collection had all but disappeared by the end of World War I. In its place were either new departments in biology or separate departments in zoology and botany. In 1899, for example, the University of Washington hired Trevor Kincaid as its first zoologist, and his position included chairing the one-person Department of Zoology. When T. C. Frye came to Seattle from the University of Chicago four years later, the institution's first Department of Botany was founded. Similar changes occurred slightly later at the University of Oregon, at the two agricultural schools, and at most of the private colleges in the region. To be sure, the early offerings in the sciences remained a secondary focus in comparison to the humanities.

The Northwest did not just attract national attention because of its extractive potential, the natural fauna and flora created national settings for the new life sciences that emerged in the twentieth century. In 1906, the Marine Station in the San Juan Islands offered the nation's first course in marine ecology, taught by the noted ecologist from the University of Chicago, Henry Chandler Cowles. From that year to the present, ecological studies have been an integral part of the zoology and botany programs at the University of Washington. When the University of Oregon began its marine station at Charleston, Oregon in the late 1930s, a similar orientation was stressed. Marine ecology was accompanied by important studies in embryology and invertebrate zoology, the two staples of American biology between 1900 and 1940.[22]

But the real change and the most dramatic transition that occurred in the sciences in the Northwest was the result of post–World War II developments in the funding of science. In general terms, the only science that was funded by the federal government prior to the war was science associated with the forests, rivers, and fields, and the actual scientific content of this application was negligible. After all, research within the fisheries and forestry communities lacked any full-scale incorporation of important ecological principles until late in the twentieth century. Philanthropic organizations often served as important sources for funding the research as both the Carnegie Institute and the Rockefeller Foundation provided critical funds for the initiation of new scientific endeavors in the 1920s and 1930s. One example of this support was the region's first oceanographic program, the Oceanographic Laboratories of the University of Washington, funded completely in 1930 by a generous grant from Rockefeller's General Education Board.[23] But both federal and private sources of funding were limited and contingent; in addition, both sources became very critical of the parochial and poorly developed nature of science on the western fringes of North America in the 1930s, a criticism that was not, in general terms, unfounded.

World War II changed this character. Massive amounts of federal funding for research about and production of war material created a large scientific and technological infrastructure in the Northwest, especially in the Puget Sound Basin and along the banks of the Columbia River.[24] Because much of this production depended on a mutualistic relationship between industry and the academy, government bureaucrats and politicians considered how to manage the necessary but unprecedented transition from a wartime effort in science and technology to peacetime efforts. From these considerations, the Truman administration, following the recommendations of Vannevar Bush, began to funnel federal appropriations through the existing but largely underfunded NIH, the new research arm of the U.S. Navy (the Office of Naval Research, ONR), and the brand new NSF. In addition, the Atomic Energy Commission (AEC) took over the peacetime activities from the Manhattan Project, the most expensive scientific research project undertaken by the federal government until the second half of the twentieth century. Much money became available to the Northwest through the clever and calculating efforts of the region's congressional leaders. A large share of this money eventually found its way into the region's colleges and universities. Often the arguments for additional federal funds were made from the perspective of preparing colleges and universities to train the large number of returning soldiers (the GI Bill, for example, was pivotal in this transition). But the actual arguments were based on the recognition of the region's needs in science.

A major factor behind the impressive development of Northwest science following the war was the indefatigable efforts of Warren Magnuson, a longtime Washington politician who eventually became the state's senior senator. (Magnuson first served in the House of Representatives and became a senator in 1944.) It was through his efforts that the University of Washington was able to receive a large federal appropriation to build the Northwest's second medical school in 1947, which quickly dominated medicine in the entire Northwest.[25] For the sixty previous years, Oregon had the only medical schools in the Northwest, the University of Oregon's school in Portland and the Medical School of Willamette University. Both were small, proprietary in nature, and poorly equipped and neither fared well in the aftermath of the important Flexner Report of 1910. Following the reforms suggested by the report, physicians and politicians in Oregon forced a merger between the two schools in 1913, consolidating both in Portland, while they also managed to block any creation of a medical school in the state of Washington for several decades.[26] However, the tremendous population growth in the Puget Sound area during the war and the increasingly apparent shortage of physicians in Washington led Magnuson to address the problem. His success with the medical school marked the first of his efforts to secure what soon became large amounts of federal funding for the development of science in his state. Joining efforts with Dixie Lee Ray, a young zoology professor at the University of Washington who worked on research projects for the Navy and then became associated with the well-funded AEC in the 1950s (she would later serve as the governor for one term), Magnuson was able to obtain new funding to add impressively to the university's Friday Harbor Laboratories, enhance the Applied Physics Laboratory for military research on the university's Seattle campus, expand the oceanography program in Seattle with funds from ONR, and provide more funding for the fisheries program along the Montlake Cut, a program that soon expanded in scope beyond the Puget Sound Basin to include the entire North Pacific, especially the Gulf of Alaska with its invaluable fishery.

For reasons that have not been examined in full detail, Oregon's congressional delegation was not as successful in obtaining federal dollars to support academic science as Magnuson was immediately following the war.[27] In fact, it was not until the 1990s, especially during Senator Mark Hatfield's last term, that Oregon benefited from the same level of federal largesse for science as Magnuson and Senator Henry Jackson provided for the state of Washington. Not surprisingly, the University of Washington soon emerged as the leading public university in the nation for acquiring federal research grants, exceeding $600 million per year in 1999. Despite the difference in the level of support from federal funds, Oregon did attract high growth technology firms, starting with Tektronix in the 1960s, Hewlett-Packard in the 1970s, and then Intel in the 1990s, all of which emphasized the importance of industrial connections to the local scientific and academic communities. To the north, Microsoft emerged as a new firm in the exciting area of microcomputing, soon becoming the world's most dominant company. Also, biotechnology found a home in Seattle, beginning with GeneticSystems in the early 1980s, but soon expanding to many firms with many genetically euphonious names. Consequently, many spheres of academic science and technology soon became more concerned with technology transfer, facilitating the development of venture-dependent research programs and patent rights, than with supporting the time-honored tradition of the academy, the basic sciences.

More importantly, these new developments may be leading to another transition in the scientific traditions in Oregon and Washington, away from the region's long-standing tie to the local environment, namely salmon, timber, and agriculture (all of which also mirrored the national interest in the region, of course), and toward "big science." The most dramatic example of this new trend is the gradual but inexorable shift within much of the science in the Northwest from individuals studying the natural world in its natural setting to large research groups slicing, dicing, and macerating nature in the laboratory. This change is exemplified by the support and growth of academic research associated with biomedical technology versus the support of the basic biological sciences. At the University of Washington, the amount of research effort and space in the former is measured in the hundreds of thousands—in square footage of research space and research dollars; in the latter, these same parameters are measured in the low double digits. Of course, this mirrors national priorities: The medical research budget of NIH exceeded $14 billion, while the budget for all the other basic sciences in the NSF barely topped $4 billion at the end of the twentieth century.

In closing, I would like to emphasize some of the wonderful opportunities for historical investigations of science in the Northwest. On a very broad level, little is known of the dynamic interactions in the Northwest between applied science and basic science, an extremely important relationship to understand because so much of the federal and state support of science in the region has been for specific purposes ranging from nuclear energy to agriculture. Furthermore, the region's valuable natural resources, especially in the fisheries and the forests, have escaped careful historical scrutiny. Some work has been done in this general arena, for example, the study that Chris Young conducted on the Forest Service in the American Southwest. He illustrated the influence of ideas pioneered in game management during the 1920s and 1930s on developments in animal ecology, an influence that has escaped the attention of many historians of ecology.[28] One might ask if there were similar influences from those involved in assisting the loggers and fishers. Finally, it would be helpful to find scholars who are interested in the study of recent history and who would direct attention to the reciprocal relationship between technology and academic science, not just to the interface between engineering and science. One intriguing example is the recruitment of Leroy Hood to the University of Washington to found a new and completely unprecedented Department of Molecular Biotechnology, funded entirely at the outset by money donated to the University by Bill Gates, the mogul from Microsoft. Shortly after Hood accepted the appointment, the local newspapers reported a new biotechnology firm founded by Gates and Hood. With the announcement in 1999 that Professor Hood has left the university to found a new research laboratory, independent from any direct academic affiliation, it appears that the transition to a new science in the Northwest has now been completed. Indeed, it seems to have come full circle, beginning outside the academy and, once again, locating itself away from the halls of academe.

Notes

1 George Basalla, "The Spread of Western Science," *Science* 156 (1967): 611-22. Admittedly, Basalla developed his thesis in reference to the more classic definition of colonial expansion than I have used. Nevertheless, he has suggested that his model of the expansion of science from the colonial power to colony might be applicable to the development of science in the United States, where the East Coast was much more developed scientifically than the West Coast (p. 612). In a recent conversation, he also expressed interest in seeing the application of his model within the United States (personal communication, 23 February 1999). In retrospect, I have attempted to do just this with the present paper.

2 The History of Science Society sponsored the formation of a new interest group, The Forum for the History of American Science, in 1984. However, most of the attention among these historians has been to the most exciting and dramatic aspects of American twentieth-century science, especially physics and genetics, areas in which Americans made many pioneering discoveries. Less attention has been directed to the natural history tradition of the first half of the nineteenth

century. Indeed, natural history is often derisively characterized as the epitome of amateur science or the type of science that needed to make room for the real developments of the modern phase of American science. Notable exceptions to this bias are the recent works of John C. Greene, *Science in the Age of Jefferson* (Ames: Iowa State University Press, 1984) and Robert V. Bruce, *The Launching of Modern American Science, 1846-1876* (Ithaca, N.Y.: Cornell University Press, 1987). But even these works pay less attention to science on the western frontier.

[3] Stephen Ambrose, *Undaunted Courage: Meriwether Lewis, Thomas Jefferson, and the Opening of the American West* (New York: Simon and Schuster, 1997).

[4] Herman J. Viola and Carolyn Margolis, eds., *Magnificent Voyagers: The U.S. Exploring Expedition, 1838-42* (Washington, D.C.: Smithsonian Institution Press, 1985); William Stanton, *The Great United States Exploring Expedition of 1838-1842* (Berkeley: University of California Press, 1975).

[5] William H. Goetzmann and Kay Sloan, *Looking Far North: The Harriman Expedition to Alaska, 1899* (New York: Viking Press, 1982).

[6] Nancy Rockafellar, "Progress, Pleasure, and Science in the Intellectual Wilderness: Dr. Albert Chase Folsom in Snohomish City, W.T., 1872-1885," (unpublished paper, Department of History, University of Washington, 1985).

[7] Robert D. Clark, *The Odyssey of Thomas Condon: Irish Immigrant, Frontier Missionary, Oregon Geologist* (Portland: Oregon Historical Society Press, 1989); Ellen T. Drake, "Horse Genealogy: The Oregon Connection," *Geology* 6 (1978): 587-91 and idem., "Pioneer Geologist Thomas Condon of Oregon: Scientist, Teacher, Preacher," in *Frontiers of Geological Exploration of Western North America,* ed. A. E. Leviton et al. (San Francisco: American Association for the Advancement of Science, 1982), 71-78.

[8] Keith R. Benson, "The Selection and Adaptation of Darwin's Evolution Theory in the American Northwest, 1870-1910," (unpublished paper, 1996).

[9] Keith R. Benson, "The Young Naturalists' Society and Natural History in the Northwest," *American Zoologist* 26 (1985): 351-61 and idem., "The Young Naturalists' Society: From Chess to Natural History Collections," *Pacific Northwest Quarterly* 77 (1986): 82-93.

[10] The only work on Kincaid is Muriel L. Guberlet, *The Windows to His World: The Story of Trevor Kincaid* (Palo Alto, California: Pacific Books, 1975), but this book is not a critical historical appraisal of his career.

[11] Rick Reed, "The Horner Museum," (master's thesis, Oregon State University).

[12] Leonard Ziontz, "The State Museum Comes of Age," *Landmarks* 4 (1985): 32-36.

[13] Joseph Taylor III, "Making Salmon: The Political Economy of Fishery Science and the Road Not Taken," *Journal of the History of Biology* 31 (1998): 33-59. This article is a publication from Taylor's "Making Salmon: Economy, Culture, and Science in the Oregon Fisheries, Precontact to 1960," (Ph.D. diss., University of Washington, 1998). It appeared in book form as *Making Salmon: An Environmental History of the Northwest Fisheries Crisis* (Seattle: University of Washington Press, 1999).

[14] Matthew Klingle, "Plying Atomic Waters: Lauren Donaldson and the 'Fern Lake Concept' of Fisheries Management," *Journal of the History of Biology* 31 (1998): 1-32.

[15] University of Washington School of Fisheries, *Commemorative: 75th Anniversary, School of Fisheries, 1919-1994, University of Washington* (Seattle: School of Fisheries, University of Washington, 1994).

[16] Barbara Kimmelman, "A Progressive Era Discipline: Genetics and American Agricultural Colleges and Experimental Stations, 1890-1920," (Ph.D. diss.,

University of Pennsylvania, 1987). To my knowledge, Kimmelman was the first historian to point out the importance of the genetics research on wheat at the Pullman station, but much more work needs to be done even on this important research center.

[17] Keith R. Benson, "The Marine Sciences along America's Western Frontier: Early Development in Marine Biology and Oceanography," in *The Pacific and Beyond: Proceedings of the Fifth International History of Oceanography Meeting,* ed. K. R. Benson and P. F. Rehbock (Seattle: University of Washington Press, 2000).

[18] Ibid. An institutional history of the University of Washington's Friday Harbor Laboratories, by Keith R. Benson, will appear before the celebration of the one hundredth anniversary of the laboratory in 2004.

[19] Richard White, *The Organic Machine* (New York: Hill and Wang, 1995).

[20] Bruce Hevly and John Findlay, eds., *The Atomic West* (Seattle: University of Washington Press, 1998).

[21] This is a point repeatedly stressed by my colleague, Professor Bruce Hevly. For example, we know very little about the science associated with the work at Hanford during the war. Perhaps it is even more striking, because Hanford was a classified government project, that we know essentially nothing about the science associated with the geological, botanical, and zoological surveys of the Columbia River prior to the building of the Grand Coulee Dam. Hevly also emphasizes how important the Naval Torpedo Station at Keyport was in the development of research into the physics of water, especially underwater acoustics, a research subject that became the focal point of the Applied Physics Laboratory (APL) when it was created on the University of Washington's campus (1943). Although there is now a museum at the Keyport facility, the Naval Undersea Museum, there has been essentially no historical investigation of the torpedo station or its relationship to the APL.

[22] Benson, "The Marine Sciences along America's Western Frontier."

[23] Richard Strickland, "Thomas G. Thompson and the Founding of the University of Washington Oceanographic Laboratories," (unpublished paper, University of Washington, 1981); James Day, "Institution Building: The University of Washington Oceanographic Laboratories, from 1929-1939, in the Context of American Marine Science," (unpublished undergraduate thesis, Program in the History of Science, Technology, and Medicine, University of Washington, 1988); Victor B. Scheffer and Richard M. Strickland, "The Origin of the Northwest's First School of Marine Science," *Columbia: The Magazine of Northwest History* 11 (1997): 20-25.

[24] Richard Kirkendall has emphasized the importance of the U.S. military decision to have Boeing build bombers in Seattle, followed by Boeing's decision after World War II to emphasize the production of commercial aircraft. See Richard S. Kirkendall, "The Boeing Company and the Military-Metropolitan-Industrial Complex, 1945-1953," *Pacific Northwest Quarterly* 85 (1994): 137-49. This article offers an important background for additional studies that should examine the developing "military-industrial-university" connection (with apologies to Professor Kirkendall) in the Puget Sound region.

[25] Shelby Scates, *Warren G. Magnuson and the Shaping of Twentieth-Century America* (Seattle: University of Washington Press, 1997). Scates, a former Seattle-area newspaper reporter, has written the most current biography of Magnuson. It includes some information about Magnuson's influential role in the development of science in the state of Washington, emphasizing his early connections with the U.S. Navy, but it also leaves much territory unexplored. For example, Magnuson was instrumental in establishing the unique arrangement the state of Washington

forged, through its medical school in Seattle, with the states of Alaska, Montana, and Idaho (and now Wyoming) to train the physicians for those states in the WAMI program. This clever scheme helped to ensure the support of no less than four (and now five) congressional delegations for federal funds dedicated to medical research and training in Seattle.

[26] Steve Ingle has written the best treatment of the early history of the medical school in Seattle, but his work is unpublished. See Steven Ingle, "From Rough Seas to the Shores of Lake Washington: The Struggle for a Medical School in Seattle," unpublished undergraduate thesis, Program in the History of Science, Technology, and Medicine, University of Washington, 1997.

[27] Scates, *Magnuson;* Robert G. Kaufman, *Henry M. Jackson: A Life in Politics* (Seattle: University of Washington Press, 2000).

[28] Christian C. Young, "Defining the Range: The Development of Carrying Capacity in Management Practice," *Journal of the History of Biology* 31 (1998): 61-83.

Northwest Climate and Culture: Damp Myths and Dry Truths

David Laskin

⇥

R AIN IS THE MASCOT AND THE SYMBOL of the Pacific Northwest. The butt of countless jokes, the target of all manner of curses and complaints, the inspiration of shimmering poems, and the trigger of black seasonal depression. *Rains all the time* is practically the region's motto, one of those tossed-off phrases that has taken on a life and a mossy, mythological patina of its own. No matter what and how much actually falls from our fabled skies, no matter how piddling Seattle's or Portland's rain buckets may look at the end of the year next to New York's or Miami's, no matter that much of the territory east of the Cascades is starved for rain. No matter. The region has been stuck for at least two centuries now with a rainy reputation that has been impossible to shake (and unnecessary too in the minds of some). In this chapter, I explore the origin of the damp myth, consider its persistence in both regional lore and literature, and present a few reasons why it has become so intimately and inextricably bound up with our regional identity.

The Invention of a Climate

Let's begin with a bit of hard data. The fact is, as Northwest boosters and apologists have been pointing out tirelessly for 150 years now, once you disregard ridiculously wet places like Astoria and Quinault, western Washington and Oregon are far drier in terms of average annual rainfall than New England, the middle Atlantic states, most of the Midwest, and almost all of the Southeast. But even more significant in the region's climatic profile than total *amount* of rain is the distribution of moisture throughout the year. The maritime Pacific Northwest has the greatest fluctuation between the wetness of the rainy season and the dryness of the nonrainy season of any region in the country. Nearly half of Seattle and Portland's total annual rain comes down in just three months: November, December, and January. Tack on October and February and you get a five-month rainy season that accounts for about 65 percent of the yearly rainfall. From June until September, in most years anyway, it's positively Mediterranean: a total of 5.0 inches of rainfall in Portland for those four months. In California, the rainy season is even more pronounced: San Francisco receives nearly 85 percent of its 20.4 inches of annual rainfall from November to March. Here on the West Coast we speak of "The Rains," a grandiose plural you never hear in the evenly moist Northeast or Midwest. In fact, in the minds of our fellow citizens who get their rain in fairly steady monthly allotments, the whole concept of a rainy season alternating with a dry season is weird, faintly suspect, and downright un-American.

This rainy season business gives people pause, shakes them up, raises red flags. You tend to forget what dry *feels* like round about January, but let's talk again in August when our lawns are brown and our cars crusted with imperishable dust. Droughts lasting thirty or more consecutive days are common in Northwest summers. In 1967, Portland had seventy-one dry days in a row and Seattle had seventy, with rainfall for July and August *combined* measuring 0.03 inch. So it doesn't really rain all that much, and for long stretches of the year it doesn't rain at all. But what burnishes the myth is that once The Rains arrives in late autumn, it rains some, usually just a little but enough to count, on lots and lots of days. Seattle and Portland have less rainfall, but more rainy days than New York City or Washington, D.C.: 150 wet days a year compared with 128 in New York and 127 in Washington. Mist, drizzle, light rain, sprinkles, liquid sunshine, heavy dew, sky weep, celestial threads: call it what you will, it happens a lot out here, enough to make folks from other places sit up and take notice. Our fabled rain, although unimpressive in volume, is capricious, fickle, full of dodges and whims. I've watched cloudbursts literally materialize out of the clear blue on a windy October afternoon and dissipate by sundown. Some of our so-called rainstorms dwindle down to mist before they've properly gotten started and others blur together so you don't know when one system has pushed through and the next one is arriving. I've seen rain over Puget Sound that seems to liquefy out of the air rather than fall from the sky, rain that eats away clouds before your eyes like a celestial backspace key, rain that looks as fat as honey and as fine as rice. Wake to a canopy of stars on a winter night, crawl back into bed convinced the next day will be sunny, rise before first light to slick pavements and weeping gray. In compensation for the recurrent moisture, we get rainbows and double rainbows and solar and lunar haloes that turn our skies into prisms. We have all of this and more out here. It's perverse. It's persistent. It hangs in.

There are enough peculiarities in our climate to foster myth and misapprehension. And circumstance, luck, and sheer human gullibility have conspired to seal this myth in place. As I discovered in reviewing the early accounts of Pacific Northwest weather, the dripping image goes all the way back to the mists of recorded history. A run of exceptionally bum weather besieged nearly every European expedition that headed this way from the mid-sixteenth century through Lewis and Clark. The Spanish mariner Bartoleme Ferrelo appears to have been the first. He got as far north as southern Oregon in February 1543 before incessant rain forced him back to California. That was enough to dampen Spanish curiosity for sixty years. Then in June 1579 came the famous exploration-cum-privateering expedition of Francis Drake, who had not yet been knighted by his queen. It was an ill-starred voyage from the start, but never more miserable than when Drake reached the California-Oregon border, where the weather turned suddenly and viciously inclement. Francis Fletcher, the ship's chaplain and the author of *The World Encompassed by Sir Francis Drake,* published in 1628 and still considered the most complete and reliable record of the voyage, gave this account of the freakish weather: On June 3, 1579 "we came into 42. deg. of North latitude, where in the night following, we found such alteration of heate, into extreame and nipping cold, that our men in generall did grievously complaine thereof, some of them feeling their healths much impaired thereby." To "the great admiration" of the entire ship's company, the next day was no warmer than the miserable night had been: "The pinching and biting aire, was nothing altered; the very roapes of our ship were stiffe, and the raine which fell, was an unnatural congealed and frozen substance, so that we seemed rather to be in the frozen Zone."

Drake buoyed up the crew's spirits as best he could with "comfortable speeches" and "other good and profitable perswasions," but to no avail. The farther north they sailed, "the more extremitie of cold did sease upon [them]," and a stiff north wind "directly bent against [them]," making progress all but impossible. Even at anchor there was no respite from the "many extreme gusts and flawes that beate upon [them]." The rare calms brought little relief, for the instant the wind ceased "there followed the most vile, thicke, and stinking fogges, against which the sea prevailed nothing, till the gusts of wind againe removed them, which brought with them such extremeity and violence when they came, that there was no dealing or resisting against them." Fletcher reported with British phlegm that in the face of such weather "a sudden and great discouragement seased upon the mindes of our men, and they were possessed with a great mislike" for the land that Drake had christened New Albion. Nonetheless, the *Golden Hinde* inched northward, possibly getting as far north as 48 degrees latitude, or just about to the border between Washington and Canada, before Drake finally gave up any hope of discovering the Northwest Passage and returned to the vicinity of present-day San Francisco. (Historians are still debating Drake's West Coast itinerary, especially the question of how far north he went and where in California he anchored.)

Fogs, even "vile, thicke, and stinking fogges," are not uncommon off the northern California and southern Oregon coasts in early June, but how do we account for the "extreame and nipping cold" that congealed water onto the ship's ropes and froze the crew's meat before they could eat it? Historians are still scratching their heads over that one.

Fletcher's history of Drake's voyage stood as the primary document of Northwest weather for two centuries. The image of the Pacific Northwest as an uninhabitable blot—remote, freezing, wet, stormy, ugly, barren— lodged itself in the English imagination. "In this place was no abiding for us," concluded Fletcher as the *Golden Hinde* retreated southward, and his countrymen saw no reason to question this. For the seventeenth and most of the eighteenth century, the region was viewed primarily as an enigmatic obstacle, a mountainous mass of green and white that stubbornly obscured the coveted Northwest Passage. The few exploring parties that did come this way sailed out of Mexico under Spanish colors. But because the Spanish preferred to keep records of their explorations to themselves, "their discoveries, as far as the rest of Europe was concerned, were scarcely discoveries at all," as historian Carlos A. Schwantes put it.

It wasn't until England's heroic circumnavigator James Cook made his third voyage around the globe starting in 1776 that we get another good account of climatic conditions in the Pacific Northwest. Again, meteorological misery prevailed. Cook named Oregon's Cape Foulweather during what he termed a "succession of adverse winds and boisterous weather" in March 1776, and the "thick and hazy conditions" may explain why Cook sailed right by the mouth of the Columbia River. (Weather, however, cannot be held responsible for Cook's famous failure to detect the opening to the Strait of Juan de Fuca, for he recorded in his journal that conditions turned fair on March 21. It was the worst navigational blunder of his distinguished career.)

If any embers of hope remained alive to rekindle the meteorological reputation of the Pacific Northwest, they were surely doused by the journals that Meriwether Lewis and William Clark kept during the winter they spent on the coast of Oregon. It's a kind of epic of rain that opens in November 1805 with muffled soggy complaints and concludes nearly six months later in mildewed, flea-bitten disgust. "Cloudy rainey disagreeable morning," Clark wrote on November 1 as their boats tossed westward down the Columbia. "Rained all the after part of last night," he wrote on November 5 as they camped near the mouth of the river, "rain continued this morning, I slept but verry little last night. . . . The day proved cloudy with rain the greater part of it, we are all wet cold and disagreeable." The word "disagreeable" begins to crop up with increasing frequency from here on, a polite euphemism covering a bottomless well of sodden gloom. So, on November 15: "from the 5th [of November] in the morng. until the 16th is *eleven* days rain, and the most disagreeable time I have experienced confined on a tempiest coast wet." Eventually Clark ceased to detail the duration or severity of the rainstorms and merely jotted down in his journal: "The rain &c." and "rained last night as usial." By winter's end, Clark made a weather tally and calculated that they'd had only twelve days without rain and only six days with sunshine (sunshine, he sniffed, is a relative term, for even "when the sun is said to shine or the weather fair[,] it is to be understood that it barely casts a shadow, and that the atmosphere is haizy of a milkey white colour.") Surely, this winter of 1805-1806 must rank with the wettest, vilest, most utterly disagreeable Northwest rainy seasons of all time.

A curious thing happened in Northwest weather history following the Lewis and Clark nadir: the emergence of what I'd like to call the antimyth. Literally out of thin air a new conception of our weather materialized and began to circulate. In place of soggy and disagreeable came words like *benign, healthful, cleansing,* and *invigorating.* Instead of leaden, dripping skies one hears of mild, snowless winters and gentle spring rains. Of course, there was a hidden political agenda behind the antimyth: Manifest Destiny. Recall that the Oregon Territory, which in those days encompassed the entire Pacific Northwest, had fallen into political limbo after the end of the War of 1812. Britain and America, in negotiating the Treaty of Ghent that ended the war in 1818, were unable to determine which side had a better claim to the region, so they agreed to leave it "free and open" country under their joint jurisdiction—sort of a demilitarized no-man's land. But as the nineteenth century wore on, American patriots began looking at Oregon with a fierce gleam in their eyes. The upper left-hand corner *must* belong to us and the best way to make this happen, they reasoned, was to see that many of us settled there and called it home. And the best way to make *that* happen was to convince unsuspecting pioneers that Oregon was heaven on earth.

The ringleader of this Oregon-as-paradise movement was a semi-addled New England schoolmaster named Hall Jackson Kelley. For mysterious reasons of his own, Kelley, after reading Lewis and Clark's journals in 1817, devoted his life to boosting Oregon and convincing his fellow citizens to relocate there. Before he ever set foot on Oregon soil, breathed a lungful of its air, or felt a drop of its rain, Kelley rhapsodized thus about the region's weather in a tract entitled *A Geographical Sketch of that Part of North America Called Oregon* (published in Boston in 1830), a marvel of invention, fantasy, and wishful thinking—the kind of prose that realtors and travel agents specialize in:

> *We are fully justified in the general remark, that no portion of the globe presents a more fruitful soil, or a milder climate, or equal facilities for*

carrying into effect the great purposes of a free and enlightened nation. . . . Providence in this gift, especially, has made Oregon the most favoured spot of His beneficence. If any part of this country is more salubrious in climate than another, it is the great plains at the foot of the mountains. These plains are less subject to rains; more remote from the sea, and better sheltered by stupendous mountains. Nevertheless it is warmer on the coast. The many lofty mountains situated in a high latitude, reflecting from their southern declivities the rays of the sun with great effect, and protecting the country from the cold winds of the North, and from the violence of the storms of the Southeast, greatly meliorate the atmosphere, and produce that surprising difference between the climates on the western and eastern sides of the American Continent.

As for the fabled rains, Kelley admitted their existence, but dismissed them as a trifling matter: "In the neighborhood of the mouth of the Columbia, rains are frequent in the winter. They commence with the South-east winds about the first of December, and terminate the last of February, when benign Spring has made some advance, 'the singing of birds has come,' and Nature dresses again in her loveliest garb. In April, a mild summer heat obtains, shrubbery is in blossom, and vegetation proceeds briskly. In June all kinds of mild fruit are ripened, and weather, delightfully pleasant, succeeds."

In Kelley's overheated prose, weather itself became a political weapon. Oregon's miraculous mildness was going to draw settlers like a magnet, and once a sufficient number of them arrived (Kelley specified "three thousand of the active sons of American freedom"), the region would fall into America's hands like a heavy, ripe apple. He was not alone in using weather to whip up Oregon fever. Missouri Senator Lewis F. Linn, for example, rhapsodized in 1838 about Oregon's almost "tropical" climate. Pamphlets and rumors about the land without a winter began circulating back to chilblained New England and the mercurial Midwest. Oregon was the place.

Settlers who came to Oregon expressly for the much-touted climate were in for something of a shock, especially if they arrived during the rainy season, as many did. One Dr. John Scouler compared the "incessant" rains he experienced in Oregon from 1824 to 1826 to equatorial downpours. John Burkhart, writing to friends back East from the Willamette, complained of the "verry disagreeable" and very long rainy season that lasted from November to March. "The climate I consider good was it not for the rains of winter which last from three to six months," wrote W. C. Dement from Oregon City to his mother back in Georgetown in July 1845. Dement added proudly that his farm has yielded a good crop of wheat, oats, and potatoes. "We may now call ourselves through, they say," wrote Amelia Stewart Knight of her family's completion of the Oregon Trail in 1853; "and here we are in Oregon, making our camp in an ugly bottom, with no home, except our wagons and tent, it is drizzling and the weather looks dark and gloomy."

Pioneer W. S. Gilliam offered a more extensive and dramatic account of the weather that greeted him and his parents upon their arrival in Oregon Territory in November 1844, some eight and a half months after departing from their home in western Missouri: "Before we reached the Cascade Falls the gates of heaven seemed to have opened and the rain came down in torrents. . . . [E]nduring hunger, drenching rains and traveling over the worst roads that I ever saw we reached Vancouver early in December. In taking a retrospect of my life I regard this trip from the Dalles to Vancouver as the severest hardship that it was ever my lot to endure. For days and nights my clothes were never dry." Lucie Fulton Isaacs, although only six in 1847 when her family emigrated from St. Joseph, Missouri to a claim in Yamhill County Oregon, never forgot her first experience of a wet Northwest winter: "Oh! how it did rain that first winter, and mother often had tears in her eyes, and child though I was I think I realized something of the sick longing she had for her old home."

It's fitting, given its rainy reputation, that the city of Seattle should have been founded on a day of wretched weather. The founding fathers and mothers who made up the Denny party, twelve adults and twelve children in all, left Illinois in the spring of 1851 and arrived in Portland 108 days later. Like most pioneers of the time, they had intended to find claims in the Willamette, but someone had told them about Puget Sound and at some point they set their hearts on settling there instead. David T. Denny and a small exploring party reconnoitered the region in September and the rest of the folks sailed up from Portland in mid-November on a schooner called the *Exact*. They disembarked near Alki Point in what is today West Seattle. The story goes that when they gathered on the shore, David Denny, emerging from the bushes, met them with the hearty greeting: "I am mighty glad to see you folks, for the skunks have eaten all my grub." That was the only gladness any of them felt that day. Historian and University of Washington luminary Edmond S. Meany conjured up the grim scene in his *History of the State of Washington*: "A dreary autumn rain was falling. There was no shelter. The schooner continued on to Olympia. The colony was alone. . . . Arthur A. Denny [David's older brother] turned to his friend and said: 'Low, white women are scarce in these parts. We had better take care of what we have.' He found his own wife sitting on a log, her back against a tree. In her arms was a babe but a few weeks old. She was weeping. 'Come, come, wife, this is no way to begin pioneering.' 'Oh, you promised when we left Illinois that we would not settle in a wilderness. Now see where we are.' The foundation of Seattle was laid in a mother's tears." Tears and rain: Arthur Denny reported in his own history of the city that the rain they encountered that first day continued, "falling more or less every day, but we did not regard it with much concern and seldom lost any time on that account." It's quite reassuring that the entrenched Seattle custom of refusing to break for rain dates back to the city's earliest days.

As reports from settlers like Gilliam, the Dennys, and Lucie Isaacs spread back East, the brief bright notion of a climatic Eden in Oregon faded behind high clouds. Nicknames like "mossback" and "webfoot" began to be affixed to Northwesterners. As Richard Maxwell Brown notes in his essay, "Rainfall and History: Perspectives on the Pacific Northwest," "By the middle of the nineteenth century, with the American flag flying over present Oregon and Washington, the image of oppressive rainfall was as well established as the homes of pioneers from Puget Sound to the Rogue River. Jokes began to circulate about the persistent precipitation."

It rains all the time. The myth that was born when the first Spanish explorers tried and failed to sail up the coast in the mid-sixteenth century took hold with a vengeance during the first generation of white settlement and has basically stuck ever since like a barnacle to a slick rock. Every now and then a glimmer of sunshine shot forth. One of the brightest rays came from the pages of Yankee sojourner Theodore Winthrop's florid but fascinating adventure-travel book *The Canoe and the Saddle* based on his trek through the Pacific Northwest during the summer of 1853. In one notable passage, Winthrop prophesied that the combined influence of "great mountains" and a climate "where being is bliss" would engender a new race of human beings in the Pacific Northwest. The people of Oregon were, in Winthrop's mind, destined to elaborate "new systems of thought and life" and give the "American Idea" its ultimate expression. This is a fairly tall order. But Winthrop was clearly intoxicated by what he describes as "the unapproachable glory of an Oregon summer sky." One hears the same swooning meteorological appreciation in the *Reminiscences of Washington Territory* by Steilacoom newspaperman Charles Prosch. An émigré from New York, Prosch settled in the south Puget Sound region in 1858, fell in love with the place and the weather at first sight, and never looked back. "It was now near the end of February," he wrote of his arrival on our shores, "and the sun never shone upon a lovelier day, in Italy or elsewhere, than that on which I quit the vessel for my new home. Nor was this charming weather confined to one or two days; weeks and months elapsed before it changed, and then for three or four days only. During the last week in June refreshing rains visited us, but the sky again cleared within a week, and we had no more rain until November. This agreeable feature of Puget Sound had much to do with making me and mine contented in our new home."

Prosch and Winthrop could effuse till they turned blue; the world was convinced that it rained all the time here, and there was nothing anyone could do about it. Even hard scientific data failed to make much of a dent. As early as 1888, a report aimed at debunking the "rains all the time" myth was prepared under the direction of Adolphus Washington Greely, the hero of the first official American expedition to the Arctic and then serving as the Army's chief signal officer, as the head of the fledgling national weather service was then known. The Greely Report makes for some interesting reading, as interesting for its *denials* as its *assertions*. One wades through only a page or two before the tone turns rather sharply defensive: "Although the rain-fall along the immediate coast of the Pacific Ocean, ranging from 70 to over 107 inches, is the heaviest in the United States, yet, contrary to the generally-received opinion, this enormous rain-fall does not cover the entire area of these states, but only 6 per centum of them." The generally received opinion that "the rain is continuous . . . during the wet season" is also false. In fact, Signal Service statistics prove that even on the coast "every other day in October and March is without rain, while in intervening months the frequency of rain is somewhat greater, rising in December to three days out of four." Away from the coast, the incidence of rainfall drops to every other day even at the height of the rainy season. Greely was equally adamant in correcting the "fallacy" that eastern Oregon and Washington are "almost rainless." In fact, "the area over which less than 10 inches of rain falls does not cover 5 per centum of either state." Putting temperature and rainfall statistics together, Greely wrapped up the introduction to the report with a glowing portrait of a meteorological Eden: "To summarize, Oregon and Washington are favored with a climate of unusual mildness and equability; while the immediate coast regions have very heavy rain falls, yet such rain occurs during the winter months of December to February, and in all cases the wet season gives place gradually to the dry season, during July and August. While the preponderating amount of rain falls during the winter, yet the spring, early summer, and late fall are all marked by moderate rains at not infrequent intervals."

Despite Greely's best efforts, the "curse of excessive rainfall," as one historian called it, has persisted, and climatologists have felt obliged to keep whacking away at it with ever more elaborate and authoritative arrays of statistics. One of the more stinging recent whacks was delivered by meteorology professor Phil Church in the December 1974 issue of *Weatherwise* magazine. Church, who had recently retired from his chairmanship of the University of Washington Department of Atmospheric

Sciences, exhaustively and ingeniously analyzed some seventy-five years of climatological records in a paper entitled "Some Precipitation Characteristics of Seattle." Right off the bat, Church established the fact that Seattle's rainy reputation is totally unjustified: From 1893 to 1970, Seattle's median yearly rainfall was just 33.83 inches, which is about the same as Dallas, Kansas City, Chicago, Cleveland, and Burlington, Vermont, and about half of what Miami and New Orleans get. But yearly totals are just the tip of the iceberg. Church proceeded to delve deeper into climatological minutiae to calibrate how many rainy *hours* we get each year, and he arrived at a rather startling conclusion: "While many visitors and a few others temporarily stationed in Seattle complain that it rains all the time, simple arithmetic shows that it rains (mean annual) a mere 11% of the time," 22 percent in January, but under 3 percent in July. But the coup de grace was Church's classification of rainfall intensities from "light drizzle" (0.01 inches and under per hour) through drizzle, light rain, and so on, all the way up to heavy rain (0.16 inches and over per hour). By Church's reckoning, 72.5 percent of Seattle's precipitation takes the form of drizzle, 19.8 percent is light rain, 6.2 percent moderate rain, and only 1.5 percent heavy rain. Thus, he summed up with a gleeful flourish, "Because of the preponderance of 'drizzle' intensities one might truthfully say that it rarely 'rains' in Seattle." It's hard to understand how "the curse of excessive rainfall" could ever recover from this deathblow, but such is the phoenix-like power of a bad meteorological reputation.

Writers' Rain

The curse mutated and multiplied fantastically once Northwest poets and novelists got into the act. Ours is a literature of meteorological extremity. Weather is not mere background or peripheral mood-setting device in our fictions: it's theme, subject, prime mover, plot twister, character maker and unmaker. Practically from the dawn of imaginative writing here in the Northwest, weather—especially big, oppressive, spirit-crushing, grandly horrible weather—emerged as a defining regional conceit. While incestuous siblings, crazed beauticians, and bellowing half-wits parade through the stories of the Deep South, we get floods, suicidal sunless winters, and punishingly low barometric pressure. Call it meteorological gothic, call it wet lit, call it what you will, foul weather quickly became an inevitable, all but compulsory, deeply conventional element in Northwest novels and poems: Rain was the "authentic" local "note." Consider this passage from H. L. Davis's Pulitzer Prize winning novel of 1935, *Honey in the Horn:* "Even to a country accustomed to rain, that was a storm worth gawking at. It cracked shingles in the roof, loaded the full-fruited old apple-trees until they threatened to split apart, and beat the roads under water belly-deep to a horse. Ten-foot walls of spray went marching back and forth across the hay-meadow as if they owned it, flocks of wild ducks came squalling down to roost in the open pasture till the air cleared, and the river boiled yellow foam over the toll bridge stumps, fence rails, pieces of old houses, and carcasses of drowned calves and horses against it."

Or listen to Betty MacDonald holding forth on the torrents of the Olympic Peninsula in her 1945 bestseller *The Egg and I*:

> *It rained and rained and rained. It drizzled—misted—drooled—spat—poured—and just plain rained. Some mornings were black and wild, with a storm raging in and out and around the mountains. Rain was driven under the doors and down the chimney, and Bob [her husband] went to the chicken house swathed in oilskins like a Newfoundland fisherman and I huddled by the stove and brooded about inside toilets. Other days were just gray and low hanging with a continual pit-pat-pit-pat-pitta-patta-pitta-patta which became as vexing as listening to baby talk. Along about November I began to forget when it hadn't been raining and became as one with all the characters in all of the novels about rainy seasons, who rush around banging their heads against the walls, drinking water glasses of straight whiskey and moaning, "The rain! The rain! My God, the rain!"*

In the tumultuous, fast-changing decades after World War II, a new strain began to appear in our literature: pride, even reverence for our notoriously poor weather. Bad weather became at once a joke and a badge of honor. "Our weather is horrendous, but we love it anyway" was one common stance. "We endure it because it nourishes us." "We soak it in until it saturates us and then we go stark raving mad" or "stark raving inspired." This strain rises to crescendo in Ken Kesey's brimming epic *Sometimes a Great Notion*. Kesey, who grew up in Oregon and graduated from the University of Oregon in 1956, pulls out all the stops as he revels in the onset of the winter rains in the grim coastal logging town he calls Wakonda:

> *Because nothing can be done about the rain except blaming. And if nothing can be done about it, why get yourself in a sweat about it? Matter of fact, it can be convenient to have around. Got troubles with the old lady? It's the rain. Got worries and frets about the way the old bus is falling to pieces right under you? It's the ruttin' rain. Got a deep, hollow ache bleeding cold down inside the secret heart of you from too many deals fallen through? too many nights in bed with the little woman without being able to get it up? too much bitter and not enough sweet? Yeah? That there, brother, is just as well blamed on the rain; falls on the*

just and unjust alike, falls all day long all winter long every winter every
year, and you might just as well give up and admit that's the way it's
gonna be, and go take a little snooze. Or you'll be mouthin' the barrel of
your twelve-gauge the way Evert Petersen at Mapleton did last year, or
samplin' snail-killer the way both the Meriwold boys did over to Sweet
Home. Roll with the blow, that's the easy out, blame it on the rain and
bend with the wind, and lean back and catch yourself forty winks—you
can sleep real sound when the rain is lullabying you.

This is weather that might have tested Job or challenged Hercules.
Weather as cosmic adversary, weather as plague, weather as the embodiment
of everything in Nature that means to thwart and mock and madden
human beings. Weather so all-encompassingly awful that nothing outdoors
matters *but* weather.

Seattle poet Richard Hugo also got a lot of metaphorical mileage out
of the Northwest's foul weather. Hugo shared with Kesey a blue-collar
perspective, a taste for the grim, and a squint-eyed respect for what Nature
dishes out. Not a whole lot of sun shines on their pages. Gray and wet are
facts of life and, as far as they're concerned, you better get used to it or
get the hell out. Like Kesey, Hugo was acutely attuned to how climate
warps the human spirit—only Hugo was less cosmic about it than Kesey.
Nobody does November better than Hugo.

In the poem called "Duwamish," Hugo conjures up the essence of
Seattle's "grim city winter" chill:

Not silver cold
like ice, for ice has glitter. Gray
cold like the river. Cold like 4 P.M.
on Sunday. Cold like a decaying porgy.

"Cruelty and rain could be expected./ Any season," he writes in the
seething "The House on 15th S.W." about his gray, violent, childhood
home. Rain falls copiously in Hugo's 1977 collection *31 Letters and 13*
Dreams, as here in "Letter to Wagoner from Port Townsend," where the
weather is wet enough to float Hugo's very soul up to the surface:

Rain five days and I love it . . . the grass explodes and trees
rage black green deep as the distance they rage in. I suppose
all said, this is my soul, the salmon rolling in the strait
and salt air loaded with cream for our breathing.

Weather is rarely the immediate subject of Hugo's poems, but the moody
damp and "wanton rain" of the Pacific Northwest seep into his verse like
an underground spring. There is something blunt, threatening, implacable

about Hugo's weather: His is not the climate of hope nor of despair, but of an irreducible, starkly strange reality.

The drumming of drops goes right on into the present. One of the finest wet lit passages of recent years comes at the climax of *The River Why*, a brilliant, freewheeling, loose-jointed, crack-pated paean to fly-fishing the wondrous rivers of western Oregon that appeared pretty much out of the blue in 1983 from then unknown Oregon writer David James Duncan. Duncan's hero, Gus Hale-Orviston, who has been fasting, praying, and abstaining from fishing for days, experiences a kind of spiritual catharsis— a cleansing of wounds, a consuming of cares, an enlightenment of mind— all precipitated by the sweet arrival of the autumn rains. It's a gorgeously sodden moment in the literature of Northwest weather:

> *For three days it rained, almost without sound, almost without ceasing. It was the first good rain since the August showers . . . a rain that hummed on the river pool and pattered on new puddles, washing the songbirds south, bringing newcomers from the north—rain birds, water lovers. . . . It was a rain that plucked the last leaves from the trees, turned stone gullies into streams, set the water ouzels singing. . . . [Y]et while the rain fell I didn't fish—only watched and rested, and I was lulled and cradled, caressed and enveloped in a cool, mothering touch that washed away the wounds of the summer; and my old, unmitigated longings—even the longings for fish, for Eddy, for the Friend—were changed from gnawing, aching dissatisfactions into a kind of sad, silent music, and the hollow place those longings had carved in me became a kind of sanctuary, an emptiness I grew used to, grew satisfied to leave unfilled. Reckoning up these transformations, watching the rain that began the day I sat at the source, I realized that I had been given a spirit-helper: I had been given this rain.*

There is no fighting a myth of this tenacity and beauty. No point in hauling out statistics, yearly averages, snapshots of sunny days. Rain is, for better or worse, our abiding badge of honor, a regional trademark indelibly imprinted on the climatic reputation of this corner of the world. As transplanted novelist Tom Robbins wrote of yet another dull autumnal dawn over the Skagit Valley: "The day was rumpled and dreary. It looked like Edgar Allen Poe's pajamas." This is just "what it's like" here, as we all know in our heart of hearts.

With weather, as with so much else outside ourselves, we perceive what we imagine and what we expect. In the end, myth is more important, more enduring than reality. No matter what it's really doing "out there," we filter the weather through the scrim of our desires, dreams, memories. And there is no question that incessant rain is essential to the dreams, memories and, yes, the desires of those who live in the Pacific Northwest. Freud might have pointed out that we wouldn't harp so much on our supposedly wretched weather if we didn't secretly—or in some cases openly—desire it, feel proud of it, identify with it. At some deep level The Rains are bound up with who we are: Mythical or actual, they are central to our private sense of self and to our regional identity.

And so I close with a pale grimace and a gray benediction: Let it rain.

Notes

This chapter draws on my book *Rains All the Time: A Connoisseur's History of Weather in the Pacific Northwest* (Seattle: Sasquatch Books, 1997).

Climate statistics come from the Portland, Oregon, and Seattle, Washington forecast offices of the National Weather Service.

The long quotations in the text come from the following sources: Francis Fletcher, *The World Encompassed by Sir Francis Drake* (London: Nicolas Bourne, 1628); Reuben Gold Thwaites, ed., *The Original Journals of the Lewis and Clark Expedition* (New York: Dodd, Mead, 1905); Hall J. Kelley, "A Geographical Sketch of that Part of North America Called Oregon" in *Hall J. Kelley on Oregon,* ed. F. W. Powell (Princeton: Princeton University Press, 1932); Edmond S. Meany, *History of the State of Washington* (New York: Macmillan, 1909); Theodore Winthrop, *The Canoe and the Saddle* (New York: J. W. Lovell, 1862); Charles Prosch, *Reminiscences of Washington Territory: Scenes, Incidents and Reflections of the Pioneer Period on Puget Sound* (Fairfield, Washington: Ye Galleon Press, 1969); General A. W. Greely, *The Climate of Oregon and Washington Territory* (Washington, D.C.: Government Printing Office, 1888); Philip Church "Some Precipitation Characteristics of Seattle," *Weatherwise* (December 1974).

Quotations from pioneers are from Robert A. Bennett, *We'll All Go Home in the Spring: Personal Accounts and Adventures as Told by the Pioneers of the West* (Walla Walla, Washington: Pioneer Press Books, 1984).

Quotations from novels and poems come from these books: H. L. Davis, *Honey in the Horn* (New York: Harper and Brothers, 1935); Betty MacDonald, *The Egg and I* (New York: J. B. Lippincott, 1945); Ken Kesey, *Sometimes a Great Notion* (New York: Viking Press, 1964); Richard Hugo, "Duwamish," "The House on 15th S.W.," and "Letter to Wagoner from Port Townsend" in *Making Certain It Goes On: Collected Poems of Richard Hugo* (New York: W. W. Norton, 1984); Richard Hugo, *31 Letters and 13 Dreams* (New York: W. W. Norton, 1977); David James Duncan, *The River Why* (San Francisco: Sierra Club Books, 1983).

The Forty-Ninth Parallel:
Defining Moments and Changing Meanings

Jeremy Mouat

⋄

A N ATTEMPT TO DESCRIBE a region or regions invites a series of questions, which are in part questions about boundaries. Where does a region begin? *When* does a region begin? In this chapter, I attempt to answer those questions by looking at a political boundary, the forty-ninth parallel, which divides the American Northwest and the province of British Columbia. The focus on European and Anglo-American settlement and colonization is in no way intended to suggest that the Pacific Northwest was *terra nullius,* an "empty land."[1] Aboriginal peoples lived throughout this area, possessing then and now their own sense of identity and region. This chapter examines the extension of British and Anglo-American hegemony and settlement. It charts the ways in which the forty-ninth parallel acquired its various meanings and uses the creation of the province of British Columbia as an example of the social construction of region within western North America.

The forty-ninth parallel functions today as a significant border, and the term is frequently used by Canadians as a shorthand phrase for the border with the United States.[2] If, as Patricia Limerick argues in *The Legacy of Conquest,* western history is "a story structured by the drawing of lines and the marking of borders," then surely the forty-ninth parallel is one of the more significant western structures.[3] Yet, it began as an imaginary line, born of Euclidean geometry and geopolitics, most notable for the way in which it imposed European definitions of space on the landscape of the Pacific Northwest. Gradually this imaginary line became real, and today one can observe at least part of its length from outer space.[4]

The forty-ninth parallel first acquired meaning in the early eighteenth century. The conclusion of the War of the Spanish Succession raised the question of where to divide British and French spheres of influence around Hudson Bay. The issue was particularly significant for the Hudson's Bay Company, because its trading operations were frequently disrupted by the ongoing wars between France and Britain. When the British government sought its advice on where to establish the boundary between the two countries' territories, the company pressed the British government to claim all the territory north of the forty-ninth parallel.[5] This demand reflected an increasingly bitter rivalry between the company and the French traders based in Montreal; the company was anxious for a border that could effectively prevent French competition. Despite the company's lobbying efforts, however, the Treaty of Utrecht (1713) and the other peace settlements following the war did not recognize the parallel as a boundary. Ironically, cartography subsequently ignored this inconclusiveness, and people began "to confuse an attempt to settle boundaries with an actual settlement."[6] By the mid-eighteenth century, British maps had begun to use the forty-ninth parallel as a boundary.

European cartographers plotted the West's size and terrain with growing precision by imposing the invisible grid of latitude and longitude, thus situating the region within their understanding of the world. However, the map widely regarded as "The single most important map in American colonial history"—Mitchell's map of 1755—contained several fundamental geographical errors.[7] Lacking accurate accounts of the topography of the continent's interior, Mitchell provided a nonexistent river link between the Lake of the Woods, which now straddles the border between the provinces of Manitoba and Ontario and the state of Minnesota to the south, with the Great Lakes. In fact, the Lake of the Woods drains north into Hudson Bay. Mitchell's map also implied that the headwaters of the Mississippi River lay northwest of the Lake of the Woods, rather than southwest. Those who negotiated the treaty ending the American War of Independence relied on Mitchell's map; consequently, these errors assumed real importance. The new nation's borders were to be the Great Lakes to the north and the Mississippi River to the west. With Mitchell's map as their guide, both sides agreed that the northwest boundary would be drawn by a border line heading west from the Lake of the Woods, which they assumed was the westernmost point of the Great Lakes drainage basin, to the Mississippi River, which they assumed rose to the north, in territory claimed by the British. In fact, such a border was impossible.

British traders with commercial interests in British North America greeted the 1783 boundary settlement with anger, arguing that the British representatives had thoughtlessly negotiated away the continent's rich resource hinterland. In the decade that followed, tensions between Britain and the new republic forced a further round of negotiations, leading to Jay's Treaty (1794).[8] The parties to this treaty agreed, among other things, to resolve the difficulties with the northwestern boundary by a survey of the source of the Mississippi. Exploration and survey work by David

Thompson several years later rendered this unnecessary, for Thompson was able to establish the real relationship of the Lake of the Woods to the Great Lakes, as well as to identify the source of the Mississippi. Alexander Mackenzie's book publicized Thompson's findings in 1801, and soon another series of negotiations were underway between British and American officials to resolve the boundary.[9] Although these negotiations led to a tentative agreement on an accurate border, which would go from the northwest corner of the Lake of the Woods to the nearest source of the Mississippi, the Louisiana Purchase soon eclipsed the importance of this agreement and initiated additional talks between representatives of the two countries.[10]

American diplomats approached British officials in 1804, hoping to secure agreement on a border between the territory acquired by the Louisiana Purchase and British territory to the north. James Monroe, the American representative, identified the forty-ninth parallel west from the Lake of the Woods as the appropriate boundary, a position that reflected the research and conclusions of President Jefferson, who held that the Treaty of Utrecht had in fact established the forty-ninth parallel as a boundary.[11] Britain and the United States did reach a tentative settlement in 1807, recognizing for the first time the forty-ninth parallel as the western boundary between the territories claimed by both governments, but the agreement was never ratified, owing to other tensions between the two countries. These tensions contributed to the War of 1812, and it was left for those negotiating a series of agreements following that war to agree finally that the forty-ninth parallel would divide the United States and British North America.

The Convention of 1818 aimed to end the longstanding ambiguity over the location of the boundary in the continent's western region. Adopting the terms of the 1807 agreement, the convention recognized the forty-ninth parallel as the border from the Lake of the Woods to the Rocky Mountains.[12] West of the Rockies, however, the boundary was left unresolved, the convention stating only that this territory would be jointly occupied.[13] The period of joint occupation lasted less than thirty years, as the quickening pace of American westward expansion and settlement rendered it untenable. Following several years of bitter wrangling in the 1840s, American and British politicians finally came to an agreement in 1846. The Oregon Treaty signed by both governments that year formally defined the border between the American Northwest and British territory to the north. Despite the passions aroused by the Oregon question—most famously, with the American slogan, "54-40 or fight"—the treaty simply extended the forty-ninth parallel as the border between American and British territory, from the Rockies west to the Pacific Ocean.[14] Too much emphasis should not be placed on this defining moment, however, for the meanings that the border was to acquire lay in the future.

Two governments far removed from the region had adopted the forty-ninth parallel as the border between the western territory that they claimed by right of discovery, exploration, and settlement. Yet, despite the controversy leading up to the 1846 treaty, the boundary at first attracted very little interest. Thirteen years passed, for example, before any effort was made to fix the line's precise location on land.[15] By this time, European colonization had reached significant proportions in the lower Columbia Valley; further south, the discovery of rich gold deposits in California attracted many thousands of people. The territory north of the forty-ninth parallel, in contrast, was much less affected by European settlement.

The first survey of the forty-ninth parallel through Washington Territory and the interior of British Columbia, 1860-61. (From volume 2 of the photographs taken by the North American Boundary Commissions, 1860-61, held at the Royal Engineers' Library, Brompton Barracks, Chatham, Kent, England. Reproduced with permission.)

The Hudson's Bay Company continued to exercise a peculiar sovereignty over much of the region, by virtue of its royal charter dating from the late seventeenth century, which had been subsequently extended by Parliament beyond the original boundaries of the Hudson Bay watershed.[16] By the mid-nineteenth century, many groups—both within and beyond its territories—disputed the company's authority. Native peoples, Métis, and others in the Red River settlement criticized the company for being an unprincipled, illegitimate, and anachronistic monopoly. The debate in Britain over granting Vancouver Island to the company as a proprietary colony encouraged a number of influential politicians, including Gladstone, to assail the company in Parliament and characterize it as a relic of an earlier era, out of place in the brave new world of free trade that Britain had embraced in 1846.[17] The company's efforts to establish viable settlements in the Columbia River Valley and the Puget Sound area had not borne fruit and few expected that it would have any greater success on Vancouver Island, once it became the company's proprietary colony in January 1849.[18] The ability of the Hudson's Bay Company to attract European settlers to the island appeared particularly doubtful, given the island's distance from Britain, the company's determination to hedge colonization with various conditions, including a relatively high price for land, and the attractions of other places, notably the American West, in general, and gold-rich California, in particular.[19] Vancouver Island, the first British colony in the Pacific Northwest, faced an uncertain future.

Gold fever broke out relatively early on the North Pacific Coast, when news came of the gold discoveries in California. "In the Spring of 1849 a vessel appeared in the harbor," recalled Roderick Finlayson, a Hudson's Bay Company official then in charge of Fort Victoria on Vancouver Island,

> *the crew of which wore red flannel shirts, and when they landed we took them to be pirates. I ordered the men to the guns, manned the bastions and made ready for defence. I then interviewed the men, from the gate, who told me they were peaceable traders, come from San Francisco, with gold, to trade for goods, as this was the only station on the northern coast where they could get the goods they wanted. Having satisfied myself that they were what they represented themselves to be, I let them in, and they then told me that gold had been discovered in California in large quantities the previous Fall, and that they had gold nuggets which they would gladly exchange for goods. . . . After this our operations here got considerably disarranged, by numbers of our men leaving for the California diggings.[20]*

As the passage suggests, the company soon had considerable difficulty retaining workers. To add to the company's anxiety, gold was also found within the region itself, on the Queen Charlotte Islands.[21] The Haida, the islands' Native people, had learned of the value that Europeans placed on gold (likely through trading expeditions to California) and brought some to a Hudson's Bay Company fort in the summer of 1850.[22] This was not placer gold, the water-borne deposits that had sparked the gold rush, but hard rock gold, recovered from a rich quartz vein. Over the next two years, Hudson's Bay Company officials and groups of American miners arrived to work the vein. None of these forays was successful, largely because of the Haida's opposition to mining. In addition, although the gold in the quartz deposit was rich, it was not extensive. Interest in the area soon faded.

The flurry of excitement over the presence of gold in the Queen Charlotte Islands raised some troubling issues for the Hudson's Bay Company and the British government. The first was simply their ability to maintain authority and sovereignty in the face of an influx of miners, a group that brought with them not only a passion for gold but also particular assumptions about their right to mine the precious metal without hindrance from government regulation and with little regard for Native rights. Complicating this was the area's uncertain political status. The sudden interest in the islands led the British government to extend the authority of the governor of Vancouver Island, James Douglas, to include the Queen Charlotte Islands as well and to fashion gold-mining regulations in a manner consistent with British law and precedent.[23] Thus, despite the fact that no significant mining developed in the Queen Charlottes, the initial excitement led to the extension of formal British sovereignty and the establishment of mining regulations based on the Australian model.

The first gold rush north of the border came in the spring of 1858. With the rapid depletion of California's richest deposits, miners fanned out along the western cordillera in search of gold. By 1855, some of these men had traveled nearly to the forty-ninth parallel, participating in a minor rush near Fort Colville during that year.[24] As this northward movement continued during the spring of 1856, Douglas advised the colonial secretary that gold discoveries had been made "within the British territory."[25]

Douglas was anxious to maintain control over events on the mainland. Although he was governor only of Vancouver Island, Douglas's second job was chief factor and head of the Western Department for the Hudson's Bay Company. Any disturbance on the mainland—an area over which the British government had granted the company exclusive trading rights with Native peoples—would jeopardize its position. A gold rush would almost certainly bring chaos; events in the Queen Charlotte Islands had demonstrated that conflicts were likely between Native and white miners. South of the border, an Indian war raged in Washington Territory during 1855 and 1856, something that Douglas was anxious to prevent on British territory. He was also well aware of the problems that the California gold rush had caused the company and no doubt expected that these difficulties would be far greater if the rush was closer to home. In addition to the possibilities of Indian wars and mass desertions by company employees, Douglas was concerned that an influx of American miners would lead to calls for annexation with the United States. In late December 1857, Douglas issued a proclamation "declaring the rights of the Crown in respect to gold found in its natural place of deposit, within the limits of Fraser's River and Thompson's River districts. . . and forbidding all persons to dig or disturb the soil in search of gold, until authorized on that behalf by Her Majesty's Government."[26]

Ironically, the rush of "adventurers from the American side" that Douglas dreaded was caused inadvertently by the Hudson's Bay Company itself, several months after his proclamation. The gold that had slowly increased in the company forts through trade with the Native population, some 800 ounces, was shipped to the San Francisco mint in February 1858.[27] This was all the encouragement needed to start the stampede from California northward; the first shipload of more than 400 miners arrived in Victoria in late April.[28] Between April and August 1858, some 25,000 to 30,000 people rushed to the Fraser River, most coming via San Francisco.[29]

Despite Douglas's anxieties, the Fraser River rush was more or less an orderly affair.[30] Considerable tension arose between European and Native miners, culminating in a series of confrontations, assaults, and murders, but actual warfare was avoided.[31] Nonetheless, the situation caused Douglas a good deal of concern and at the height of the tensions between the two groups, in August 1858, he traveled to the mining district to act as a mediator.[32] Overall, however, the rush was not particularly lucrative for the participants. Harsh conditions and meager returns left many with no desire to remain on the river bars and soon the exodus began. But the gold rush did have a substantial impact on the region. It forced British authorities to declare mainland British Columbia a British colony and caused far more Europeans to settle in the region north of the forty-ninth parallel than the Hudson's Bay Company had managed to entice to Vancouver Island during the preceding ten years.

British Columbia's gold rush encouraged what was to become a common dichotomy, one that would be used often in subsequent years to characterize the difference between the Canadian West and American West and to give meaning to the forty-ninth parallel. This was the assumption that life on the northern side of the border was more peaceful and orderly, that Canadian society was somehow more law-abiding and less violent than American society. Such an analysis forces one to consider why the behavior of the same group of people might differ so radically depending on their location, whether they happened to be on the gold fields of California or on the banks of the Fraser River. To the extent that any significant difference did exist, the following diary entry gives some clue as to its meaning. It was written by a British soldier who was briefly in Victoria on Vancouver Island in the summer of 1858, at the height of the gold rush: "July 31st. Last night we were roused by a message from the Governor to say that a riot had broken out at Victoria, & our presence was instantly required. The men were soon turned out & got on board the *Plumper* (one of our Men of War here) which carried us around. It was very exciting when we came in sight of the town & the order was given to load & the ship's guns run out & cleared for action."[33] To maintain the rule of law, authorities in Victoria were prepared to shell the town with the mid-nineteenth-century equivalent of heavy artillery. However law-abiding the people of Victoria may have been, what stands out is the willingness of British authorities to use force to suppress what was in fact a fairly trivial disturbance.[34] Unlike the relatively weak government presence in California in 1848-1849, British authority on Vancouver Island was well-established and unwilling to permit any challenge to its position.

Whatever the accuracy of the lawful/lawless dichotomy, gold discoveries in British Columbia did lead to the establishment of a distinctive legal system north of the forty-ninth parallel, a system that in some ways differed fundamentally from the one taking shape south of the border. Following the Australian precedent, authorities in British Columbia enshrined in law the Doctrine of the Royal Metals, which embodied assumptions about the state ownership of resources that persist to this day.[35] The nascent state also opted to invest relatively heavily in the construction of transportation routes to facilitate east-west traffic across the mountain ranges running north and south. The rationale was straightforward: the fledgling government needed ready access to the interior if it was to exercise political authority over the distant interior. Merchants on the coast were also keen to encourage traffic into the area, hoping that this would enable them to earn substantial profits. The point of the Cariboo Road and the Dewdney Trail— both built during the 1860s to provide access from the coast to inland mining regions—was to establish communications and trading networks confined to the northern side of the border.

British Columbia's ambitious road program was expensive and servicing the resulting debt was difficult. Dwindling returns from placer mining became a major economic problem for a government that had begun to rely on the revenues that it derived from gold production.[36] In 1866, the two separate colonies, Vancouver Island and the mainland colony that had been created in the wake of the Fraser River gold rush, united to form the colony of British Columbia to rationalize the expenses of government.

Five years later, in 1871, British Columbia opted to join Canada as a province.

British Columbia's absorption into the four-year-old Canadian state was very different from the manner in which western territory came under the authority of the American government. In British North America, considerable geographical, social, and cultural distance separated the province of Canada (today's southern Ontario and southern Quebec) from the other British possessions further west. Very little direct communication occurred between the regions prior to the coming of the transcontinental railways in the 1880s. As a result, the creation of the new Dominion of Canada in 1867, which united the province of Canada with the maritime colonies of Nova Scotia and New Brunswick, had almost no impact in the west. Unlike the experience in the United States, no groundswell of western migration and political rhetoric informed by a sense of mission accompanied British Columbia's entry into the confederation in 1871, or that of the province of Manitoba the year before.[37] In the latter region, news of the Canadian government's purchase of the Hudson's Bay Company's territory sparked an uprising in 1869, forcing the Canadian government to renegotiate the terms of confederation with the local population. For its part, the colony of British Columbia was bribed into Canada in 1871, notably with the promise of a transcontinental railway connection within ten years of joining the new country.[38]

British Columbia's entry into Canada turned out to be a Faustian bargain, for the Canadian Pacific Railway, which was finally completed through the new province in 1885, did far more than simply move people and freight east and west.[39] The steel rails tied the new province firmly to an emerging transcontinental economy, an economy dominated by the business interests of a powerful commercial elite based in central Canada. These interests underwrote Canada's "National Policy," a development strategy first articulated in the late 1870s that was based on state-sponsored railway construction and facilitating European settlement in western Canada. The policy also created a protective tariff that enabled the establishment of American branch plants, or subsidiaries, in central Canada, but that also effectively prohibited those in western Canada from purchasing manufactured goods directly from American suppliers.[40] As the Canadian political economist Harold Innis argued more than seventy-five years ago, "Western Canada has paid for the development of Canadian nationality, and it would appear that it must continue to pay. The acquisitiveness of eastern Canada shows little sign of abatement."[41]

Canadian scholars have tended to view the construction of the Canadian Pacific Railway in the 1880s as a metaphor for the nation's coming of age.[42] The tale becomes an epic in which the railway/the country surmounts the opposition of shortsighted politicians, skeptical financiers, and, of course, nature itself (in the form of a hostile northern climate as well as daunting geographical obstacles). The completion of the Canadian Pacific Railway through to the Pacific Coast is seen as a moment of triumph, as tangible evidence of an emerging transcontinental nation, as the justification of a particular national vision, and so on. Few historians have regarded the railway's completion as an index of industrialization or as the agent of metropolitan capital, although those perspectives make a good deal more sense than those that see steel rails and locomotives as mystical symbols of national destiny.

Canada's first transcontinental railway was a transportation corridor with a very specific sense of the forty-ninth parallel. The Canadian government explicitly prohibited the construction of any competing lines south of the Canadian Pacific Railway on the prairies, to prevent any north-south lines from crossing the border and weakening the east-west orientation of the new railway.[43] In 1883, federal authorities also prevented the construction of a short portage railway in southeastern British Columbia, which would have linked Kootenay Lake with the Columbia River. By this time, the Northern Pacific stretched across the northern states, while north of the border, the promised Canadian transcontinental was still two years away. The proposed portage railway would have linked British Columbia's interior with the American transcontinental, via steamboats operating on the Columbia River. Although the provincial government supported the idea, the federal government disallowed the railway, pointing out that "the company consists almost wholly of American capitalists, and . . . notwithstanding the representations made that the proposed railway will connect by steamer with the Canadian Pacific Railway, and thus bring traffic to that road and to the Canadian seaboard, . . . the road under consideration would in all probability eventually become a feeder to the Northern Pacific Railway."[44] The move angered the provincial government, but it could do little other than express its indignation. The British North America Act, which set out the division of powers between the federal and provincial governments, gave federal politicians considerable control over economic development and they were intent on imposing their own interpretation of the forty-ninth parallel's meaning.

The southeast corner of British Columbia experienced a series of mining booms in the 1890s. The prospect of considerable rail traffic caught the attention of both the American and Canadian transcontinental railways, running just to the south and to the north. The region became a much contested borderland, one in which the forty-ninth parallel functioned as a critical divide. Although some people argued that economic growth could only be achieved with free trade (or "reciprocity") across the border, this was a minority view. Others insisted that the natural resources of the region ought to benefit Canada, and that such benefit demanded not free trade or a weakening in the protective tariff that followed the forty-ninth parallel, but an improved transportation link directly into the Kootenays from central Canada. In a letter to the prime minister written in 1896, for example, the Canadian Pacific Railway's vice president described the need for a railway into the Kootenays from the east as "the most important railway work if not indeed the most important work of any kind now requiring the attention of Government. . . . To answer the purpose for which it is intended, viz., to preserve for Canada the business incident to the mining of the precious metals copper and coal in that section of Canada by building up smelting enterprises and smelting towns, it is essential that the railway be an integral part of the Canadian system without any interest South of the International Boundary."[45] Less than a year later, the Canadian Pacific Railway received government assistance to build the line.

The new railway line into the Kootenays from southern Alberta was completed in 1898. It underlined the Canadian government's willingness to subsidize economic development in such ways as to strengthen the east-west axis and, consciously or not, to encourage the commercial dominance of central Canada. Such initiatives provoked a good deal of protest on the Pacific Coast, where members of the business community felt that they too ought to be able to tap into the mineral wealth of the Kootenays, rather than see it flow either south through Spokane or east to central Canada. They were unable to exert sufficient influence to force the federal government to change its policies.

The Canadian Pacific Railway's economic power, its political influence, and its east-west focus had profound implications for British Columbia. Any attempt to diversify the local economy that might affect the railway's position was actively discouraged. A minor episode in the Kootenays illustrates this point. In the early 1900s, the smelter city of Trail, located on the banks of the Columbia River, was emerging as an industrial complex, based on the extensive mineral resources of the region, a ready supply of hydroelectricity, and a crude but effective regional transportation network. The smelter itself was the property of the Canadian Pacific Railway, but in 1904 it was managed by an American, W. H. Aldridge. He found it ludicrous that the Trail plant produced lead, only to ship it to central Canada where it was turned into pipe and subsequently shipped back to western Canada. The solution seemed obvious: Aldridge decided to make a modest investment in equipment and manufacture lead pipe in Trail. The railway's head office responded immediately:

> We must not lose sight of the fact that the men who are interested in this lead pipe business in the East are amongst the largest shippers over our

*line, and any advantage that you would receive from the utilization of
your lead product in the manufacture of pipe would be a mere bagatelle as
compared with the loss of revenue to the Company if these important
interests were antagonized. . . . There is, as you say, a manifest
incongruity in the fact that pig-lead is shipped from Trail to Montreal,
then manufactured into pipe and shipped west again, but this occurs with
a great many other articles. . . . I recognise your anxiety to make the most
of the situation at Trail, but it is of vital importance that our other
interests should not be overlooked.*[46]

Aldridge was forced to close the lead plant.

The 1890s and early 1900s have been described as "the directly formative
birth-time of basic institutions, social relations, and political divisions of
United States society as it evolved toward and beyond the mid-twentieth
century," and they were equally important in Canada for many of the same
reasons.[47] An influential cross-section of Canadian society began to interpret
"Canadian" nationality as closely aligned with Britain's new imperialism.[48]
Such attitudes influenced a growing number of British Columbia's
European residents and gave new meaning to the border with the United
States.

Recent scholarship emphasizes the complexity of such notions as
nationalism and national identity.[49] During the late nineteenth century,
there was much defining and redefining of national identities, and the
border's shifting significance reflects this volatility. It can also be discerned
in what might at first seem a rather trivial affair: a fight that broke out
during the summer of 1903 in Rossland, then the leading city in booming
southeastern British Columbia. A Vancouver newspaper's rather bemused
account described how an angry citizen had attacked and bitten one of
Rossland's newspaper editors.[50] Although the dispute seemed straightforward enough—the editor had printed a satirical piece that had infuriated
his assailant—it also revealed the changing meaning of the forty-ninth
parallel and the national identities that it was coming to define.

In the spring of 1903, the mayor of Rossland traveled south to Spokane,
Washington with a group of other mayors from his region. The purpose
of their trip was to meet President Theodore Roosevelt. Upon his return
to Canada, the mayor decided that the American holiday of the Fourth of
July should be celebrated that year in Rossland. Such celebrations were
common in earlier years, when many among the mining communities of
the region hailed from the United States, and this had not been
controversial. In fact, overshadowing the town was Spokane Mountain, a
name that acknowledged the significant role played by that American city
in Rossland's early years. But residents' loyalties were changing. During

the Anglo–Boer War, Spokane Mountain was renamed Mount Roberts to commemorate Lord Roberts's taking of Pretoria in June 1900.[51] And so the editor of Rossland's *Evening World,* reflecting the new mood of imperialism and staunch loyalty to Britain, characterized the mayor's plan to celebrate American independence on Canadian soil as bordering on treason and published a sarcastic program for the event that Rossland's mayor was proposing. This column provoked an angry reader to assault the editor.

Such currents were not confined to Rossland, but increasingly influenced public debate across Canada. The 1911 federal election brought this debate into sharp focus. The government of the day, Laurier and the Liberal Party, campaigned on a platform of free trade with the United States. The Conservatives denounced the idea, charging that the government was betraying Canada with the suggestion of closer economic ties with the United States. It was revealing of the public mood that although Laurier had been a very popular prime minister, the male electorate rejected his platform and the Conservatives assumed power in Ottawa.[52]

The border acquired additional meanings in the region during World War I, largely because of the neutrality of the United States for the first three years of the war.[53] Munitions production for the British forces was concentrated in Canada and the country's reliance on American smelters for its supply of copper, nickel, and zinc troubled British and Canadian strategists. Two commissions investigated the situation, amid growing rumors of covert German metal purchases through agents in the United States.[54] To end the country's reliance on American smelters and refineries, they recommended establishing new Canadian metallurgical plants and diversifying the capacity of others. As a consequence, the Trail smelter grew and expanded considerably, growth that was later to raise the troubling issue of cross-border pollution.[55]

Many Canadians were relieved when the United States joined the war in 1917, although there was also considerable consternation when President Wilson objected to Canada having an independent voice at the Versailles peace conference following the war's end.[56] Tensions between Canada and the United States were not unknown: the Alaska boundary dispute following the Klondike gold rush had produced a good deal of anger.[57] In fact, the Canadian army did not scrap Defence Scheme No. 1, which envisaged war with the United States, until 1931, although the plan had been largely discredited much earlier. In similar fashion, the U.S. military occasionally imagined that Canada might join a hostile coalition against the United States. When an American official testified to this effect in 1935, to the Military Affairs Committee of the House of Representatives, President Franklin D. Roosevelt quickly repudiated the idea.[58]

The years between the two world wars saw the emergence of a continental economy, as American finance capital assumed a much more active role in the Canadian economy. At the same time, the American cultural presence in Canada grew increasingly dominant, particularly in the new media of radio and motion pictures. The situation preoccupied a number of Canadian intellectuals, although the general view seems to have been that the American presence was largely benign.[59] In part, this was a legacy of the carnage of World War I, which encouraged a sense in Canada that Europe was a place of ancient antagonisms and the war a conflagration into which Canadians had needlessly been drawn. North America, in contrast, was a place of peace. A Canadian politician epitomized this view in 1924, while addressing the League of Nations: "Not only have we had a hundred years of peace on our borders, but we think in terms of peace, while Europe, an armed camp, thinks in terms of war. . . . We live in a fireproof house, far from inflammable materials. A vast ocean separates us from Europe."[60]

Two politicians contributed to the growing rapprochement between Canada and the United States. Mackenzie King, Prime Minister of Canada for much of the interwar years, had studied at the University of Chicago and during World War I was active as a labor-relations consultant for Rockefeller and numerous other American business interests. In contrast, President Roosevelt had few Canadian connections, but had a genuine respect for his country's northern neighbor. These two men presided over the era in which the present close ties between Canada and the United States were forged. Roosevelt set the tone in the summer of 1938 when, in Canada to receive an honorary doctorate, he declared unequivocally, "I give to you assurance that the people of the United States will not stand idly by if domination of Canadian soil is threatened by any other empire."[61] This was music to the ears of nervous Canadian politicians, who were anxiously watching the growing might of Nazi Germany in Europe. The theme of continental defense that Roosevelt had raised in his speech culminated two years later when he and Mackenzie King met at Ogdensberg, New York and laid the basis for the Permanent Joint Board of Defense. This was followed by a second agreement eight months later, the Hyde Park Declaration of April 1941, which enabled American purchases of war material in Canada, a critical agreement for the cash-strapped Canadian economy. Then, after the bombing of Pearl Harbor, came the construction of the Alaska Highway, a concrete symbol of the common interests of the two countries and their commitment to joint defense.[62] Even the atomic weapons that brought the war to an end in the summer of 1945 had a cross-border dimension, for they were developed in part with heavy water from the Trail smelter in the Kootenays.[63]

Given the growing convergence of the two countries, it is scarcely surprising that by the end of World War II, the forty-ninth parallel was re-imagined in a more benevolent light. It had become an informal boundary between two friendly nations, two allies with shared interests and values. The centenary of the Oregon Treaty in June 1946 was an occasion for celebrating this fact, with many expressions of good will. The British Columbia, Washington, and Oregon Historical Societies worked together to fashion a suitable ceremony at the Blaine border crossing, on the highway between Seattle and Vancouver.[64] The speeches that day were broadcast on radio on both sides of the border and a new marker unveiled, with appropriate commemorative plaques, on the line itself. Similar ceremonies were held at other crossings along the length of the British Columbia-Washington border. But the celebrations also implicitly acknowledged the fact that in the hundred years since the signing of the treaty, the forty-ninth parallel had become a significant boundary, evidence of just how contingent the process was—and is—of where and when regions begin, evidence of how the imaginary can become real.

Notes

[1] *Terra nullius* was a legal fiction sometimes used by Europeans to deny Aboriginal people legitimate title to their traditional territories. The concept is described in Shirley V. Scott, "*Terra Nullius* and the *Mabo* Judgment of the Australian High Court: A Case Study of the Operation of Legalist Reasoning as a Mechanism of Political-Legal Change," *The Australian Journal of Politics and History*, 42, no. 3 (1996): 385-401; Gerry Simpson, "*Mabo*, International Law, Terra Nullius and the Stories of Settlement: An Unresolved Jurisprudence," *Melbourne University Law Review* 19 (June 1993): 195-210; cf. J. A. Andrews, "The Concept of Statehood and the Acquisition of Territory in the Nineteenth Century," *Law Quarterly Review* 94 (July 1978): 408-27.

[2] For example, in Ian Lumsden, ed., *Close the 49th Parallel Etc.* (Toronto: University of Toronto Press, 1973); Richard J. Gwyn, *The Forty-Ninth Paradox: Canada in North America* (Toronto: McClelland and Stewart, 1985). In the 1980s, a 49th Parallel Institute operated out of the University of Montana.

[3] Patricia Nelson Limerick, *The Legacy of Conquest: The Unbroken Past of the American West* (New York: W. W. Norton and Company, 1987), 55.

[4] See the photograph of the Alberta/Montana boundary taken by the LANDSAT-3 satellite in 1978, reproduced in Brian Banks, *Canada from Space: Satellite Photographs* (North York, Ontario: Camden House, 1995), 43. Note also the discussion of this extraordinary image by Richard Manning in "The Sweet Smell of Subsidies," *Harper's Magazine* 292, no. 1751 (April 1996): 64-65.

[5] For a thorough discussion of these negotiations and the issues at stake, see Max Savelle, "The Forty-Ninth Degree of North Latitude as an International Boundary, 1719: The Origin of an Idea," *Canadian Historical Review* 38, no. 3 (September 1957): 183-201; E. E. Rich, "The Hudson's Bay Company and the Treaty of Utrecht," *Cambridge Historical Journal* 11, no. 2 (1954): 183-203. Cf. Charles O. Paullin, "The Early Choice of the Forty-Ninth Parallel as a Boundary Line," *Canadian Historical Review* 4 (December 1923): 127-31; E. E. Rich,

Hudson's Bay Company 1670-1870. Vol. I. *1670-1763* (Toronto: McClelland and Stewart Ltd., 1960), 483-85; Norman L. Nicholson, *The Boundaries of the Canadian Confederation* (Ottawa: Carleton Library, 1979), 18-19. The line that the Hudson's Bay Company sought as a boundary extended from the Atlantic Coast of Labrador southwest through today's northern Quebec and then west along the forty-ninth parallel; see the map in Savelle, "The Forty-Ninth Degree of North Latitude as an International Boundary, 1719," 198.

[6] Paullin, "The Early Choice of the Forty-Ninth Parallel as a Boundary Line," 128.

[7] On Mitchell's map, see William E. Lass, "How the Forty-Ninth Parallel Became the International Boundary," *Minnesota History* 44 (Summer 1975): 209-19, esp. 211-12; J. P. D. Dunbabin, "Red Lines on Maps: The Impact of Cartographical Errors on the Border between the United States and British North America, 1782-1842," *Imago Mundi: The International Journal for the History of Cartography* 50 (1998): 105-25, esp. 108-10; Map 59, in John Goss, *The Mapping of North America: Three Centuries of Map-making 1500-1860* (Secaucus, N.J.: The Wellfleet Press, 1990), 130-31; Matthew H. Edney, *John Mitchell's Map: An Irony of Empire,* a web site designed and prepared to accompany the exhibit of John Mitchell's map at the Osher Map Library and Smith Center for Cartographic Education at the University of Southern Maine, available via http://www.usm.maine.edu/%7Emaps/mitchell/ The web site includes a digitized image of the map as well as an annotated bibliography.

[8] For the 1783 treaty, see George W. Brown, "The St. Lawrence in the Boundary Settlement of 1783," *Canadian Historical Review* 9, no. 3 (September 1928): 223-38. On Jay's Treaty, see Samuel Flagg Bemis, *Jay's Treaty: A Study in Commerce and Diplomacy,* rev. ed. (New Haven, Conn.: Yale University Press, 1962); E. E. Rich, *Hudson's Bay Company 1670-1870.* Vol. II. *1763-1820* (Toronto: McClelland and Stewart Ltd., 1960), 197-204; Samuel Flagg Bemis, "Jay's Treaty and the Northwest Boundary Gap," *American Historical Review* 27, no. 3 (April 1922): 465-84.

[9] Lass, "How the Forty-Ninth Parallel Became the International Boundary," 212-14; Dunbabin, "Red Lines on Maps," 110-11.

[10] See the discussion in Jesse S. Reeves, *American Diplomacy under Tyler and Polk* (1907; reprint, Gloucester, Mass.: Peter Smith, 1967), 192-201. For a map showing the route of the proposed line from the northwest corner of the Lake of the Woods to the nearest source of the Mississippi, see Lass, "How the Forty-Ninth Parallel Became the International Boundary," 214.

[11] See Thomas Jefferson, "The Limits and Bounds of *Louisiana,*" in *Documents Relating to the Purchase and Exploration of Louisiana* (New York: Houghton, Mifflin and Co., 1904), esp. "P.S. The Northern Boundary of *Louisiana,* Coterminous with the Possessions of *England,*" 40-45. For a useful discussion of Jefferson's changing views on the northern boundary, see Thomas Maitland Marshall, *A History of the Western Boundary of the Louisiana Purchase, 1819-1841* (Berkeley: University of California Press, 1914), 1-16; Lass, "How the Forty-Ninth Parallel Became the International Boundary," 215-16; Dunbabin, "Red Lines on Maps," 111. More generally, see Binger Hermann, *The Louisiana Purchase and Our Title West of the Rocky Mountains with a Review of Annexation by the United States* (Washington, D.C.: Government Printing Office, 1898), 55-58; Reeves, *American Diplomacy under Tyler and Polk,* 193-201.

[12] The convention has been described as "a tacit agreement to divide North America along the forty-ninth parallel to the Pacific," Reginald C. Stuart, *United States Expansionism and British North America, 1775-1871* (Chapel Hill: University of North Carolina Press, 1988), 103. On the agreement itself, see Frederick

Merk, "The Oregon Question in 1818," in *The Oregon Question: Essays in Anglo-American Diplomacy and Politics* (Cambridge, Mass.: Belknap Press of Harvard University Press, 1967), 30–45; Donald A. Rakestraw, *For Honor or Destiny: The Anglo-American Crisis over the Oregon Territory* (New York: Peter Lang, 1995), 9–14.

[13] The convention explicitly stated that its purpose was only "to prevent disputes and differences" between the United States and Britain, not to settle any conflicting claims that the two might have for the territory. The relevant article (no. III) stated that the point of the convention was not to resolve border issues, "it being well understood, that this agreement is not to be construed to the prejudice of any claim which either of the two High Contracting Powers may have to any part of the said Country," quoted in Robert E. Cail, "The Oregon Treaty: Finis to Joint Occupation," *British Columbia Historical Quarterly* 10, no. 3 (July 1946), 222–23.

[14] For the Oregon dispute and its resolution, see Norman A. Graebner, *Empire on the Pacific: A Study in American Continental Expansion* (New York: Ronald Press, 1955); Merk, *The Oregon Question;* David Mitchell Pletcher, *The Diplomacy of Annexation: Texas, Oregon, and the Mexican War* (Columbia: University of Missouri Press, 1973); Rakestraw, *For Honor or Destiny;* Howard Jones and Donald A. Rakestraw, *Prologue to Manifest Destiny: Anglo-American Relations in the 1840s* (Wilmington, Del.: SR Books, 1997). On the genesis of the slogan "54-40 or fight," see Edwin A. Miles, "'Fifty-four Forty or Fight'—An American Political Legend," *Mississippi Valley Historical Review* 44 (September 1957): 291–309.

[15] For an engaging first-hand account of the activities of the British boundary survey, see George F. G. Stanley, ed., *Mapping the Frontier: Charles Wilson's Diary of the Survey of the 49th Parallel, 1858-1862, while Secretary of the British Boundary Commission* (Seattle: University of Washington Press, 1970); cf. Herman J. Deutsch, "A Contemporary Report on the 49 Boundary Survey," *Pacific Northwest Quarterly* 53, no. 1 (January 1962): 17–33; Kathleen Weeks, "Monuments Mark the Boundary," *Canadian Geographical Journal* 31 (September 1945): 120–33. Little evidence of the American survey appears to have survived, but see Marcus Baker, *Survey of the Northwestern Boundary of the United States, 1857-1861,* Bulletin of the United States Geological Survey, no. 174 (Washington, D.C.: Government Printing Office, 1900). Both the British and American official accounts of the survey were misplaced, which perhaps reflects the significance that the two governments attached to them. A Canadian later discovered the British documents in Greenwich in 1898: see Don W. Thomson, *Men and Meridians: The History of Surveying and Mapping in Canada.* Vol.1, *Prior to 1867* (Ottawa: Information Canada, 1966), 262; Otto Klotz, "The History of the Forty-ninth Parallel Survey West of the Rocky Mountains," *The Geographical Review* 3, no. 5 (May 1917): 382–87. Efforts to establish the water boundary through the Gulf Islands, between Vancouver Island and the mainland, became deadlocked, and were ultimately resolved by international arbitration; see F. W. Howay, W. N. Sage, and H. F. Angus, *British Columbia and the United States: The North Pacific Slope from Fur Trade to Aviation* (1942; reprint, New York: Russell and Russell, 1970), 218–27. British and American survey teams did not track the forty-ninth parallel on the other side of the Rockies until the early 1870s; see Don W. Thomson, "The 49th Parallel," *Geographical Journal* 134, pt. 2 (June 1968): 209–15.

[16] See esp. E. E. Rich, *Hudson's Bay Company 1670-1870.* Vol. III. *1821-1870* (Toronto: McClelland and Stewart Ltd., 1960), 401–5; Willard E. Ireland, "The Evolution of the Boundaries of British Columbia," *British Columbia Historical Quarterly* 3, no. 4 (1939), 268–69.

[17] The parliamentary debate on the grant of Vancouver Island to the Hudson's Bay Company took place on 18 August 1848; see *Hansard's Parliamentary Debates: Third Series.* Vol. 101, 263-307 (Gladstone's lengthy speech is on pp. 268-89). In his section on colonies in *The Wealth of Nations,* Adam Smith had criticized the role of monopolistic companies such as the Hudson's Bay Company: "Of all the expedients that can well be contrived to stunt the natural growth of a new colony, that of an exclusive company is undoubtedly the most effectual," a quotation that Gladstone used in his own speech attacking the company; see Adam Smith, *An Inquiry into the Nature and Causes of the Wealth of Nations* (New York: Modern Library Edition, 1937), 542; *Hansard's Parliamentary Debates,* Vol. 101, 18 August 1848, 270.

[18] For the debate surrounding the company's colonization of Vancouver Island, see Paul Knaplund, "James Stephen on Granting Vancouver Island to the Hudson's Bay Company, 1846-1848," *British Columbia Historical Quarterly* 9, no. 4 (1945): 259-71; Knaplund, "Letters from James Edward Fitzgerald to W. E. Gladstone Concerning Vancouver Island and the Hudson's Bay Company, 1848-1850," *British Columbia Historical Quarterly,* 13, no. 1 (1949): 1-21; John S. Galbraith, "The Hudson's Bay Company under Fire, 1847-62," *Canadian Historical Review* 30 (1949): 322-35; Galbraith, "James Edward Fitzgerald Versus the Hudson's Bay Company: The Founding of Vancouver Island," *British Columbia Historical Quarterly* 16, no. 3 (1952): 191-207; Galbraith, *The Hudson's Bay Company as an Imperial Factor, 1821-1869* (Berkeley: University of California Press, 1957); Barry Cooper, *Alexander Kennedy Isbister: A Respectable Critic of the Honourable Company* (Ottawa: Carleton University Press, 1988).

[19] On the early colonizing efforts of the Hudson's Bay Company, see Richard Mackie, "The Colonization of Vancouver Island, 1849-1858," *BC Studies* no. 96 (Winter 1992-93): 3-40; Mackie, "Colonial Land, Indian Labour and Company Capital: The Economy of Vancouver Island, 1849-1858," (master's thesis, University of Victoria, 1984), as well as the works in the preceding footnote.

[20] Finlayson, *Biography of Roderick Finlayson,* 21-22. Note also Helmcken's comments in *The Reminiscences of Doctor John Sebastian Helmcken,* ed. Dorothy Blakey Smith (Vancouver: University of British Columbia Press, 1975), 293-94. The gold rush had a similar impact in the Columbia River Valley, where the company still maintained its fort, as James Douglas described in a letter to a friend who lived east of the mountains: "The Company's servants are distracted at the idea of losing so rich a prize and have deserted to the number of 30 from this establishment [Fort Vancouver on the Columbia River], the others so far steady, but we cannot depend upon them one hour." James Douglas to Donald Ross, 8 March 1849, File 39, Microfilm A-831, Donald Ross Collection, British Columbia Archives, Victoria.

[21] For detail on the Queen Charlotte gold discovery and subsequent events, see Margaret Ormsby, "Introduction," in *Fort Victoria Letters 1846-1851,* ed. Hartwell Bowsfield (Winnipeg: Hudson's Bay Record Society, 1979), xci-xciv; Drew W. Crooks, "Shipwreck and Captivity: The Georgiana Expedition to the Queen Charlotte Islands," *Columbia* VIII, no. 2 (Summer 1994): 17-23; Bessie Doak Haynes, "Gold on Queen Charlotte's Island," *The Beaver* (Winter 1966): 4-11; Patricia Vaughan, "Cooperation and Resistance: Indian-European Relations on the Mining Frontier in British Columbia, 1835-1858," (master's thesis, University of British Columbia, 1978), 29-42. Much official documentary evidence may be found in two parliamentary papers: Great Britain, *Copies or Extracts of Correspondence Relative to the Discovery of Gold at Queen Charlotte's Island,* "Ordered by the House of Commons to be printed 19 July 1853" (London:

Eyre and Spottiswoode, 1853); Great Britain, *Copies or Extracts of Correspondence Relative to the Discovery of Gold at Queen Charlotte's Island,* "Ordered by the House of Commons to be printed 9 August 1853" (London: Eyre and Spottiswoode, 1853). Note also the comments in R. C. Mayne, *Four Years in British Columbia and Vancouver Island: An Account of their Forests, Rivers, Coasts, Gold Fields, and Resources for Colonisation* (London: John Murray, 1862), 43-44.

22 Vaughan, "Cooperation and Resistance," 29. She notes that "There is evidence to suggest that the Haida were looking for new trade items."

23 See Sir John Pakington to James Douglas, 27 September 1852, reprinted in Great Britain, *Copies or Extracts of Correspondence Relative to the Discovery of Gold at Queen Charlotte's Island,* "Ordered by the House of Commons to be printed 19 July 1853" (London: Eyre and Spottiswoode, 1853), 12-14; Barry M. Gough, "'Turbulent Frontiers' and British Expansion: Governor James Douglas, The Royal Navy and the British Columbia Gold Rushes," *Pacific Historical Review* 41 (1972), 16-17; Clarence Karr, "James Douglas: The Gold Governor in the Context of His Times," in *The Company of the Coast,* ed. E. Blanche Norcross (Nanaimo, British Columbia: Nanaimo Historical Society, 1983), 56-78.

24 William J. Trimble, *The Mining Advance into the Inland Empire: A Comparative Study of the Beginnings of the Mining Industry in Idaho and Montana, Eastern Washington and Oregon, and the Southern Interior of British Columbia; and of Institutions and Laws Based Upon that Industry* (1914; reprint, New York: Johnson Reprint Corporation, 1972), 15-23.

25 Douglas to Labouchere, 16 April 1856, in *Copies or Extracts of Correspondence Relative to the Discovery of Gold in the Fraser's River District, in British North America,* "Presented to both Houses of Parliament by Command of Her Majesty, July 2, 1858" (London: Eyre and Spottiswoode, 1858), 5.

26 Douglas to Labouchere, 29 December 1857, op. cit., 8. Douglas candidly admitted to Labouchere that he had exceeded his authority in issuing the proclamation.

27 Howay et al., *British Columbia and the United States,* 14; "The Discovery of Hill's Bar in 1858," *British Columbia Historical Quarterly* III, no. 3 (July 1939), esp. 217 (this is the reminiscences of James Moore, one of the discoverers); R. E. Gosnell, "First Gold Excitement," in *The Year Book of British Columbia and Manual of Provincial Information* (Victoria, British Columbia: s.n., 1897), 88 (another account based on Moore's recollections); Walter N. Sage, *Sir James Douglas and British Columbia* (Toronto: University of Toronto Press, 1930), 203.

28 See Douglas to Labouchere, 8 May 1858, *Correspondence,* 12-14; also *The Reminiscences of Doctor John Sebastian Helmcken,* 154-55.

29 As a recent study notes, estimates vary from a low of 10,000 to a high of 100,000; see Daniel P. Marshall, "Rickard Revisited: Native 'Participation' in the Gold Discoveries of British Columbia," *Native Studies Review* 11, no. 1 (1997): 91-108.

30 The best account of the rush is Morley Arthur Underwood, "Governor Douglas and the Miners, 1858-1859," (bachelor's thesis, University of British Columbia, 1974), but see also the recent book by Netta Sterne, *Fraser Gold 1858! The Founding of British Columbia* (Pullman: Washington State University Press, 1998).

31 For an opposing view that argues explicitly that there was a "Fraser River War," see Marshall, "Rickard Revisited." My approach is largely drawn from Vaughan's "Cooperation and Resistance: Indian-European Relations on the Mining Frontier in British Columbia, 1835-1858," esp. 43-55.

32 See Vaughan, "Cooperation and Resistance," 54; Sage, *Sir James Douglas and British Columbia,* 225-28.

[33] Stanley, *Mapping the Frontier,* 27.

[34] See the account in Mayne, *Four Years in British Columbia and Vancouver Island,* 52-54. Mayne's much repeated anecdote, involving "a blustering Yankee" and Douglas is also revealing of British attitudes and the invention of the Canadian tradition. When the American allegedly demanded to know how British authorities would treat those prepared to defy and resist the law, Douglas is supposed to have responded, "We should cut them to mince-meat, Mr. _____; we should cut them to mince-meat,"55.

[35] For a succinct account of the doctrine, see T. A. Rickard, *Historic Backgrounds of British Columbia* (Vancouver: Wrigley Printing Co., 1948), 297; also, Robert Foster MacSwinney, "Property in Mines Royal," in *The Law of Mines, Quarries, and Minerals* (London: W. Maxwell and Son, 1884), 40-41. Today's system of tree farm licenses that underpins the B.C. forest industry reflects the same principle, and continues to generate acrimonious disputes under the North American Free Trade Agreement.

[36] See Paul Phillips, "Confederation and the Economy of British Columbia," in *British Columbia and Confederation,* ed. W. George Shelton (Victoria: Morriss Printing Company Ltd., 1967), 43-65, esp. 47-48.

[37] There was, however, a keen sense in Canada West (today's southern Ontario) of the need to incorporate the prairie west into a greater Canadian state. See Doug Owram, *Promise of Eden: The Canadian Expansionist Movement and the Idea of the West, 1856-1900* (Toronto: University of Toronto Press, 1980); note also the American interest in the same territory, described in James G. Snell, "The Frontier Sweeps Northwest: American Perceptions of the British American Prairie West at the Point of Canadian Expansion (circa 1870)," *Western Historical Quarterly* 11, no. 4 (October 1980): 381-400. Suzanne Zeller's work deconstructs scientific speculation about and exploration in the prairie west: see her book, *Inventing Canada: Early Victorian Science and the Idea of a Transcontinental Nation* (Toronto: University of Toronto Press, 1987), passim; Zeller, "Classical Codes: Biogeographical Assessments of Environment in Victorian Canada," *Journal of Historical Geography* 24, no. 1 (1998): 20-35.

[38] For useful accounts of the events at Red River, see Gerald Friesen, *The Canadian Prairies: A History* (Toronto: University of Toronto Press, 1984), 91-128; J. M. Bumsted, *The Red River Rebellion* (Winnipeg: Watson and Dwyer, 1996). British Columbia's entry into Confederation has attracted little noteworthy scholarship, but see the essays in W. George Shelton, ed., *British Columbia and Confederation* (Victoria: Morriss Printing Company Ltd., 1967). Canadian politicians had wanted to call the country created in 1867 "the Kingdom of Canada," but were forced to accept the "dominion" of Canada ("dominion" was adopted from the Seventy-second Psalm: "He shall have dominion also from sea to sea and from the river unto the ends of the earth."). As Sir John A. Macdonald, Canada's first prime minister and one of the architects of Confederation, later recalled, "the change of the title from Kingdom to Dominion . . . was made at the insistence of Lord Derby, then Foreign Minister, who feared the first name would wound the sensibilities of the Yankees." Letter of Sir John Macdonald, 18 July 1889, quoted in Joseph Pope, *Memoirs of the Right Honourable Sir John Alexander Macdonald* . . . (1894; reprint, Toronto: Musson Book Co., 1930), 332. Cf. the discussion of American politicians' opposition to the "Kingdom of Canada" in Lester Burrell Shippee, *Canadian-American Relations, 1849-74* (1939; reprint, New York: Russell and Russell, 1970), 195-203.

[39] See Norbert MacDonald, "The Canadian Pacific Railway and Vancouver's Development to 1900," in *British Columbia: Historical Readings,* ed. W. Peter Ward

and Robert A. J. McDonald (Vancouver: Douglas and McIntyre Ltd., 1981), 396-425; Robert A. J. McDonald, "Victoria, Vancouver, and the Economic Development of British Columbia, 1886-1914," in *British Columbia: Historical Readings,* ed. Ward and McDonald, 369-95; Robert A. J. McDonald, *Making Vancouver, 1863-1913* (Vancouver: University of British Columbia Press, 1996), esp. 33-89.

40 For various perspectives on this (enormous) topic, see Ronald Radosh, "American Manufacturers, Canadian Reciprocity, and the Origins of the Branch Factory System," *CAAS Bulletin* 3, no. 1 (1967): 19-54; Michael Bliss, "Canadianizing American Business: The Roots of the Branch Plant," in *Close the 49th Parallel Etc.: The Americanization of Canada,* ed. Ian Lumsden (Toronto: University of Toronto Press, 1970), 26-42; Thomas William Acheson, "The Social Origins of Canadian Industrialism: A Study in the Structure of Entrepreneurship," (Ph.D. diss., University of Toronto, 1971); Craig Heron, "The Second Industrial Revolution in Canada, 1890-1930," in *Class, Community and the Labour Movement: Wales and Canada 1850-1930,* ed. Deian R. Hopkin and Gregory S. Kealey (Aberystwyth, Wales, U.K.: Llafur, 1989), 48-66.

41 Harold Adams Innis, *A History of the Canadian Pacific Railway* (1923; reprint, Toronto: University of Toronto Press, 1971), 293-94. Similarly, "to a very large extent the net earnings and total receipts of the Canadian Pacific Railway have been directly obtained from western Canada," Innis, *A History of the Canadian Pacific Railway,* 269. Interestingly enough, the book's review in the *Canadian Historical Review* drew attention to this: "Throughout, Dr. Innis has endeavoured to preserve an objective attitude, and to abstain from judgments as to the wisdom or unwisdom of the polices discussed. One interesting and highly controversial exception is the repeated assertion of the 'acquisitive' attitude of eastern Canada," O. D. Skelton, *Canadian Historical Review,* 4, no. 2 (June 1923): 180. For an introduction to Innis's work and its influence, see Harold A. Innis, *Staples, Markets, and Cultural Change: Selected Essays of Harold Innis,* ed. Daniel Drache (Montreal: McGill-Queen's University Press, 1995).

42 For an account of this theme in the historiography, see Jeremy Mouat, "Nationalist Narratives and Regional Realities: The Political Economy of Railway Development in South-Eastern British Columbia, 1895-1905," in John M. Findlay and Ken Coates, eds., *Parallel Destinies: Canadians, Americans, and the Western Border* (Seattle: University of Washington Press, 2001).

43 See T. D. Regehr, "Western Canada and the Burden of National Transportation Policies," in *The Prairie West: Historical Readings,* 2d. ed., ed. R. Douglas Francis and Howard Palmer (Edmonton: Pica Pica Press, 1992), 264-84; more generally, Friesen, *The Canadian Prairies,* 162-94.

44 "Report of a Committee of the Privy Council," 14 June 1883, reprinted in *British Columbia Sessional Papers,* 1884, 175; cf. the discussion of this episode in Patricia E. Roy, "Railways, Politicians and the Development of the City of Vancouver as a Metropolitan Centre 1886-1929," (master's thesis, University of Toronto, 1963); Ronald Howard Meyer, "The Evolution of Railways in the Kootenays," (master's thesis, University of British Columbia, 1970).

45 T. G. Shaughnessy to Prime Minister Wilfrid Laurier, 12 September 1896, no. 6990, quoting an earlier memorandum to Sir Charles Tupper, 15 April 1896; reproduced on microfilm, "Papers Relating to British Columbia from the Laurier Collection in the Public Archives of Canada," Reel 1 (copy in University of British Columbia Library).

46 Thomas G. Shaughnessy to W. H. Aldridge, 12 October 1904, Shaughnessy Letterbook 83, M.G. 28, III 20, Reel 111, 459-460, National Archives of Canada;

see also W. H. Aldridge to Thomas G. Shaughnessy, 22 September 1904, and Shaughnessy to Aldridge, 19 December 1904, both in Shaughnessy Letter Register no. 19, 1904, File 76913, CPR Archives, Montreal.

[47] Martin J. Sklar, *The Corporate Reconstruction of American Capitalism, 1890-1916: The Market, the Law, and Politics* (New York: Cambridge University Press, 1988), 1; cf. Alfred Dupont Chandler, *The Visible Hand: The Managerial Revolution in American Business* (Cambridge, Mass.: Belknap Press, 1977), passim. For an overview of the Canadian context, see Robert Craig Brown and Ramsay Cook, *Canada 1896-- 1921: A Nation Transformed* (Toronto: McClelland and Stewart, 1974); Kenneth Norrie and Douglas Owram, *A History of the Canadian Economy,* 2d. ed. (Toronto: Harcourt Brace Canada, 1996), 217-90; Christopher Armstrong and H.V. Nelles, *Monopoly's Moment: The Organization and Regulation of Canadian Utilities, 1830- 1930* (Philadelphia: Temple University Press, 1986). (The last is a very useful analysis despite the narrow focus suggested by the title.)

[48] On the significance of Britain and Empire in fin de siècle Canada, see Carl Berger, *The Sense of Power: Studies in the Ideas of Canadian Imperialism, 1867-1914* (Toronto: University of Toronto Press, 1970); Douglas Cole, "Canada's 'Nationalistic' Imperialists," *Journal of Canadian Studies* 5, no. 3 (August 1970): 44-49 (a thoughtful review of Berger's book); Douglas Cole, "The Problem of 'Nationalism' and 'Imperialism' in British Settlement Colonies," *Journal of British Studies* 10 (1971): 160-82; Robert J. D. Page, "Canada and the Imperial Idea in the Boer War Years," *Journal of Canadian Studies* 5, no. 1 (February 1970): 33-49. More generally, see John Eddy and Deryck Schreuder, eds., *The Rise of Colonial Nationalism: Australia, New Zealand, Canada and South Africa First Assert Their Nationalities, 1880-1914* (Sydney: Allen and Unwin, 1988).

[49] The literature on nationalism is large and growing, but important works include Benedict Anderson, *Imagined Communities: Reflections on the Origin and Spread of Nationalism,* rev. ed. (London: Verso, 1991); Eric Hobsbawm and Terence Ranger, eds., *The Invention of Tradition,* (Cambridge: Cambridge University Press, 1983); Linda Colley, *Britons: Forging the Nation, 1707-1837* (New Haven, Conn.: Yale University Press, 1992); Geoff Eley and Ronald Grigor Suny, eds., *Becoming National: A Reader* (New York: Oxford University Press, 1996); Geoffrey Cubitt, ed., *Imagining Nations* (Manchester: Manchester University Press, 1998).

[50] See "Bitten, But Unconvinced," Vancouver *Daily Province,* 27 June 1903, 1.

[51] See J. D. McDonald and Joyce Austin, comps., *Rossland Centennial Photo Album, 1897-1997* (Rossland, B.C.: Rossland Historical Museum, 1996), 120; also, the contemporary comment (from a diary kept through the summer of 1900) by "Col. D. Streamer" (Harry Graham), *Across Canada to the Klondyke,* ed. Frances Bowles (Toronto: Methuen, 1984), 140. For Spokane's influence on Rossland's growth, see John Fahey, *Inland Empire: D. C. Corbin and Spokane* (Seattle: University of Washington Press, 1965), passim; Jeremy Mouat, *Roaring Days: Rossland's Mines and the History of British Columbia* (Vancouver: University of British Columbia Press, 1995), 12-32.

[52] See the account of the campaign in J. M. Beck, *Pendulum of Power: Canada's Federal Elections* (Scarborough, Ontario: Prentice-Hall of Canada, 1968), 120-35; W. M. Baker, "A Case Study of Anti-Americanism in English-Speaking Canada: The Election Campaign of 1911," *Canadian Historical Review* 51, no. 4 (December 1970): 426-49; Stephen Scheinberg, "Invitation to Empire: Tariffs and American Economic Expansion in Canada," *Business History Review* 47, no. 2 (Summer 1973): 218-38; Robert E. Hannigan, "Reciprocity 1911: Continentalism and American Weltpolitik," *Diplomatic History* 4 (Winter 1980): 1-18; Gordon T. Stewart, *The American Response to Canada since 1776* (East Lansing: Michigan State University Press, 1992), 101-26.

[53] See, for example, John Herd Thompson and Stephen J. Randall, *Canada and the United States: Ambivalent Allies* (Athens: University of Georgia Press, 1994), 92-98.

[54] See Ontario, *Report of the Royal Ontario Nickel Commission* (Toronto: King's Printer, 1917); Canada, Imperial Munitions Board, *A Record of the Investigation, Report and Subsequent Action of the Commission . . . to Investigate the Feasibility of Refining Copper and Producing Metallic Zinc on a Commercial Scale in the Dominion of Canada* (Ottawa: Dominion Printing and Loose Leaf Co., 1916); O. W. Main, *The Canadian Nickel Industry: A Study in Market Control and Public Policy* (Toronto: University of Toronto Press, 1955), esp. 82-89; Viv Nelles, *The Politics of Development: Forests, Mines and Hydro-electric Power in Ontario, 1849-1941* (Toronto: Macmillan of Canada, 1974), 326-35, 349-61; Jeremy Mouat, "Creating a New Staple: Capital, Technology and Monopoly in B.C.'s Resource Sector, 1901-1925," *Journal of the Canadian Historical Association* New Series, 1 (1990): 215-37.

[55] This was the famous (or notorious) Trail Smelter case, which revolved around damage that the smelter's sulfur dioxide fumes caused south of the border. The U.S. government referred the issue to the International Joint Commission in 1928; it was not resolved until 1941. See John E. Read, "The Trail Smelter Dispute," *Canadian Yearbook of International Law/Annuaire Canadien de Droit International,* 1 (1963): 213-29; Alfred P. Rubin, "Pollution by Analogy: The Trail Smelter Arbitration," *Oregon Law Review* 50 (1971): 259-98; D. H. Dinwoodie, "The Politics of International Pollution Control: The Trail Smelter Case," *International Journal* 27, no. 2 (Spring 1972): 219-35; Keith A. Murray, "The Trail Smelter Case: International Air Pollution in the Columbia Valley," *BC Studies* 15 (Autumn 1972): 68-85; James Robert Allum, "Smoke across the Border: The Environmental Politics of the Trail Smelter Investigation," (Ph.D. diss., Queen's University, Kingston, Ontario, 1995); John D. Wirth, *Smelter Smoke in North America: The Politics of Transborder Pollution* (Lawrence: University Press of Kansas, 2000).

[56] L. F. Fitzhardinge, "Hughes, Borden, and Dominion Representation at the Paris Peace Conference," *Canadian Historical Review* 49, no. 2 (June 1968): 160-69; C. P. Stacey, *Canada and the Age of Conflict: A History of Canadian External Policies.* Vol. 1. *1867-1921* (Toronto: University of Toronto Press, 1984), 240-49.

[57] See Stacey, *Canada and the Age of Conflict,* Vol. 1, 85-103; Thompson and Randall, *Canada and the United States: Ambivalent Allies,* 66-69.

[58] For Defence Scheme No. 1, see James Eayrs, *In Defence of Canada: From the Great War to the Great Depression* (Toronto: University of Toronto Press, 1964), 70-78, 323-38 (which reprints extracts from the plan); Richard A. Preston, *The Defence of the Undefended Border: Planning for War in North America 1867-1939* (Kingston: McGill-Queen's University Press, 1977), 213-33; C. P. Stacey, *Canada and the Age of Conflict: A History of Canadian External Policies,* Vol. 2. *1921-1948, The Mackenzie King Era* (Toronto: University of Toronto Press, 1981), 155-58; Galen Roger Perras, *Franklin Roosevelt and the Origins of the Canadian-American Security Alliance, 1933-1945: Necessary, But Not Necessary Enough* (Westport, Conn.: Praeger, 1998), 16, 29, n. 98. For the comment from the U.S. military and Roosevelt's reaction, see Perras, *Franklin Roosevelt,* 12-16; Preston, *The Defence of the Undefended Border,* 217-28; Stacey, *Canada and the Age of Conflict,* 2, 154.

[59] See Thompson and Randall, *Canada and the United States: Ambivalent Allies,* 127-50; and more generally, Carl C. Berger, "Internationalism, Continentalism, and the Writing of History: Comments on the Carnegie Series on the Relations of Canada and the United States," in *The Influence of the United States on Canadian Development: Eleven Case Studies,* ed. Richard A. Preston (Durham, N.C.: Duke University Press, 1972), 32-54; Phillip Buckner, "How Canadian Historians

Stopped Worrying and Learned to Love the Americans!" *Acadiensis* 25, no. 2 (Spring 1996): 117-40; Allan Smith, *Canada—An American Nation? Essays on Continentalism, Identity and the Canadian Frame of Mind* (Montreal: McGill-Queen's University Press, 1994), esp. 57-58, 99-101. More speculative, but also valuable are W. H. New, *Borderlands: How We Talk about Canada* (Vancouver: University of British Columbia Press, 1998); John Grey, *Lost in North America: The Imaginary Canadian in the American Dream* (Vancouver: Talonbooks, 1994).

60 Senator Raoul Dandurand, quoted in Stacey, *Canada and the Age of Conflict: A History of Canadian External Policies,* Vol. 2, 61.

61 Quoted in Perras, *Franklin Roosevelt,* 43-44; Stacey, *Canada and the Age of Conflict: A History of Canadian External Policies,* Vol. 2, 226; cf. the description in James Eayrs, *In Defence of Canada: Appeasement and Re-armament* (Toronto: University of Toronto Press, 1965), 183.

62 On World War II and its impact on Canadian-American relations, see Perras, *Franklin Roosevelt,* passim; Eayrs, *In Defence of Canada: Appeasement and Re-armament,* passim; J. L. Granatstein, *Canada's War: The Politics of the Mackenzie King Government, 1939-1945* (Toronto: Oxford University Press, 1975), passim; Thompson and Randall, *Canada and the United States: Ambivalent Allies,* 150-78; Stacey, *Canada and the Age of Conflict: A History of Canadian External Policies,* Vol. 2, 194-373.

63 See Jeremy Mouat, *The Business of Power: Hydro-Electricity in Southeastern British Columbia, 1897-1997* (Victoria: Sono Nis Press, 1997), esp. 121-25; C. D. Andrews, "Cominco and the Manhattan Project," *BC Studies* no. 11 (Fall 1971): 51-62. Note, however, that Andrews focuses exclusively on events at Trail and consequently overlooks much important information. For the bigger picture, see Brian L. Villa, "Alliance Politics and Atomic Collaboration, 1941-1943," in *The Second World War as a National Experience,* ed. Sidney Aster (Ottawa: Canadian Committee for the History of the Second World War, 1981), 148-62; Robert Bothwell, *Nucleus: The History of Atomic Energy of Canada Limited* (Toronto: University of Toronto Press, 1988), ch.1. Heavy water production was possible at Trail largely as a consequence of the pollution control mechanisms that had been put in place to reduce cross-border pollution.

64 See the account in "Centenary of the Signing of the Oregon Boundary Treaty, June 15, 1846," *British Columbia Historical Quarterly* 10, no. 3 (July 1946): 242-44.

The View from Above:
Alaska and the Great Northwest

Stephen W. Haycox

↭

H OW GREAT IS THE PACIFIC NORTHWEST? Because of historical accidents of political geography, commentators usually describe its limits as the states of Washington, Oregon, and Idaho.[1] But cross-border and ecosystem paradigms have suggested that it might better be defined as Cascadia, an area that includes the Georgia Basin and possibly the lower Fraser River Valley.[2] Perhaps the region needs to be still larger. Is it great enough to include the Caledonia Department of Hudson's Bay Company or even the Athabaska Country, as in the artist Paul Kane's "Great Nor-West"?[3] To push the limits even farther, is Alaska part of the Pacific Northwest? Is Alaska a place that should be included in the region that Americans, at least, recognize with intuitive carelessness as the upper, outer corner of their country? And to ask a western historian's question, if Alaska is to be included or excluded, would that be an old or a new Northwest?

Thinking intuitively, the answer to my basic question must surely be "No, Alaska should not be included." If British Columbia is, as Jean Barman has it, "the west beyond the west," then Alaska must be "the America beyond America," of but not *in* the country because outside the familiar and conversational boundaries.[4] Alaskans themselves recognize this intuitive separation by referring to the lower forty-eight states as "Outside," as in "We don't give a damn how they do it outside," the sagebrush rebellionist bumper sticker of the 1970s. And if one purpose of a volume on the regionalism of the Pacific Northwest is to nurture a sense of region, an attempt to include Alaska is surely counterproductive and perhaps inappropriate.

Alaska is a remarkable place. And because *place* can be defined as an integration of nature and human culture, I wish for the moment to focus on the first of these, the landscape.[5] Environmentally, Alaska is actually a number of regions, or, as Robert Bailey might call them, domains.[6] These include the southeast rain forest, the maritime south-central coast, the interior plain, the heavily watered southwest lowland, the Arctic slope, the Aleutian Island archipelago, and several dominating mountain systems, including the Alaska Range, the Wrangell Mountains, and the Brooks Range.

Certainly Alaska has many features that distinguish it as a separate natural region, or environment. Alaska is big, nearly four times as large in land area as California. Alaska has more ecoregions than just about any macroregion. It is America's last wilderness, quite literally, in addition to containing the largest expanses of undeveloped land: Alaska's 50 million acres of designated wilderness equal the total designated wilderness in the rest of the country. In terms of its land area, Alaska is nearly roadless; there are less than 3,000 miles of improved, interurban highway. More than 150 settlements in Alaska are not connected by road to other places. Most of those settlements are Native villages. Alaska is remote; it is not contiguous with the lower forty-eight states, and it is the only U.S. state situated in the high latitudes. Being in the high latitudes (Anchorage lies just north of 60°N latitude), the state has long winters characterized by few hours of daylight and short summers with long daylight hours. Alaska is home to America's largest populations of many species, including brown and black bear; caribou; moose; such marine mammals as orca (killer whale), sea lion, sea otter, and a variety of seals; migratory and nonmigratory waterfowl, including geese, ducks, swan, murres, murrelets, guillemots, and puffins; a number of raptors, including eagles and falcons; and raven, lots and lots of ravens. Some of these, especially moose, bear, and geese are encroaching on the built environment in ever-increasing numbers, because that environment offers resources, shelter, and protection. These mostly unique features of the natural environment do distinguish Alaska somewhat from the rest of America and are the largest attractor of the more than 1 million tourists who visit annually.

Ninety thousand Native Americans live in Alaska: Eskimos, Aleuts, and Indians. There are 211 Native villages. In many of these, subsistence harvesting of natural resources constitutes a major portion of the daily diet and the use of daily time and energy. In 70 of those villages, there is no indoor plumbing. In American terms, all of these are extraordinary statistics by any standard; they make Alaska a unique area and many of the settlements within it unique places.

If human culture is an essential element for defining place, however, analysis of Alaska's population and its place in the region generates a very different image of the state. The notion of exceptionality begins quickly to fade, for the human population is not widely dispersed across the region. There are vast spaces of Alaska with no human population and little human imprint. Today, the total human population of Alaska is about 621,000; Alaska is the second least populated state in the nation. Most of that population has very little interaction with most of Alaska's environment, a phenomenon contrary to the image many Outsiders have of Alaskans, and, remarkably, what many Alaskans imagine of themselves. In 1931, Robert

Marshall wrote that the people of the Koyukuk in Wiseman, Alaska, on the slopes of the Brooks Range, were the happiest people he had ever encountered or could imagine, happy because they lived in and at one with the wilderness, freed from the artificialities of consumerism and social prestige.[7] But few have taken the message to heart, for almost no one lives in Bob Marshall's Alaska.

As they have done historically throughout the West and through all of Alaska's history, most non-Native, immigrant Alaskans live in towns. According to the Alaska Department of Labor, 70 percent of Alaska's population is urban.[8] The principal towns are located in a long north-south string, all along the Pacific Coast from Ketchikan to Seward, and then along a rail corridor from Seward to Fairbanks. About 475,000 people (76 percent) live in that highly concentrated and restricted strip of Alaska. From an environmental perspective, this line of human habitation might be compared to a knife driven into the heart of Alaska along the Susitna and Nenana Rivers, with the handle (complete with indentations for fingers) lying along the Pacific Coast.

Some brief demographic analysis is useful: 260,000 people live in the municipality of Anchorage, crowded together on a tongue of mountain detritus a few feet above Cook Inlet; another 50,000 live in the nearby Matanuska Valley, which has become an Anchorage bedroom community; this is exactly half the state's population.[9] Anchorage's population includes more than 20,000 Alaska Natives, 8 percent of the city's residents, 23.5 percent of all the state's Natives. Another 60,000 urban Alaskans live in the coastal rain forest communities of Southeast, Ketchikan, Petersburg, Wrangell, Sitka, Juneau, Haines, and Skagway, and a number of smaller places. These towns are easily supplied by barge and ferry from Tacoma, normally a two- or two-and-a-half-day journey. In addition to the 310,000 people in the Anchorage area, another 25,000 live in the coastal communities of the Kenai Peninsula and Prince William Sound: Cordova, Valdez, Seward, Kenai/Soldotna, Homer, and Kodiak just beyond the end of the Kenai Peninsula. More than 80,000 people live in Fairbanks and environs, North Pole, Salcha, Harding Lake, and along the rail corridor between Anchorage and Fairbanks. All of these communities also are easily supplied by freight carriers from Tacoma, a four-day trip, or by the Alaska Railroad, which runs from Seward through Anchorage to Fairbanks. It is the transportation link to Seattle/Tacoma that makes life possible in all of these places, that is, the kind of life the people there wish to live.

That is not a life characterized by any intimate, dependent relationship with wilderness or the land. In fact, it is the very independence from the land (or the appearance of independence) that defines the lifestyle and the *desideratum* of these people. Alaska's urban population is comprised of people who desire, demand, all the amenities, entertainments, conveniences, comforts, distractions, and distortions of contemporary urban life in America. More fundamentally, these people want jobs, and the jobs are in these communities. The jobs are necessary to pay for the amenities, entertainments, and the rest, without which the people who hold the jobs would not tolerate the climate and the remote nature of the place.[10] For this reason, I choose to call the narrow strip of human habitation running from Ketchikan to Fairbanks the "replication corridor." Susan Orlean, a writer who addresses social conditions in America, wrote in *The New Yorker* several years ago of a culture of trailer courts, bowling alleys, one-story warehouses, and small fundamentalist Christian churches that begins "somewhere on the Great Plains, skips over cities like Portland and Seattle, and then jumps up to Alaska."[11] There are a number of cultures in the replication corridor, but the central idea I wish to suggest by the term is captured well by Orlean's image. The bottom end of the Alaska corridor is anchored at Seattle, anchored by culture and by economy. I will return to this image.

Many people who live in that replication corridor believe themselves to be living in a unique place, exotic by the norms of American experience. Particularly when the winter temperature sinks well below 0° Fahrenheit for weeks at a time, exposing weaknesses in auto batteries, house seams, and certain parts of the soul, exoticism sometimes takes on a blunter meaning. But, in fact, there is little truly exotic about the lives they lead, especially their relationship to the environment. Life in Alaska's large and smaller urban centers is nearly indistinguishable from life in the cities and towns that dot the landscape across the rest of the western United States.

Virtually all of the people in the replication corridor live what is essentially an imitative lifestyle, one that is feasible only because the cost of shipping goods 1,500 miles to the north can be kept within reasonable limits. These low freight rates facilitate settlement in Alaska, because few would live in the state if they could not enjoy the chief features of mainstream American culture. And few could afford to live that lifestyle in any location substantially distant from the coast–railbelt axis. Even a nominal distance from the coast and rail corridor inflates the cost of living dramatically, limiting settlement and non–Native population accordingly. The farther one goes from the habitation axis, the fewer non–Natives there are and the more the population is composed of Natives depending to some degree, usually a large degree, on subsistence for their livelihood.

Few of Alaska's people are self-sufficient. They work at traditional urban jobs for regular wages. Their work places are as likely to be glass monoliths with central heating and indoor-outdoor carpet as in any other part of America, or if in a smaller town, the framed, more cozy structures of the

American hinterland. Most drive ordinary cars on asphalted streets to platted subdivisions of framed houses with unruly grass and unruly children. They shop for groceries in modern supermarkets and for fashionable clothing in typical variety stores. In the larger towns, Alaskans have their choice of warehouse stores or upscale clothing shops. Their lives and lifestyles are the same as those of mainstream America because, as consumers and as developers, they have imported the culture they know and with which they are comfortable. Few have come to the state to live an alternative lifestyle, hunting their own food, hewing their own wood, and carrying their own water. Rather, they have come to prearranged jobs, having been assured first of adequate housing, good schools, and a favorable tax climate. They would not have come at all without the guarantee of job security. Even in a recreational sense, these people have little tangible connection to the unbuilt environment. Saturday afternoon is more likely to find them at Home Depot and at Nordstrom's than anywhere in the wilderness. Thus, in the human culture of the replication corridor, there is little to distinguish the places as Alaskan.

This is a historical phenomenon as well as a contemporaneous one. Immigrants to Alaska have always quickly formed traditional communities characterized by all of the technologies and amenities that characterized the places they left to go north. In 1890, for example, Juneau and Douglas already boasted between them five hotels (with restaurants) and three lodging houses, two free-standing restaurants, thirty-six saloons, two drug stores, thirteen general merchandise stores, two grocery stores, two barbers, a steam laundry, two stove and tin-ware stores, a shoe shop, two breweries, two jewelers, two fur and curio shops, two cigar factories, a slaughterhouse, a meat market, a newspaper, a photographer's studio, a confectioner, several blacksmith shops, and a lumber yard.[12] This was when the total non-Native population of the territory was about 5,000 and there were several other towns in the region, including Sitka and Wrangell. Going to Alaska then (and ever since) has been much like moving from one familiar setting to another.

Other aspects of the cultural environment fail to manifest much distinction. The various analytical criteria that new western historians apply to the West to interpret its overall history fit Alaska quite well. Clyde Milner identified these as nonvanishing Native Americans, the impact of the federal government, exploitation of a golden land, and global population of an international borderland.[13] Patricia Limerick's list, which appeared in *Trails: Toward a New Western History,* also fits: "fuzzy" regional boundaries, a historical process defined in terms other than frontier, the convergence of diverse peoples and their encounters with the environment, a continuitous history, a lack of illusion about negative aspects of the history, and suspicions about objectivity.[14]

Taking these roughly in order, Alaska Natives have not vanished and never thought of doing so. Throughout the twentieth century, the Alaska Native Brotherhood ably represented Alaska Native concerns and staunchly defended Native rights. They worked effectively to bring both the Indian Reorganization Act to Alaska in 1936 and a land claims jurisdiction act the year before.[15] The monumental Alaska Native Claims Settlement Act of 1971 was a culmination of decades of Native political focus and the beginning of an era of extraordinary Native empowerment.

In regard to federal presence, the federal government holds 60 percent of Alaska's land in conservation, military, and resource reserves; 32 percent of the federal land, 72 million acres, is public domain, managed by the Bureau of Land Management. Historically, the federal government vigorously and comprehensively supported non-Native settlement and economic development in Alaska from the purchase to today. The exploitation of each new resource led to a substantial increase in federal largesse, the symbol of which is the Alaska Railroad. This was the only federally owned and operated railroad in an American territory in the nation's history, built to compete with the Guggenheim-owned Copper River and Northwestern Railway (that is, free enterprise).[16] From 1940 to 1970, when Alaska's proximity to the Soviet Union was of extreme importance, the federal government was the biggest employer and biggest spender in Alaska. Today, Alaska is at the top of the list in per capita federal spending by state.[17]

In common with other high-latitude places, Alaska's economy is nearly exclusively based in resource extraction, in the case of Alaska, first gold, then salmon, copper, and oil. Today, taxation of petroleum production contributes about 73 percent of general fund revenue; investment earnings and other resource tax revenue contribute another 20 percent.[18] Capital for extraction investment must come from outside the region, of course, thus creating tension within the state over dependence on the outside sources for continued residence and sustenance within the region. In regard to global population in a borderland, there were always minorities in Alaska to discriminate against and to fear when their successful land claims took potential resources out of non-Native control.

Alaska's history reads much better as a continuitous process than as a triumphalist saga, although many residents have convinced themselves that it is their mission to triumph over nature. Most non-Natives went to the region as what Richard White has called "modern migrants," that is, to acquire wealth that could be liquefied and transferred out of the region, to warmer and more familiar climes. The transiency rate has always been high in Alaska and is one of the highest in the nation still.

Much of this reality has been ignored in framing the historical meaning of Alaska, however, as it has been ignored in much of the history of the American West. The Canadian historian Desmond Morton captured well the problem of writing history in the face of fiercely held historical mythologies: "History is a study of the past, pursued by those who try to get things right, even if they almost never succeed. Heritage is our attempt to exploit the past for present tastes, and therefore, by definition, has nothing to do with what actually happened."[19] Richard White has emphasized that myth denies historical change, and thus is, in the final analysis, unhistorical.[20] As in the rest of the West, mythologized history plays a significant role in Alaska modern consciousness.

An unabashed history of Alaska would find dependence, racism, and significant environmental despoliation and alteration. This history would include the overturning and denuding of the earth and the manipulation of its water everywhere there was mineralized rock, inundation of game populations and the introduction of exotic species for sport and trophy hunting, favorable reaction to federal subsidies of the harvest of old growth stands in the Tongass National Forest, and jealousy that absentee investors reaped the capital rewards for salmon and crab harvesting rather than those who might get themselves classified as locals by meeting residency requirements. This history would also find the gleeful embrace of each new magnitude of technological advance, including the Atomic Energy Commission's megaton nuclear-device testing program on Amchitka Island, a wildlife refuge; the same agency's plan for "peaceful use of the atom" to create an artificial harbor at Cape Thompson on the western Arctic coast; and the U.S. Army Corps of Engineers scheme to dam the Yukon River to create a reservoir the size of the state of Connecticut over the breeding grounds of hundreds of thousands of migratory waterfowl.

The history of environmental regulation in Alaska also mimics what has taken place in the West. Three wilderness issues became environmental battlegrounds as national policy shifted from Progressive-era conservationism to modern environmentalism: the Alaska Pipeline, the Alaska Lands Act, and the Tongass National Forest. Alaska was but the venue for these battles; the issues were national and so was the leadership.[21] The Alaska Coalition, formed to lobby Congress and rally national support for a permanent protection of Alaska wilderness, was comprised of national representatives and spokespersons from all of the major environmental groups working for the change in national policy. Most of them were fresh from environmental battles in the American West.[22]

But all of these aspects of western commonality pale when compared to the mythologizing of the past that passes for an Alaska history. Gold-pan-toting sourdoughs, awed Matanuska colonists, grimly determined statehood campaigners, and rugged Carhart-padded pipeline construction laborers speak a heroic saga in countless tourist videos that manifest a single-minded, exclusivist preoccupation with triumph over a hard, resistant, and unforgiving natural environment, all dedicated to regional economic development and Alaskan progress. These images owe more to Jack London and flattering historians than they do to serious scholarship and comprehensive analysis. But these images manifest an imagined past that contemporary Alaskans believe produced the place they live today and the people they would like to become.

All historians of the American West will recognize these various interpretive historical paradigms: the nonvanishing Native American, the impact of the federal government, the exploitation of the golden land, a global population in a borderland, the repetitive mythologizing of the region's history. They are now stock in trade in western scholarship. What perhaps has not been well recognized is their application to Alaska. They seem fully applicable, providing a more balanced, realistic, and useful explanation of what things were and how they have become what they are.

Identifying such commonalities relates Alaska to the history of the American West, places Alaska history nicely within the context of western history, and helps to lodge Alaska in the American West. Virginia Scharff would perhaps be as horrified in the way I have expanded the West to include Alaska as she was at what had been taken out of the West, writing in "Honey, I Shrunk the West," her review of the *Atlas of the New West*.[23] But the Alaska of the replication corridor is virtually indistinguishable from the broader West that Scharff and others have called for. As the tourists so often say when they step off the plane in Anchorage and look around, "Where's Alaska? This looks like the place I just left."

To say that Alaska should be included in the West does not erase those aspects of its history and character that are unique. But the historical mythology or heritage of Alaska has from the beginning focused on exceptionality. And the rhetoric of exceptionality has emphasized independence, despite historical realities to the contrary. Economically, for example, Alaska has always been slavishly dependent; in fact, Alaska has been called an economic appendage of Seattle. Before the development of "big oil" in Alaska, little economic activity, aside from that stemming from federal subsidies and support, did not involve Seattle. Virtually all histories of that city recount the economic leap provided by the Klondike and subsequent gold rush era. The Alaska Bureau of the Seattle Chamber of Commerce sought to capitalize on Alaska by planning the Alaska-Yukon-Pacific Exposition in 1908, which developed the grounds that became the University of Washington campus.[24] When they dedicated the Alaskan Way

Viaduct along Seattle's waterfront in 1955, the city fathers acknowledged the "seminal role Alaska has played in the economic growth and advance of this metropolis. We must recognize the central role played by the Klondike gold rush and the mining industry of Alaska in laying a foundation for Seattle's business community."[25]

The Alaska Bureau built well, for Seattle never relinquished its role as Alaska's port. The city continues to be Alaska's principal supplier (that is, creditor). "Virtually everything that is consumed or used in Alaska, from staples like beans and rice to luxuries like BMWs and Rivieras, passes through the ports and airports of Puget Sound," a journalist wrote recently.[26] "We have an umbilical-cord connection to the Northwest," the head of the AFL-CIO Alaska chapter asserted. Sea-Land Service, Inc. and Totem Ocean Trailer Express move 70 percent of all Alaska tonnage through their terminals at Tacoma, which represents 35 percent of the port's container business. The remainder of Alaska freight moves by barge from Seattle. Indeed, 90,000 Puget Sound-area jobs are related to the northern state.[27]

Alaska fishing has always been a Seattle- and Puget Sound-based enterprise. The principal packers of Alaska salmon are Seattle companies. A dominating portion of the salmon and crab fishing fleet comes from Seattle, Bellingham, and other Puget Sound ports and Anacortes, as Patrick Dillon's story about crabbers in the Bering Sea, *Lost at Sea,* recalls.[28]

An estimated 1.4 million visitors came to Alaska in 1999; the volume of tourist business was up 4 percent from the previous year, a phenomenon that has repeated for over half a decade. Most of those visitors came through Seattle to get to Alaska, even those who started from Vancouver, B.C. Westours, Grayline, and Alaska Airlines, the biggest players, are all based in Seattle. Although the tourist industry creates a number of low-wage jobs in Alaska, most of the profits go to Seattle.

Much of Alaska's history was written by Washington state's political patriarchs, Henry M. Jackson and Warren G. Magnuson. From his seat on the Senate Interior Committee, Jackson directed a presidential committee to find a way to solve the Alaska Native land claims dilemma in 1965. The committee had just produced a solution when Prudhoe Bay oil was discovered in 1967. The monumental claims settlement act in 1971 was very much Jackson's project.[29] Magnuson wrote the Fishery Conservation and Management Act of 1976 that established the 200-mile economic enterprise zone off Alaska's western coast and virtually created the Alaska bottom-fishery industry. Other Washington political magnates earlier in the century handled Alaska patronage and used their legislative power to benefit Seattle-based businesses. Wesley Jones, of the sometimes-infamous Jones Act, leaps to mind.

These historical realities demonstrate Alaska's position as economic hinterland to Seattle's function as distribution, service, and investment center.[30] Indeed, the dependence is so complete that it ought not to be possible to write the history of Seattle and Tacoma, at least, and to a lesser degree Portland and Spokane, without an awareness of the economic relationship of those places to Alaska. A history of the political economy of the Pacific Northwest that does not include an analysis of Alaska's role would be incomplete. Of all the places in Virginia Scharff's broader West, Alaska is tied most closely to Puget Sound country.

I return, now, to Susan Orlean's image of a hapless West strewn across the Great Plains to the Pacific Northwest and jumping over Portland and Seattle to a terminus in Alaska. This image carries with it a sense of movement, of successive false starts, perhaps, finally reaching the end of the line at the end of the road. "End of the road" worked for long time as a migration metaphor in the American West. As the West increasingly lost its isolation in the last half of the twentieth century, the metaphor transferred nicely to Alaska. Jon Krakauer used it recently in his chilling book on Christopher McCandless, *Into the Wild*.[31] Kevin Coughlin, a University of Oregon journalism graduate student, is using it for a book about Louis Hastings, who on March 1, 1983, lured his few neighbors to a friend's cabin near the airstrip at McCarthy, Alaska and shot nine of them to death, almost half the population of that wilderness cul-de-sac.[32] Tom Bodett gave it a comic turn in his first major collection, *As Far as You Can Go without a Passport: The View from the End of the Road*.[33] Alaska today has supplanted the American West, and perhaps the Pacific Northwest, as the end of the line. The far corner of the country is no longer Seattle or Point Roberts; it's probably Bethel, Alaska, which has been described as "Sin City, USA."[34] If "end of the road" were only a detritus metaphor, I suspect Seattleites would be happy to be rid of it.

But Orlean captures only half of the imagery. Writing in his 1966 Turnerian analysis of the twentieth-century West, *America's Frontier Heritage,* Ray Allen Billington used psychological terms to identify motives for westward movement, "deficiency motivation" and "abundancy motivation."[35] Those characterized by deficiency motivation were running away, Billington suggested; abundancy motivation meant curiosity for something more. The publishing market seems to have less room for Alaska success stories than for northern tragedy, but there are some. Jay Hammond's *Tales of Alaska's Bush Rat Governor: The Extraordinary Autobiography of Jay Hammond, Wilderness Guide and Reluctant Politician* is one of the few, the title of which seems fair warning regarding the writer's interpretation.[36] One has to return nearly to the gold rush to find an abundance of migratory triumphs, as in the recently republished memoir of William B. Haskell, who spent 1897 and 1898 in the north and came home with gold.[37]

The corridor to the gold fields started in Seattle. Through Seattle's port, and to a lesser degree Portland's and Victoria's, poured all the men and women headed north, the material they thought they needed, their energies and aspirations, their anxieties and shortcomings, and most fundamentally, their culture. Somewhat surprisingly, about half of the number who came in that first wave stayed. Seattle nurtured their determination to recreate as quickly and as wholly as possible the culture they feared they might leave behind. Seattle did its work so well that not only did the Alaskans replicate all that they had known, but economies of scale made them permanently dependent on Seattle produce, durable goods, and even ideas. Today, no city rivals Anchorage as disciple of the corner and midblock coffee stand. Names such as Coho Cafe, Motor Mocha, Raven's Roast, and Latte-Dah are so ubiquitous that one can create the illusion of actually being in Seattle simply by their recitation.

At least culturally, then, I would suggest that Alaska's replication corridor, despite its more remote location and the potential within it for an embrace of wilderness values, manifests little that is different from most of the rest of the American West, particularly the corner of it closest to Alaska, the Pacific Northwest. Exceptionality as an interpretive paradigm has played well as heritage, but it works poorly as history, a reality that I hope students of Alaska history will take increasingly to heart.

Notes

[1] Carlos Schwantes, *The Pacific Northwest: An Interpretive History* (Lincoln: University of Nebraska Press, 1989), 1–16.

[2] See, for example, J. Kingston Pierce et. al., with photographs by Morton Beebe, *Cascadia: A Tale of Two Cities, Seattle and Vancouver, B.C.* (New York: Harry N. Abrams, 1996); Robert D. Kaplan, *An Empire Wilderness: Travels into America's Future* (New York: Random House, 1998), 314–24; an older suggestion appears in Joel Garreau, *The Nine Nations of North America* (Boston: Houghton-Mifflin, 1981).

[3] Diane Eaton and Sheila Urbanek, *Paul Kane's Great Nor-West* (Vancouver: University of British Columbia Press, 1995).

[4] Jean Barman, *The West Beyond the West: A History of British Columbia* (Toronto: University of Toronto Press, 1991).

[5] Dan Flores, "Place: An Argument for Bioregional History," *Environmental History Review* 18 (Winter 1994): 1–18.

[6] Robert G. Bailey, *Ecoregions of the United States* (Washington, D.C.: Department of Agriculture, U.S. Forest Service [prepared by the U.S. Geological Survey], 1976).

[7] Robert Marshall, *Arctic Village* (New York: H. Smith and R. Haas, 1933), 375–79.

[8] Alaska Department of Labor, *Alaska Population Overview* (Juneau: ADL, June 1998), 97; U.S. Bureau of the Census, *Statistical Abstract of the United States 1998: The National Data Book* (Washington, D.C.: Government Printing Office, October 1998), 46. The Bureau of the Census defines urban as places with a population of 2,500 or more. Fifty-four percent of Alaska's population lives in places with 10,000 or more people. The 1990 census reported that 67 percent of Alaska's

population was urban, 93 percent of California's, 70 percent of Oregon's, 76 percent of Washington's, and 57 percent of Idaho's.

9 Compare other western states, Washington, for example, with the Bellingham-Seattle-Tacoma-Olympia corridor accounting for most of the population, or Oregon, with the Portland-Salem-Corvallis-Eugene corridor.

10 The jobs are of two kinds, generally: those connected to the principal economic activity of the region, resource extraction, and those that provide the amenities, entertainments, and the like, including basic sustenance and the replication of the materialist consumerism that has characterized American life through the twentieth century.

11 Susan Orlean, "Figures in a Mall," *The New Yorker,* 21 February 1994, 49-63.

12 U.S. Department of the Interior, Census Office, *Eleventh Census of the United States, Economics* (Washington, D.C.: Government Printing Office, 1891), 238.

13 Clyde A. Milner II, *Oxford History of the American West* (Oxford: Oxford University Press, 1994), 5-6.

14 Patricia Nelson Limerick, Clyde A. Milner II, and Charles E. Rankin, eds. *Trails: Toward a New Western History* (Lawrence: University of Kansas Press, 1991), 85-87.

15 Donald Craig Mitchell, *Sold American: The Story of Alaska Natives and Their Land, 1867-1959: The Army to Statehood* (Hanover, N.H.: The University Press of New England, 1997), 243; Gerald A. McBeath and Thomas A. Morehouse, *Alaska Politics and Government* (Lincoln: University of Nebraska Press, 1994), 267-68.

16 William H. Wilson, *Railroad in the Clouds: The Alaska Railroad in the Age of Steam, 1914-1945* (Boulder, Colo.: Pruett Publishing Co., 1977).

17 "Alaska Gets More from Uncle Sam Than Just About Anybody," *Anchorage Daily News,* 28 June 1992, B2; "Alaska Tops Uncle Sam's Financial Handout List," *Anchorage Daily News,* 4 April 1994, A3.

18 McBeath and Morehouse, *Alaska Politics,* 2, 55, 58, 68, 71, 183.

19 Desmond Morton, *Toronto Star,* 15 January 1998, B1.

20 Richard White, *It's Your Misfortune and None of My Own: A History of the American West* (Norman: University of Oklahoma, 1991), 661.

21 Peter Coates, *Trans-Alaska Pipeline Controversy: Technology, Conservation, and the Frontier* (Bethlehem, Penn.: Lehigh University Press, 1991), 316-23.

22 Peter Coates, "Project Chariot: Alaskan Roots of Environmentalism," *Alaska History* 4 (Fall 1989): 1-31.

23 Virginia Scharff, "Honey, I Shrunk the West," *Pacific Historical Review* 67 (August 1998): 409-20.

24 Schwantes, *Pacific Northwest,* 193, 216-17. Between 1900 and 1910, Seattle's population increased 294 percent, Tacoma's 222 percent.

25 Seattle *Post-Intelligencer,* 12 November 1955, 2.

26 Al Gibbs, "Trade in the Shade," *Anchorage Daily News,* "We Alaskans," 24 March 1996, 12-13.

27 If Alaska were an independent nation, it would rank third highest as an export destination for products from Washington state.

28 Patrick Dillon, *Lost at Sea: An American Tragedy* (New York: Dell Publishing, 1998).

29 Robert D. Arnold with Janet Archibald, *Alaska Native Land Claims* (Anchorage: Alaska Native Foundation, 1976).

30 See Schwantes, *Pacific Northwest,* 382-86, on Seattle's transition from being a hinterland to servicing one.

31 Jon Krakauer, *Into the Wild* (New York: Villard, 1996).

32 Kevin Coughlin, "Works in Progress," *Oregon Quarterly* 78 (Autumn 1998): 9-10.

[33] Tom Bodett, *As Far as You Can Go without a Passport: The View from the End of the Road* (Reading, Mass.: Addison–Wesley, 1985).

[34] Wendell H. Oswalt, *Bashful No Longer: An Alaskan Eskimo Ethnohistory, 1778-1988* (Norman: University of Oklahoma Press, 1990), 187.

[35] Ray Allen Billington, *America's Frontier Heritage* (New York: Holt, Rinehart and Winston, 1966), 26.

[36] Jay Hammond, *Tales of Alaska's Bush Rat Governor: The Extraordinary Autobiography of Jay Hammond, Wilderness Guide and Reluctant Politician* (Fairbanks: Epicenter Press, 1994).

[37] William B. Haskell, *Two Years in the Klondike and Alaskan Gold-Fields, 1896-1898: A Thrilling Narrative of Life in the Gold Mines and Camps* (1898; reprint, Fairbanks: University of Alaska Press, 1998).

Nature's Northwest: In Search of a Pacific Region

William G. Robbins

↩

The West is several different regions . . . all so different in their history and ethnic compositions, that I think trying to make a unanimous culture out of them would be a hopeless job. It would be like wrapping five watermelons.[1]

WALLACE STEGNER

HUMAN CULTURES OF THE PACIFIC NORTHWEST are vivid expressions of the region's geography and history. Both natural events and cultural activity are interwoven across its vast landscape, initiating changes that we are only now beginning to understand. Because they possess geographical agency and are continually in the process of transforming the Earth, humans have always enjoyed a reciprocal relationship with the world around them. This is certainly the case with the Northwest, where the human imprint on the landscape, even by conservative estimates, dates at least to the late Pleistocene. And by all indications, that influence was a considerable one, especially through the use of fire, a widespread and general feature of Indian practice.[2] While humans in the region were in the process of altering their physical surroundings, those culturally induced changes have in turn influenced the behavior of the successive peoples who have settled in the Northwest. In the postindustrial age, in fact, natural and cultural processes have become so intertwined that it is sometimes difficult to distinguish between the two.[3] If global warming is affecting climatic patterns and changes in precipitation eventually alter floral and faunal compositions, conventional distinctions between culture and nature will become even more blurred.

In the sense that humans have provided a geographic description for the Northwest, the region conforms roughly to the vast Columbia River watershed, the 259,000-square-mile drainage of the River of the West. For the last several millennia, the Columbia has sliced through sharply differing climatic zones and ecosystems and a myriad of human cultures along its winding passage to the Pacific Ocean. The river has its source in British Columbia's inconspicuous Columbia Lake, 2,650 feet above sea level, and its largest tributary, the 1,038-mile Snake River, begins at the roof of the continent in two small lakes on Wyoming's Two Ocean Plateau. The extensive Columbia River system has provided the great physical artery, linking the interior reaches of the Pacific slope with the oceanic highways to the west. To a considerable degree, geography has served as a regionalizing influence for the Northwest, with *Nch'i-wána,* the Yakama word for "the Big River," providing a connecting thread during both the prehistoric and historic periods.[4] As Richard White points out, we must reckon with the Great River: "The Columbia runs through the heart of the Northwest in ways we have never imagined. It flows along the numerous divisions of our fractured society."[5]

By the 1840s, a half century or more after the onset of Euro-American influences, the watershed came to define a larger geographic region known as the Oregon Country, a vast area loosely described as extending from the border with Mexico at the forty-second parallel north to the Russian settlements in Alaska and east to the Continental Divide. Canadian scholar Alan Artibise argues that the current globalist effort to promote a Cascadia region is remarkably similar in description to the physical outlines of the old Oregon Country.[6] Despite a few disclaimers, today the greater Pacific Northwest embraces Oregon, Washington, and Idaho, Montana west of the Continental Divide, and southern British Columbia and northern California, contiguous areas with comparable ecosystems and economies. A powerful argument can also be made that historical ties of economics, culture, and passage require that Alaska be considered an extension of the Northwest. Although it is seldom acknowledged, Alaska shares a common boundary with British Columbia (as do Washington, Idaho, and the northwestern corner of Montana). And irrespective of political allegiance, all of those places share a collective reckoning with Pacific waters as well as time and spatial associations with wider geographical spheres. The broad outline of this Pacific Northwest confirms William Ferris's observation that the most important definitions of regions are geographical—illustrated statements that can be seen on a map.[7]

To know something about the physical geography of the greater Pacific Northwest and to know something about the successive human groups that have occupied its storied landscape is to recognize that the great Columbia system, the Fraser, and other streams in the region have been significant forces in human as well as geological history. In addition, the American Northwest shares historical experiences with contiguous areas in Canada: common traditions in dispossessing Native peoples; simultaneous early commercial development centered in the fur trade; the appearance of sawmills and then fish canneries on both sides of the border at the same time; the concurrent extension of transcontinental railroads to Portland, Tacoma, and Vancouver, British Columbia; similar technological environments in mining and logging throughout the natural resource districts of Oregon, Washington, Idaho, and north of the border in British Columbia; shared immigrant/ethnic traditions, including Alaska, that transcend the international boundary; and, finally, both the Canadian and American Northwests front on the "Pacific flank of North America."[8]

But there are problems with cross-border inquiries. Canadian historian Robin Fisher views the international boundary as "an insurmountable object" to defining a larger Pacific Northwest. Only First Nations people, he maintains, effectively ignored the forty-ninth parallel after the Oregon Treaty of 1846. Moreover, historians on both sides of the border have been consumed by imperial and national perspectives and have been more interested in how their respective western portions compare with the east than with comparisons of places north and south of the international boundary. Distinctions between east and west rather than north and south have dominated scholarly discourse. If one takes *la longue duree,* a 10,000-year perspective, a period dominated by First Nations' people, cultural divisions run north and south rather than east and west. The basic differences among Native people were between coastal and interior groups. Canadian historian Ken Coates agrees—the Pacific Northwest enjoyed both cultural and economic integrity during the aboriginal period: "Trade goods moved extensively up and down the coast and from coastal zones into the interior (and along several key interior routes, including the Columbia and Snake rivers)." But when the imperial powers extended their two empires westward, cross-border relations became more limited and citizens reckoned increasingly with their respective nation-states.[9]

"We perhaps do not read enough of each other's history," Fisher suggests. Among other problems, he sees differences in historical interpretations north and south of the border; British Columbia historians have had only a limited interest in ideas, whereas Americans have been obsessed with Frederick Jackson Turner, even while they agree that his ideas no longer hold explanatory power. It should also be remembered, Fisher cautions, that the boundary represents no more than a brokered deal between imperial bargainers. Although historical actors rather than geographic realities dictated the boundary settlement, British Columbia scholar Allan Pritchard remarks that "a strong sense early developed in B.C. that those which separated it from the American northwest marked a division between two different social orders." Different polities and cultures evolved on each side of the border that shaped distinct but adjoining regions. And even in the United States, journalist Mark Trahant observes that territorial and state boundaries were seemingly "drawn by Congress in fits of compromise, greed, and political expediency."[10]

From the formation of the Hudson's Bay Company's Columbia Department in the 1820s to the development of the Bonneville Power Administration's extensive grid system after 1940, the Pacific Northwest has been purposefully defined to serve a variety of corporate, institutional, administrative, and professional purposes. For the United States, those constructions took on added importance early in the twentieth century when Congress created a variety of federal agencies and bureaus with regional offices to administer the nation's resources more efficiently. The academic world, too, joined this regionalizing tendency at the turn of the century when Joseph Schafer at the University of Oregon and Edmund Meany at the University of Washington began teaching the History of the Pacific Northwest.[11] As such, Schafer and Meany were following in the footsteps of the great regionalist, Frederick Jackson Turner, who first gave scholarly credibility to the study of "regions and sections" and subsequently became the icon for an earlier version of American regionalism. One should add to this mix of research the pioneering regional ethnographic work of James G. Swan, Franz Boas, Melville Jacobs, Leslie Spier, Edward Sapir, and Luther Cressman.[12]

✦

There would also appear to be a temporal quality to Pacific Northwest regionalism, because the Northwest is an anomaly among North American regions in one important respect: Its historic period is *very* recent, comprising a relatively brief two centuries of time. Until the early years of the nineteenth century, the Northwest was beyond the reach—or at best on the periphery—of the great demographic, economic, and cultural changes taking place in the great global centers of commerce. Because the historical transformation that has taken place in the region is so recent, those circumstances present unique opportunities to inquire into and explore the *cultural* meaning of what can only be described as dramatic and systemic change over a very brief period of time.[13] To a greater extent than in much of the United States, for example, Native people in the Pacific Northwest still have a living and meaningful presence across the landscape because of their significant holdings in land and resources and their treaty-guaranteed rights to resources away from reservations. And unlike more recent arrivals in the Northwest, its Native American residents live amid the thick cultural meanings of long-inhabited places.[14]

In the study of regions, it is also important to focus attention on questions that contribute to some larger understanding of the relationship between regional and national history. In their thoughtful book, *The Midwest and the Nation,* Andrew Cayton and Peter Onuf contend that the upper Mississippi Valley states of the "Old Northwest" were nurtured and molded "with the ascendancy of commercial capitalism." White, Protestant, and middle-class values permeated the region during its formative period to about the 1850s. When conflict and disagreement arose, it took place within the ideological framework of the social and political values of liberal capitalism; the inherent viability of the system itself was not questioned. "The rise of middle-class values and the institutions of capitalism," they argue, "were synonymous with the rise of the Northwest.[15]

The initial construction of the Pacific Northwest took shape with the ascendancy of the great fur-trading firms: first the Northwest Company and then, after 1821, the Hudson's Bay Company. The increasing reference to the Oregon Country during the 1840s, and after the resolution of the boundary issue in 1846 between England and the United States, the formal designation of Oregon Territory (1848) gave greater physical clarity to the region. The rise of industrial capitalism in the eastern United States was accompanied by the extension of railroads and other symbols of industrialism to the Northwest. Railroads were physical symbols of a technological revolution in production and a dramatic representation of change. As a consequence, it can be argued that a different kind of society developed in the resource-dependent communities of the Pacific Northwest. The coming of industrialism to the region brought different cultural groups, new people, new forms of dependency, and some questioning of bourgeois values.[16]

The physical and cultural worlds of the Pacific Northwest, therefore, harbor fascinating stories. For a century or more following European American occupation and settlement, the American and Canadian Northwests suffered the consequences of economic colonialism: lack of regional autonomy in the control of natural resources and the appropriation of the wealth gleaned through the processing of those resources by capitalists outside the Northwest. There is an additional caveat: The wonderful natural abundance that provided subsistence for Native peoples and that has attracted newcomers to the Northwest for more than a century still has a powerful hold on the region. Although high-tech industries and the attractions of outdoors amenities have surpassed agriculture, mining, logging, and fishing as the Northwest's most visible economic indicators, what we might call "nature's industries," are still at the heart of its cultural landscape. Themes rooted in the material and cultural worlds of natural resource exploitation continue to inspire the best regional writers—Mary Clearman Blew, William Dietrich, Annie Dillard, Ivan Doig, Timothy Egan, David Guterson, Ken Kesey, William Kittredge, Craig Lesley, Native American authors Sherman Alexie and Elizabeth Woody, and many others.[17] As those totems of nature, salmon and old forests, become threatened or disappear altogether, they will continue to be powerful points of conflict and to hold cultural cachet for residents of the region.

"Reality does not come to us in neatly labeled packages," the writer Garry Wills observed. "We impose the labels." As literary constructs, the idea of regionalism and regional identity is a state of mind, a condition where image and cultural belief are as important as substance; moreover, humans also tend to be interested in the lore of the places they inhabit.[18] Katherine Morrissey argues that regionalism is appealing as an intellectual construct, in part, because it is so thoroughly malleable. "What defines a region?" she asks. "What are its boundaries?" To add to this confusion, the manner in which people make attachments and identify with particular places is often difficult to comprehend. "The Nature of a 'region,' " Merrill Jensen pointed out nearly fifty years ago, "varies with the needs, purposes, and standards of those using the concept."[19] Moreover, the Pacific Northwest, the "newest" of American regions, admittedly lacks the deep-rooted and rich cultural life of, say, New England, the South, the Gulf region, the Midwest, or for Canada, the Atlantic and prairie provinces.[20] Appalachia, the Mississippi Valley, and the Sunbelt all resonate with certain meaning to large numbers of people. Carlos Schwantes, author of the most popular history of the Northwest, admits the futility of looking for definitive borders to the region: "Any search for commonly agreed upon boundaries for the Pacific Northwest will prove fruitless. . . . The regional perimeter, except along the Pacific Ocean, remains as indistinct as a fog-shrouded promontory." Schwantes reasons, however, that the Northwest should include the "generally accepted" states of Oregon, Washington, and Idaho, "because of the logic of geography, economics, and history."[21]

The great Columbia River country is obviously a bifurcated physiographic province; it is divided east and west by the north-south trending Cascade Mountain range, with different cultural and political worlds inhabiting each of these sectors. For most of its history, definitions of the Northwest have tended to identify the region with the green, forested lands and metropolitan areas west of the Cascades, with the latter dominating the region's political economy. John Gunther's 1946 classic, *Inside U.S.A.,* defined the Northwest as Oregon and Washington, because they were an integral unit and "fit together like chunks of a well-constructed jigsaw puzzle." The two states shared similar historical, geographical, climatic, and natural resource features, "with Idaho as a sort of pendant." Raymond Gastil's 1975 study, *Cultural Regions of the United States,* regarded the Northwest as an expression of physical geography, "very close to being the American portion of the Columbia River drainage basin," with Puget Sound and a slice of coastal Oregon included. And in a fascinating 1976 article, "The Pacific Northwest," published in *Atlantic Monthly*, Thomas Griffith focused his essay on the three conventional American states, Montana west of the Continental Divide, and coastal British Columbia.[22]

These varying and contradictory definitions of the Pacific Northwest suggest that the region embraces contingent and ambivalent historical, political, and cultural meaning. Because the subject implies definitions of physical geography, the intentional bounding of a place invites controversy and conflict.[23] The purpose of this essay is to inquire into the inherent regional meaning attached to the varying representations of the Northwest, to probe the fascinating and multiple historical/cultural voices that tell stories about occupation and conquest, common patterns to life on the land (farming, mining, logging, town-building), the changing technological landscape particular to the region and that describe the Northwest's various ethnic identities. The frenetic pace of population/demographic change in one of the fastest growing of all American regions and the erosion of regional differences by the media and consumer culture (spurred on by the globalization of economic activity) poses an obvious threat to all regional cultures. The great danger, in my view, is that regionalism will become little more than the worship of the quaint, exotic, and fanciful fringes of antiquated cultural forms and that it will lose its significance for particular places. I do not believe, however, that regionalism represents an antimodernist tendency that romanticizes rural and traditional phenomenon. And although we should resist claims to a crude exceptionalism, we also need to give credence to the special qualities of local meaning.[24]

✤

The threat to regional cultures, even when they are dynamic and changing, is real and the dangers are everywhere. In their book, *Many Wests: Place, Culture, and Regional Identity*, editors David Wrobel and Michael Steiner note that an inexorable cultural leveling appears to characterize American life and that citizens themselves have been implicated in the process.[25] Regional distinctions have tended to crumble as Americans moved ever more aggressively to transform nature since World War II and as information-age technology has increasingly obliterated time and space. The accelerating pace of change across the United States today threatens to reduce the cultural distinctiveness of all regions to a common flavor. According to cultural historian Jackson Lears, to argue that regionalism is still a powerful force denies the tremendous influence of corporations in reshaping culture at every level of human consciousness. To ignore this fact trivializes the ability of this "enormous concentrated power" to communicate its ideas. "America," the writer Donald Snow observes, "is a cuisinart culture that homogenizes as it goes." In such an acquisitive and hyperactive culture, both humans and capital easily transport themselves to places of greater advantage. The consequences of this perpetual motion, he concludes, is that regions once possessing distinctive qualities "are blended down into a pablum of commercial culture . . . in which place is mostly irrelevant, and, increasingly, so is community." Much has changed in our present age; we are now tied globally to a new level of interrelatedness and participation in a world culture and global system.[26]

In a breezy essay for *The Atlantic* on the position of the Pacific Northwest in the new global economy, Robert Kaplan asks his readers to imagine a future in which the dominant culture is internationalized, "in which loyalty is an economic concept." His argument centered on a binational meeting in 1989 when sixty legislators from British Columbia, Washington, and Oregon formed the loosely structured Pacific Northwest Economic Region. Kaplan viewed this strategic alliance of the region's business elite as a "giant high-tech trading block." Warren Gill, an urban geographer at Vancouver's Harbor Centre campus of Simon Fraser University, told Kaplan that "a dynamic and highly educated population and strategic transportation links" were the only requirements for sovereignty "in the phase of history we are entering." Gill then went on to describe Vancouver as "a generic, modern-postmodern" city and especially trendy in the sense that it looks outward to the Pacific world.[27]

But it is the very placelessness suggested in Kaplan's writing that prompted William Leach to point out that American business culture has always been indifferent to place and has been especially so in the last two decades. Place-insensitive bankers and financial managers, he contends, have asserted themselves everywhere and have created a "landscape of the temporary" in which a huge floating population moves about impervious to long term commitments to communities. The consequence is "the weakening of place as a centering presence in the lives of ordinary people." Leach sees the erosion of "a healthy connectedness to place" as a dangerous precedent. The greatest threats to the contemporary world, he believes, are powerful global pressures that are unconcerned about provincial needs, "forces that have ripped to shreds local commitments" and have driven millions of people "into unwanted dispossession and exile." The greatest danger to daily life today is the absence of strong provincial commitments.[28]

Other scholars, however, are persuaded that historical connections and cultural interaction in the Pacific Northwest continue to provide unique forums for discussion. Canadian historian Ken Coates believes that regional cultures and societies, even those that transcend international borders, still exist despite the awesome power of the modern nation-state. "The impressive economic weight of the United States" notwithstanding, Coates thinks the greater Pacific Northwest provides a useful case study because of historic ties and connections between neighbors: "It would be folly to argue . . . that cultural distinctiveness is disappearing." Alan Artibise also describes the Northwest (he uses the term *Cascadia*) as a transboundary province. Beginning with the earliest European presence, people recognized the Northwest as a region unto itself with its common natural resources, maritime industries, mineral discoveries, and interior agricultural sectors. And, Artibise adds, for most of the European American period, boom-and-bust resource exploitation has characterized Cascadia's economy. Artibise notes that the key issue of debate today is between those who see the region as a strategic player in the emerging global and continental economy and those interested in the study of a bioregion. He sees mutual antipathy between the bioregionalists and the free traders. Although they downplay with one voice the significance of the nation-state, "their visions for Cascadia are diametrically opposed."[29]

❧

The study of regions remains a messy proposition and is hotly contested. Those who examine the larger historical and social forces that have directed the course of change during the modern era tend to seek out common threads, unifying causal factors to explain what they see as the underlying catalyst guiding that transformation. In *Colony and Empire: The Capitalist Transformation of the American West,* I used precisely such a strategy in search of a general model to illustrate the distinctive features, the dynamics common to change in western America from the late nineteenth century to the present. The more plausible and convincing explanations for historical change, I argued, were vested in the material world: "in the economic relationships among people; in the ever-changing dynamics of particular economies; and in the set of values and assumptions, the mode(s) of production, inherent in what we call capitalism, the basic organizing principle for much of the global economy from the onset of the Industrial Revolution to the present." I concluded, in short, that capitalism provided coherency, structure, and an organizational theme for addressing change in the American West during the last 200 years.[30]

The evidence for such an interpretive framework seemed overwhelming. I was persuaded by the convincing arguments of my colleague and friend, William Appleman Williams, the writings of Fernand Braudel, Raymond Williams, and a host of others that the world-view and values associated with capitalism explained the way people behaved in the world about them and that economic and political decisions were always components of a larger rational scheme. For North America, particularly its western reaches, the argument *is* convincing. The characteristic behavior of capitalism fit the region well: its inclination to always expand its theater of operations, its perpetual move toward ever-increasing accumulation, its favoritism toward urban centers, its propensity toward unceasing technological change, and its incessant dynamism in destroying and creating new forms of capitalist relations. This inherently revolutionary and volatile system, I contended, affected all and left nothing untouched in its wake.[31]

To be sure, that is a significant part of the story and explains much about the evolution of the modern West. But as friends and critics alike have indicated, there is much more to explaining the historical process than a singular focus on the hegemony of capitalism. On one level it works wonderfully as an all-encompassing explanatory model. And yet, viewing capitalism as the singular reality of the social and political order does not explain *everything*. It fails to reckon with human ingenuity and difference and it overlooks the efforts of those who sought to build a society that promised something more than the reduction of all behavior to market transactions. The human spirit has always possessed an insurgent mood that has contested cultural conformity and political orthodoxy. In a delightful series of essays on the American South, social historian Jack Temple Kirby refers to such resistance as "noncollaboration with the hegemonic national (as well as regional) culture of capitalist individualism."[32] Moreover, those counter-cultural expressions of difference usually manifested themselves at the local and regional level, where intimate associations with place are deeply lived experiences.[33]

Historically, expressions of dissidence in opposing various orthodoxies across the greater Pacific Northwest assumed a variety of political and cultural forms. The region has enjoyed its fair share of religious and political utopian communal experiments of varying kinds.[34] Wilhelm Keil escorted a party of German Christian communists from Missouri to Washington and then to Oregon, where the group established Aurora Colony in 1857. From the late 1880s through the first part of the twentieth century, utopians established several ethnic and communal socialist experiments in the region. Although the numbers involved in these settlements were never large, the new settlers brought a refreshingly multicultural ethnic cast of people to the Northwest—Germans, Swedes, Finns, Russians, Danes, and many others. A small group of young Jewish refugees established a short-lived community known as New Odessa, near Roseburg, Oregon in the 1880s. Because Astoria developed as an important center for the salmon canning industry, it first attracted a sizable Chinese and then a Finnish settlement, with the latter eventually creating a vibrant socialist tradition in the community. And in the quiet farming community of Junction City, Oregon an enterprising realtor and immigrant from Denmark, A. C. Nielsen, established a significant colony of Danes during the first two decades of the twentieth century. Neilson's avowed purpose in establishing the colony was to "to preserve our Christian life and our cultural uniqueness."[35]

But the most significant and memorable of the resistance cultures were associated with the region's great geography of resources: minerals, timber, fish, and rich valley-bottom land. "For the better part of its recorded history," according to Carlos Schwantes, "life in the Pacific Northwest revolved around supplying the world with raw materials." With its "hinterland status" as a "supplier of raw material," residents of the region had to struggle through decades of economic colonialism. According to Ann Markusen, an important source of historical differentiation in the Pacific Northwest has been its function as a producer of primary products. Economic instability and the unbridled exploitation of natural and human resources were the consequences of what can best be described as the uninhibited extraction of nature's wealth.[36] The boom-and-bust economies so characteristic of mining, logging, and other industrial activities in the Northwest brought its rewards with the emergence of vibrant, if episodic, labor protests and violence across the region.

The *regional* distinctiveness of militant labor traditions in the Northwest should not be exaggerated, because mining districts in Montana, Colorado, and Arizona and agricultural tracts in California's great Central Valley experienced similar conditions. But labor insurgency in the Northwest was conspicuous both in the number of natural resource industries affected and in the magnitude of some of its worker protests. Radical crusades, militant unions, and turbulence occurred in Butte, Montana, the Coeur d'Alene, Idaho, and Rossland, British Columbia mining districts and in the lumber mill towns of Everett and Centralia and in the great railroad center of Spokane. The Western Federation of Miners, founded in Butte, quickly swept westward through the Coeur d'Alenes and beyond and thereby established a profoundly radical stamp on a sizable segment of the labor movement in the Northwest. The region's boom-and-bust extractive economies, seasonal employment, and distance from markets helped to forge these volatile conditions. From the 1880s through World War I, Carlos Schwantes points out, the Pacific Northwest labor force was "composed predominantly of young single males who depended upon the major extractive industries of the West for jobs." Moreover, the most notable aspect of the region's work force during those years was its mobility and apparent rootlessness.[37] Those mercurial conditions ultimately provided fertile recruiting ground for the most radical of all labor unions, the Industrial Workers of the World (IWW).

Although the IWW had its roots in the western mining industry, it played a more active role in the Pacific Northwest, especially in the region's logging camps and lumber mills. In addition to the wood products industry, Wobbly organizers also worked hard to organize hard rock miners and migratory harvest hands. Those distinguishing features of the Northwest work force—overwhelmingly centered in nonfactory, industrial manual labor—provided fertile recruiting grounds for industrywide organization. While the IWW was active in other sections of the country, Carlos Schwantes argues that "they appeared more at home in the region than elsewhere." Although the IWW's grandiose ambition was to organize the nation's entire working class into "One Big Union," Robert Tyler observes that the Wobbly organization found its "most hospitable reception in the economies of the post-frontier West." To underscore its influence in the Pacific Northwest, one of its two principal newspapers, *The Industrial Worker,* was published in Spokane before it moved to Seattle in 1910. Moreover, several of the IWW's epic heroes—Jack Walsh; Frank Little; William D. "Big Bill" Haywood; Wesley Everest; Ralph Chapin; and Elizabeth Gurley Flynn, the "Rebel Girl"—were natives of the region or important to IWW activity in the Northwest. Finally, the IWW enjoyed "a taste of power" in the summer of 1917 when widespread strikes in the logging camps and mill towns across the Northwest brought lumber production to a standstill.[38]

The resurgence of IWW influence in the Northwest began in 1916 when the organization stepped up its organizing activity in the forests of the Inland Empire, the Douglas fir country west of the Cascades, and among harvest hands in the fruit orchards, hop fields, and wheat districts of Oregon and Washington. As they had elsewhere across the United States, Wobblies turned dissatisfaction among loggers and sawmill workers in the Northwest into a full-blown industrial revolt by the summer of 1917. "Familyless, womanless, overworked, underpaid, poorly treated," according to Melvyn Dubofsky, the land of the "timber beasts" appeared to be ideal recruiting grounds for IWW organizers. Taking advantage of a tight job market and American mobilization for the European war, IWW strikes in the Northwest paralyzed the lumber industry, seriously disrupted orchard and wheat harvests, and threatened copper production in Butte (and in the Utah and Arizona copper regions as well). The consequences of this widespread insurgency in the Northwest and elsewhere were government raids of IWW offices, the arrest of its leadership, and, in the lumber industry, the formation of a quasi-government/company union, the Loyal Legion of Loggers and Lumbermen. Although the government move destroyed the IWW threat, workers gained shortened and uniform working hours, better wages, and improved living conditions.[39]

Other regionally distinct protest movements that span decades of time are the efforts of various tribal groups in the Northwest to assert their treaty-guaranteed rights to hunt and fish "in their usual and accustomed grounds and stations." Although the legal struggles between states and Indian fishers date from the early years of the twentieth century, those conflicts began to escalate in the 1950s when Indians ignored state fish-and-game laws and began to fish in off-reservation waters. Race, politics, and Marlon Brando were involved, and in the end, a major shift in rights took place that greatly increased the influence of American Indian treaty tribes. Two key Federal District Court cases, one in 1969 and a second in 1974, affirmed the Indian treaty fishery. The latter decision, handed down by George H. Boldt of the Federal District Court in Tacoma and subsequently upheld twice by the Supreme Court, confirmed the treaty-guaranteed rights to fish irrespective of state regulations. A good argument can be made that the storm over the Indian fishery question and the later environmental protests over timber cutting were the two most contentious public disputes in the region during the last quarter of the twentieth century.[40]

❧

Although they may be more symbolic than substantive, Navajo and cowboy poetry; the veneration of the rodeo; the celebration of open spaces; seeing beauty in cactus, sagebrush, and the night desert sky; and reverence for magnificent redwood forests are *all* manifestations of particular places in the American West. For the greater Pacific Northwest, I would argue that few symbols more powerfully represent the essence and meaning of the region than salmon.[41] The basis for such a claim is vested in both history and how the region is culturally constructed. Over millions of years of time, salmon have inhabited the region unlike any other animal. Chinook salmon, for example, breed in the densely forested streams along the North Pacific littoral as well as in Rocky Mountain-fed streams that flow through the arid interior. Although they are a threatened and endangered species today, salmon are survivors, according to fisheries biologist Jim Lichatowich, "living through volcanic eruptions, ice ages, mountain building, fires, floods, and droughts." As the region moves into the next millennium, he contends, "the salmon's problem . . . has truly become everyone's problem."[42]

Salmon, therefore, are more than a dwindling species at the center of a regional crisis; they have been an integral part of the Northwest for 10 million years, and for the last 10,000 years, native people have enjoyed an intimate relationship with the fish. Salmon literally swim everywhere through the historical and cultural worlds of the greater Pacific Northwest. From the Native period to the present, salmon have been cultural icons, testimony to the fecundity and natural abundance of the region. Historically, salmon spawned in great numbers in North American watersheds from the San Joaquin and Sacramento Rivers in California to streams in British Columbia and Alaska as well as Asian river systems from the Russian far east to North Korea and Japan. To one observer, salmon were "the totem of the North Pacific Rim."[43] Although salmon also reproduce in Canadian, Alaskan, and Russian rivers discharging into the Arctic, they have much greater historical, cultural, and political significance in the more heavily populated Pacific Northwest.

The once prodigious salmon runs in Northwest streams provided sustenance for native people, and for most of the 150 years since European American settlement, salmon (and the vast stands of timber) were symbols of security and permanence, physical manifestations of nature's bounty in the region. "To be a Northwesterner," *New York Times* correspondent Timothy Egan contends, "was to be a salmon-eater."[44] Salmon that were once abundant, however, have now become scarce; they are already extinct in some watersheds and threatened in many others. The Pacific Northwest is now confronted with the unthinkable. What one writer has called "the heart and soul of the Northwest," a species that has "defined its history and culture" may disappear entirely from the region's numerous waterways.[45] A casual glance at the headlines in the morning newspaper or an impromptu look at the evening news suggests the degree to which endangered salmon have become the focus of contentious political debate. Science and politics have now become entangled in an intricate dance, vying for influence in determining the best strategy for saving salmon. In the process, blame is being liberally directed at virtually every constituency in the region.

Salmon have been important symbols of regional identity from the onset of the historical period in the Northwest. On the hot August afternoon in 1805 when the U.S. Army Corps of Discovery stumbled through Lemhi Pass in the Bitterroot Range, they happened on a group of Shoshones who befriended the party and offered them "a small morsel of boiled antelope and a piece of fresh salmon fresh roasted." The latter was a great source of satisfaction to Captain Meriwether Lewis, who confided to his journal, "this was the first salmon I had seen and perfectly convinced me that we were on the waters of the Pacific Ocean." When the Corps of Discovery reached the main stem of the Columbia and floated toward the Cascades, Lewis and Clark sketched a dramatic picture of abundance centered in the consumption of salmon.[46] The fur traders who followed were the first to suggest that salmon could be turned to account in the marketplace. Alexander Ross, on the river in 1811 for John Jacob Astor's Pacific Fur Company, thought Columbia River salmon "as fine as any in the world," and his partner Robert Stuart embellished the commodity value of the fish when he reported the existence of "a first rate salmon fishery" at the Long Narrows where a competent person could catch 500 fish per day during the season. And a committee of the U.S. House of Representatives, reporting about the prospects of colonizing the region a few years later, remarked that the Columbia was "of the utmost importance" commercially, especially "the fisheries on that coast" and "the vast quantities of furs."[47]

Two years after the establishment of Fort Vancouver, John McLoughlin asked Hudson's Bay Company officials for permission to trade salted salmon. In what turned into perceptive insight, he added: "It is certain if the Americans come they will attempt something in this way." Boston merchant Nathaniel Wyeth conceived the most ambitious of the early American efforts to establish a commercial fishery on the Columbia in 1834. Although that effort failed, Lieutenant Charles Wilkes and the U.S. Exploring Expedition investigated the Columbia River area in 1842 and gave unstinting praise to the region's extensive fishery. The rivers and coast, he reported, "abound in salmon of the finest flavor and appear inexhaustible." Of all the rivers in the Northwest, Wilkes thought the Columbia produced the finest salmon and in greatest numbers.[48] Geographic distance from world markets and a limited technology for preserving salmon, however, prevented entrepreneurs from capitalizing on those earlier reports about the region's abundant salmon runs. But when Maine natives Andrew Hapgood and the Hume brothers established the first salmon cannery on the lower Columbia in 1866, the rush was on.

From beginning to end, the Pacific Northwest salmon industry was a tremendously productive and efficient operation, yielding huge quantities of salmon for the numerous canneries located on the Columbia, Puget Sound, lower British Columbia and Vancouver Island, and the region's myriad coastal streams. Despite noticeably declining fish runs well before the turn of the twentieth century, an aura of unlimited abundance prevailed. Whereas the salmon take for all species in the Columbia River reached a high point of 46.6 million pounds in 1911, Puget Sound fishers produced an even larger output, one that did not peak until 1917. The Alaskan fishery, which got off to a later start, eventually surpassed both.[49] Subsequently, industrial practices, especially the introduction of mechanized and more intrusive logging and agricultural activities, quickened the pace of environmental change in the region and contributed to a steady and appreciable decline in the salmon catch. Those practices, along with the building of dams on major salmon-bearing streams in the region, have now imperiled the future of all salmon runs. "Things go wrong with rivers," the naturalist Robert Pyle remarked, "and much of what could go wrong with the Columbia already has."[50] With the exception of northern British

Columbia and Alaskan streams, the same could be said for most salmon-producing waters in the Northwest.

Writing for *The Atlantic* in 1976, Thomas Griffith drew attention to the depleted runs of salmon and the intensifying quarrel over the remnant runs in the Pacific Northwest. "The story of salmon," he concluded, "makes the Northwest vividly aware of the limits of what once seemed nature's unending bounty." But even in decline, Richard White notes, "salmon remain culturally as powerful as when they passed upriver in a flood of abundant life"; everywhere along the North Pacific slope they continue to hold great meaning as symbols of nature's abundance.[51] Those remarks come at the close of nearly two centuries of reckoning with the significance of the anadromous fishes to the greater Pacific Northwest. Although I do not believe that salmon provide an *essentialist* and definitive grounds for explaining the Northwest, I would insist that they are an important conceptual symbol for framing *historical* questions about the region.

Timothy Egan's glib comment, "The Pacific Northwest is simply this: wherever the salmon can get to," *does* have more than a semblance of validity. Speak to any native spokesperson from northern California to Alaska's Bristol Bay, Egan contends, "and you hear the story of a god that lives deep in the middle of the ocean. It's the same story, this mythic explanation of salmon."[52] Salmon are both historical representations of nature in the Northwest, I would argue, and an important regional cultural icon that has transcended the ages. Oregon's Governor John Kitzhaber underscored the centrality of salmon in an unusual June 1999 appearance before the Northwest Power Planning Council, the agency created by Congress in 1980 and charged with managing salmon and hydroelectric power in the Columbia River Basin. Kitzhaber told the council that it had "an extraordinarily pivotal role" and that its success or failure would "truly shape the future of the region."[53]

❧

Although the representations are whimsical and seemingly less significant, there have always been offbeat characterizations of regional cultures, portrayals that elevate the seemingly fatuous and inane to levels of serious discussion.[54] The stoic and dry humor of northern New England, especially residents of rural Maine and Vermont, reflects a drab folk, usually dressed in bib overalls, who are as spare in language as they are gaunt in frame. In similar fashion, the rural Great Plains has a long tradition of exaggerated humor usually centered in the extremes of climate, of drought, wind, blizzards, and vast distances. In the American South, rural Southerners have long been referred to by outsiders and Southerners alike as "rednecks" and "hillbillies," pejorative references that have helped build a historical stereotype of common white folk. Jack Temple Kirby, who has written thoughtfully and sympathetically about class in the South and the white southern underclass in particular, portrays the popular typecast in stark terms as "quaint premoderns, prone to taking the law into their own hands, but entertaining despite their doleful delinquencies in discipline and taste."[55]

Although northern Idaho's hate-mongering Aryan Nations and other right-wing fringe groups in the Pacific Northwest have captured national headlines in the last two decades, the region has also generated a cluster of quirky images centered around climate, scenery, quality of life, and pioneering legislation.[56] In an address to the Oregon Cattlemen's Association in 1984, Richard Nixon's Secretary of Agriculture, Earl Butz, remarked that the Northwest had "more kooks per square mile than any other place in the U.S." He later clarified that he was speaking about "environmentalists" and the state's reputation "a few years ago for no-growth."[57] The year before Butz made his visit to the region, the writer Sherry Stripling described Northwesterners as "conservative, provincial but tolerant, fiercely protective of the area's natural beauty and chauvinistic about its appeal." Writing for the *Seattle Times,* she conducted a host of interviews with newcomer and native residents alike, including the author Tom Robbins. "Being a Northwest native is a state of mind as much as indigenous birth," Robbins told Stripling. "I'm a Northwesterner who was born on the East Coast as the result of a genetic accident. As soon as I was old enough, I corrected the mistake." Humor aside, Stripling found common themes repeated favorably in all of her interviews: lifestyle, unpretentiousness, casual dress, concerns about uncontrolled growth, and scenic splendors that belie the region's often gray weather.[58] The point to this discussion is *not* to hang regional meaning on wackiness or contrariness, but to suggest that the Northwest cultural milieu, like that of other regions, embraces a strain of popular tradition and mores that may be unique to this corner of the United States.

That sense of quirky Northwest chauvinism, especially the Oregon variety, may have reached a peak during (and after) the governorship of Tom McCall (1967-1975). Along with his compatriot state executives, Washington's Dan Evans and Idaho's Cecil Andrus, McCall was a person with a considerable national reputation. Tall, eloquent, and with a bastardized accent that commingled upper-class Boston English with a western drawl, McCall's famous advice to visitors, "Come visit us again and again. . . . But for heaven's sake, don't come here to live," served up rich material for political opponents and editorial pundits alike. The euphemistic James G. Blaine Society, the erstwhile creation of the deceased writer Stewart Holbrook, gained tongue-in-cheek notoriety for discouraging immigration to the Northwest. Advertising the region's sun lamps that drizzle, saw tooth rain worms, electric trees, and the Oregon epidermis (a skin rash caused by rain), writers accentuated the negative about the region. Observing this aspect of Oregon's wackiness, a California writer still acknowledged that he was "a patsy for Oregon's natural endowments" and the state's livability. The Northwest, the home of "the decent middle," Thomas Griffith wrote just as McCall was leaving office, "is for people more interested in being than in achieving."[59]

A former Oregonian who moved to Indiana in the 1980s remarked that, unlike the Northwest where diversity in cultural and character types reigned supreme, everybody was the same in her newly adopted home. "Everybody looks alike, talks alike, thinks alike," she lamented. Such divergent views about the Northwest prompted Jeff Kuechle to ask, "Who are we?" in a 1987 article published in the Portland *Oregonian:* "Why, we're Northwesterners. The few. The Proud. Rugged. Outdoorsy. Absolute individuals. Healthy. Environmentally virtuous. The envy of our fellow countrymen. Dwellers in God's own corner of America. We're different. Or are we?" Although identifying the characteristics that frame regional identity "is a slippery task," he believed that *"something"* tied Northwesterners together. Statistics, survey research, scholars who generalize about human behavior, and ideas that "just float around as part of the Northwest's collective wisdom," according to Kuechle, provide sufficient grounds for identifying the Northwest as a distinct place. There is, he insisted, "a tie that binds." It can be found in the fact that the Northwest is statistically the most secular of American regions, its people cherish quality of life over material success, its residents favor the environment over the corporate world, Northwesterners purchase more books *and* sunglasses (per capita) than other Americans, and business matters take a hind seat to quality-of-life issues. Kuechle concluded that the rest of America may see residents of the region as "the slightly addled inhabitants of a paradise that isn't for everybody. Unique? Not so much as we might think. But enviable in a strange sort of way."[60]

The Northwest has a sizable constituency that prides itself in believing that residents of the region march to a different drummer, to what we might call a kind of Northwest noir. How does one explain popular television shows of the recent past that were filmed in the region—*Northern Exposure, Twin Peaks*—or television's *The Simpsons,* the creation of former Portlander and Evergreen College graduate, Matt Groening. And then there are the offbeat novels such as Ken Kesey's *One Flew over the Cuckoo's Nest* (1962) and *Sailor's Song* (1992) and Katherine Dunn's *Geek Love* (1989), which deals with the breeding habits of circus dwarfs. Add to this list the work of comic-strip creator/journalist/playwright Lynda Barry, the dark and off-center productions of filmmaker Gus Van Sant (*Drugstore Cowboy*, 1989; *My Own Private Idaho*, 1992; and *Even Cowgirls Get the Blues*, 1994) or the iconoclasm and individuality of Seattle's Pearl Jam and Nirvana. And the most zany of them all may be Gary Larson's wonderful creation, "The Far Side," perhaps the most famous comic strip ever crafted. A Seattle resident, some of Larson's insight to animal and bug behavior may be attributed to the fact that he attended the state's land-grant university, Washington State University in Pullman.[61]

Admittedly, artists, writers, and other creative specialists approach regional culture from a very different perspective. Katherine Dunn sees her work as a writer as a "process of looking at the unusual, but from two steps to the side." She believes that the "metaphor of the subterranean is at work in a lot of Northwest writers and artists," and suggests that the work of filmmakers Gus Van Sant and David Lynch (the creator of *Twin Peaks*) have that quality. According to one writer, Van Sant has had a great influence in how Northwesterners see themselves and how those from outside view its residents. Van Sant especially likes the kind of people who are slightly off-center; they provide him with ideas for characters and plots. "People in the Northwest," he observes, "tend to be more eccentric than people elsewhere. This place is full of people who disdain the things that you might go to Los Angeles for: a big house, a lot of money, ego." David Lynch, who grew up in Spokane and Missoula and was a member of the Boy Scouts, used a prototype logging town in the region to develop the crazy characters and dark humor voiced in *Twin Peaks*. "Do any of these characters really exist?" Seattle-based *New York Times* correspondent Timothy Egan asked in 1991. "Well, you can wonder what sort of Boy Scout troop David Lynch belonged to in Missoula." For those who think Matt Groening's and Lynda Barry's drawings have no basis in reality, Egan reminds his readers that both were classmates at Olympia's Evergreen College, whose mascot is an obscene-looking, five-foot-long geoduck clam.[62]

That "light" and "dark" commentary on Northwest culture did not originate in the last two or three decades. Although it is not the purpose of this essay to survey the region's wealth of creative fiction, one novel stands out as a kind of representative archetype for the off-center view of the world that is featured in regional writing of the present moment. H. L. Davis's 1935 Pulitzer-Prize winning novel, *Honey in the Horn* is the prototypical fictional account of early twentieth-century life in rural Oregon, of less-than-heroic characters, losers who muddle their way through life in the absence of any larger, more consuming ambition. Davis's characters belch, break wind, pick their noses. A married couple living amid lichen- and moss-covered buildings in Oregon's coastal mountains never speak to each other during the long, rainy winter months. The novel centers on Clay and Luce, flawed teenagers, whose lives drift among itinerant workers, horse traders, and nondescript backcountry settlers. The humor, in historian Edwin Bingham's words, "is raucous, indelicate, and drawn-out," and the characters are "unconventional and sometimes grotesque."[63] But the important qualities to be remembered, I believe, are that the differences between *Honey in the Horn* and the iconoclastic fictional works of the last two decades are generational and matters of degree rather than substance.

⌁

The disparate ideas discussed in this essay suggest that the study of regionalism is something less than a clinically forged, scientifically motivated exercise. William Ferris, Chair of the National Endowment for the Humanities during the Clinton administration, put it best when he remarked that whereas all disciplines offer insights to regions, our attachment to place is ultimately emotional and irrational and "is revealed in the romantic vision of nature and man's relation to it." Regionalism, in his view, treats American culture as a vibrant laboratory upon which to draw a portion of our expansive landscape. To study a region, Ferris believes, is to discover something about America. Regionalism is more than simply nostalgic "local color" stories. It embraces a dynamic interplay of cultural, political, and psychological components. According to geographer Terry Jordan, humans also possess mental maps of the places they inhabit, "vernacular regions" or exercises in the self-consciousness of place. "That is, the inhabitants believe that the region exists."[64]

In the end, however, the study of regions is more than a descriptive exercise; it is an analytical tool for making sense of a seemingly incomprehensible and chaotic world. Regions exist in proximity to one another and they should never be studied in isolation. Even "functional" bureaucratic regions represent rationalized efforts to mark, bound, and impose reasonable human scale on landscapes.[65] It may seem redundant, but it is important to recognize that the special dynamics of the places we inhabit affect us directly. Change can be disruptive to our sense of well-being. For the Pacific Northwest, sharply diminished salmon runs and severe environmental restrictions on timber harvests have been harmful to traditional resource communities, contributing to economic dislocation and social disorder. In some cases, it has pitted members of a community against each other; in still others, it has put urban and rural people on opposing sides of environmental issues. In the end, however, physical landscapes— cascading and meandering waterways, forested slopes, sprawling grasslands, sagebrush deserts, and rockbound seacoast—are the centerpiece of our regional iconography.

There is a common feature, an essential focus to this discussion of the Pacific Northwest, of its once prodigious salmon runs, and the region's trove of offbeat stories. It rests, I suggest, in the intimate association between humans and geography, the ties that bind people to particular places. I use this relationship, what I call our affinity and affection for place, to underscore its potential as a moral force to guide and shape social and environmental policies.[66] It is appropriate for us to acknowledge that our collective behavior toward the world around us and toward each other has been less than benign. We live amid landscapes that are far different from the ones that existed two centuries ago. If we are to be caring trustees for the special qualities of the Pacific Northwest, there will be no better test of our will than the stewardship we exercise toward the world about us and toward each other.[67]

Notes

[1] Quoted in David M. Wrobel and Michael C. Steiner, eds., *Many Wests: Place, Culture, and Regional Identity* (Lawrence: University Press of Kansas, 1997), v.

[2] Carl O. Sauer, "A Geographical Sketch of Early Man in America," *Geographical Review* 34 (1944): 529-73; Sauer, "The Agency of Man's Role on Earth," in *Man's Role in Changing the Face of the Earth*, ed. William I. Thomas (Chicago: University of Chicago Press, 1956), 1, 54-56; Stephen J. Pyne, *Fire in America: A Cultural History of Wildland and Rural Fire* (Princeton: Princeton University Press, 1982), 75.

[3] The discussion here reflects, in part, my reading of Robert David Sack, *Homo Geographicus: A Framework for Action, Awareness, and Moral Concern* (Baltimore, Md: Johns Hopkins University Press, 1997), 1-26.

[4] For a description of the Columbia River system, see Carlos A. Schwantes, *The Pacific Northwest: An Interpretive History*, rev. ed. (Lincoln: University of Nebraska Press, 1996), 12-13.

[5] Richard White, *The Organic Machine: The Remaking of the Columbia River* (New York: Hill and Wang, 1995), 113.

[6] Alan F. J. Artibise, "Canadian Adventures: Shared Visions, Strategic Alliances, and Ingrained Barriers in a Transborder Region" (paper presented at the conference On Brotherly Terms: Canadian-American Relations West of the Rockies, University of Washington, 14 September 1996). Copy in the author's possession.

[7] William Ferris, "Region as Art," in *Regional Studies: The Interplay of Land and People*, ed. Glen E. Lich (College Station: Texas A&M University Press, 1992), 5. Writing for *New York Times Magazine* at the close of World War II, journalist Richard Neuberger defined the region to include Oregon, Washington, Idaho, British Columbia, and Alaska. See *New York Times Magazine,* 9 December 1945.

[8] The ideas discussed here are adapted from Cole Harris, banquet address, Pacific Northwest History Conference, Victoria, British Columbia, 16 April 1999.

[9] Robin Fisher, "Defining the Region: Is There a Pacific Northwest?" (paper presented at the Pacific Northwest History Conference, Bellingham, Washington, 25 March 1994) and Ken Coates, "Border Crossings: Pattern and Process in the History of the Pacific Northwest," (plenary address to the conference On Brotherly Terms: Canadian-American Relations West of the Rockies, University of Washington, 12 September 1996), both copies in the author's possession; Mark

Trahant, "In Altered States, Cascadians Could Dream of Living in Oz," Portland *Oregonian,* 26 November 1995.

[10] Allan Pritchard, "The Shapes of History in British Columbia Writing," *BC Studies,* no. 93 (Spring 1992): 48.

[11] For the first professional history of the Pacific Northwest, see Joseph Schafer, *History of the Pacific Northwest* (New York: The Macmillan Company, 1905).

[12] For only a few works by these authors, see James G. Swan, *The Northwest Coast: or, Three Years' Residence in Washington Territory* (1857; reprint, Seattle: University of Washington Press, 1972); Franz Boas, *Chinook Texts,* U.S. Bureau of American Ethnology Bulletin, no. 20 (Washington, D.C.: Government Printing Office, 1894); Boas, *Contribution to the Ethnology of the Kwakiutl* (New York: Columbia University Press, 1925); Boas, *Kwakiutl Culture as Reflected in Mythology* (New York: American Folklore Society, 1935); Melville Jacobs, *The Content and Style of an Oral Literature: Clackamas Chinook Myths and Tales* (Chicago: University of Chicago Press, 1959); Jacobs, *Coos Myth Texts* (Seattle: University of Washington Press, 1940); Jacobs, *Kalapuya Texts* (Seattle: University of Washington Press, 1945); Leslie Spier, *Klamath Ethnography*, University of California Publications in American Archaeology and Ethnology, vol. 30 (Berkeley: University of California Press, 1930); Edward Sapir, *Takelma Texts*, University of Pennsylvania Anthropological Publications of the University Museum, vol. 2, no. 1 (Philadelphia: University of Pennsylvania Press, 1909); Sapir, *A Sketch of the Social Organization of the Nass River Indians,* Geological Survey of Canada, Victoria Memorial Museum Bulletin, no. 19 (1915); Luther Cressman, *An Approach to the Study of Far Western North American Prehistory: Early Man,* Bulletin of the Museum of Natural History, University of Oregon, no. 20 (1973); and *Early Man in Oregon: Archaeological Studies in the Northern Great Basin*, University of Oregon Monographs, Studies in Anthropology, no. 3 (August 1940).

[13] For an extended version of this discussion, see William G. Robbins, *Landscapes of Promise: The Oregon Story, 1800-1940* (Seattle: University of Washington Press, 1997), 28-29.

[14] See Sack, *Homo Geographicus,* 8.

[15] Andrew R. L. Cayton and Peter S. Onuf, *The Midwest and the Nation: Rethinking the History of an American Region* (Bloomington: Indiana University Press, 1990), xviii, 84-85, 118. Cayton and Onuf point out that the emergence of industrialism in the Midwest brought a similar questioning of republican, middle-class values and assumptions. For other studies of the Midwest, see John R. Borchert, *America's Northern Heartland: An Economic and Historical Geography of the Upper Midwest* (Minneapolis: University of Minnesota Press, 1987); William E. Mallory and Paul Simpson-Housley, *Geography and Literature: A Meeting of the Disciplines* (Syracuse, N.Y.: Syracuse University Press, 1987); James Madison, *Heart Land* (Bloomington: Indiana University Press, 1988); James P. Shortridge, *The Middle West: Its Meaning in American Culture* (Lawrence: University Press of Kansas, 1989).

[16] For the influence of industrialism in the Pacific Northwest, see Robbins, *Landscapes of Promise,* 180, and *Colony and Empire: The Capitalist Transformation of the American West* (Lawrence: University Press of Kansas, 1994), 121-42.

[17] Selected books by these authors pertinent to the Northwest include: Blew, *Circle of Women: An Anthology of Contemporary Western Women Writers* (New York: Penguin Books, 1994); Dietrich, *Final Forest: The Battle for the Last Great Trees in the Pacific Northwest* (New York: Simon and Schuster, 1992); Dietrich, *Northwest Passage: The Great Columbia River* (New York: Simon and Schuster, 1995); Dillard, *The Living: A Novel* (New York: Harper Collins, 1992); Doig, *Winter Brothers: A*

Season at the Edge of America (New York: Harcourt Brace Jovanovich, 1980); Doig, *Mountain Time* (New York: Scribner, 1999); Duncan, *The River Why* (New York: Bantam Books, 1984); Egan, *The Good Rain: Time and Terrain across the Pacific Northwest* (New York: Knopf, 1990); Guterson, *Snow Falling on Cedars* (San Diego: Harcourt Brace, 1994); Kesey, *One Flew over the Cuckoo's Nest* (New York: Viking Press, 1962); Kesey, *Sometimes a Great Notion* (New York: Viking Press, 1964); Kittredge, *Owning It All* (St. Paul, Minn.: Graywolf Press, 1987); Kittredge, *Hole in the Sky: A Memoir* (New York: Alfred A. Knopf, 1992); Lesley, *Winterkill* (New York: Dell Publishing, 1984); Lesley, *River Song* (New York: Dell Publishing, 1989); Alexie, *The Lone Ranger and Tonto Fistfight in Heaven* (New York: Atlantic Monthly Press, 1993); Woody, *A Circle of Nations: Visions and Voices of American Indians* (Hillsboro, Oregon: Beyond Words Publishers, 1993).

[18] Garry Wills, "A Reader's Guide to the Century," *New York Review of Books,* 15 July 1999, 24; Eugene Victor Walter, *Placeways: A Theory of the Human Environment* (Chapel Hill: University of North Carolina Press, 1988), 1.

[19] Katherine G. Morrissey, *Mental Territories: Mapping the Inland Empire* (Ithaca, N.Y.: Cornell University Press, 1997), 12. Jensen quoted in Lich, ed., *Regional Studies,* x.

[20] For an interesting study of the Corn Belt region in the upper Midwest, see John C. Hudson, *Making the Corn Belt: A Geographical History of Middle-Western Agriculture* (Bloomington: Indiana University Press, 1994). Hudson argues that the Corn Belt, established by 1850, is an agricultural region where physical environment and human decisions have been of primary importance (see pp. 1-2).

[21] Schwantes, *The Pacific Northwest,* 1-2. I reviewed these same questions and issues at the Teachers' Institute, sponsored by the Oregon Council for the Humanities at Reed College, 22 June 1999.

[22] John Gunther, *Inside U.S.A.* (1946; reprint, New York: Book-of-the-Month Club, 1997), 85; Raymond Gastil, *Cultural Regions of the United States* (Seattle: University of Washington Press, 1975), 265; Thomas Griffiths, "The Pacific Northwest," *The Atlantic Monthly* (April 1976): 54.

[23] Katherine Morrissey makes this point in *Mental Territories,* 165.

[24] At the same time, I recognize that provincial contexts provided the cornerstone for the earliest expressions of American culture. See Charles Wilson Reagan, ed., *The New Regionalism* (Jackson: University of Mississippi Press, 1998), ix.

[25] Wrobel and Steiner, *Many Wests,* 5.

[26] Jackson Lears in quoted in Peter Applebome, "Out from under the Nation's Shadow," *New York Times,* 20 February 1999; Donald Snow, "A Fierce Devotion," *Northern Lights* 12 (Spring 1997): 13; Sack, *Homo-Geographicus,* 8.

[27] Robert D. Kaplan, "Travels into America's Future," *The Atlantic Monthly* (August 1998): 37, 52, 58.

[28] William Leach, *Country of Exiles: The Destruction of Place in American Life* (New York: Pantheon Books, 1999), 6-7, 180.

[29] Coates, "Border Crossings," 8; and Artibise, "Canadian Adventures."

[30] Robbins, *Colony and Empire,* ix.

[31] Ibid., xii-xiii.

[32] Jack Temple Kirby, *The Countercultural South* (Athens: University of Georgia Press, 1995), 1.

[33] Yi-Fu Tuan, *Space and Place: The Perspective of Experience* (Minneapolis: University of Minnesota Press, 1977), 136-48.

[34] For the history of utopian communities in western Washington, see Charles P. LeWarne, *Utopias on Puget Sound, 1885-1915* (Seattle: University of Washington Press, 1975).

[35] Schwantes, *The Pacific Northwest,* 353; Paul George Hummasti, *Finnish Radicals in Astoria, Oregon, 1904-1940: A Study in Immigrant Socialism* (New York: Arno Press, 1979); Gerald Rasmussen and Otto N. Larsen, *Oregon Danish Colony: Ethnic Assimilation in Junction City, 1902-1952* (Junction City, Oregon: Danish American Heritage Society, 1998), 23-27.

[36] Schwantes, *The Pacific Northwest,* 2-3; Ann Markusen, "The Economics and Politics of Regionalism," in Lich, ed., *Regional Studies,* 51.

[37] Ibid., 328-30; Schwantes, *Radical Heritage: Labor, Socialism, and Reform in Washington and British Columbia, 1885-1917* (Seattle: University of Washington Press, 1979), 15-21.

[38] Schwantes, *The Pacific Northwest,* 339-40; Robert L. Tyler, *Rebels of the Woods: The IWW in the Pacific Northwest* (Eugene: University of Oregon Books, 1967), 5-11; Melvyn Dubofsky, *WE SHALL BE ALL: A History of the Industrial Workers of the World* (Chicago: Quadrangle Books, 1969), 186-87, 318-19.

[39] Dubofsky, *WE SHALL BE ALL,* 318-19, 324, 333-36, 359-64, 412-14.

[40] *Seattle Times,* 7 February 1999. Even though it is dated, the best source is Fay G. Cohen, *Treaties on Trial: The Continuing Controversy over Northwest Indian Treaty Fishing Rights* (Seattle: University of Washington Press, 1986).

[41] On this point, I disagree sharply with John Findlay, who argues that the adoption of salmon as a regional icon is "a recent invention." See John M. Findlay, "A Fishy Proposition: Regional Identity in the Pacific Northwest," (paper presented at the Pacific Northwest History Conference, Tacoma, Washington, 25 April 1997), copy in the author's possession. Also see the published version, "A Fishy Proposition: Regional Identity in the Pacific Northwest," in Wrobel and Steiner, eds., *Many Wests,* 37-70.

[42] Jim Lichatowich, *Salmon without Rivers: A History of the Pacific Salmon Crisis* (Washington, D.C.: Island Press, 1999), 5-7.

[43] The information regarding the extent of salmon spawning habitat and the quotation is in Findlay, "A Fishy Proposition," 39.

[44] Timothy Egan, *The Good Rain: Across Time and Terrain in the Pacific Northwest* (New York: Alfred A. Knopf, 1990), 183.

[45] Will Stelle, Director, National Marine Fisheries Service, quoted in Joan Laatz, "The Salmon's Decline," *Oregonian,* 29 January 1995.

[46] Gary E. Moulton, ed., *The Journals of Lewis and Clark,* vol. 5 (Lincoln: University of Nebraska Press, 1988), 83, 287-88, 327, 335.

[47] Alexander Ross, *Adventures of the First Settlers on the Oregon or Columbia River, 1810-1813* (1859; reprint, Lincoln: University of Nebraska Press, 1986; Oregon State University Press, 2000), 108; Philip Aston Rollins, ed. *The Discovery of the Oregon Trail: Robert Stuart's Narrative* (New York: Charles Scribner's Sons, 1935), 52; "Occupation of the Columbia River, A Report of the Committee to Inquire into the Situation of the Settlements upon the Pacific Ocean," *Oregon Historical Quarterly* 8 (1907), 62.

[48] David Johnson, "Salmon: A Legacy of Abundance," *What's Happening* (Eugene, Oregon), 31 January 1991, 6; Anthony Netboy, *Columbia River Salmon and Steelhead Trout: Their Fight for Survival* (Seattle: University of Washington Press, 1980), 19; Charles Wilkes, "Report on the Territory of Oregon," *Oregon Historical Quarterly* 12 (September 1911): 286-87.

[49] Schwantes, *The Pacific Northwest,* 164; Netboy, *Columbia River Salmon and Steelhead Trout,* 34-36, 150-55.

[50] Robert Michael Pyle, *Wintergreen: Rambles in a Ravaged Land* (New York: Scribners, 1986), 41.

[51] White, *The Organic Machine,* 90; Griffith, "The Pacific Northwest," 81.

[52] Egan, *The Good Rain*, 22.

[53] Kitzhaber is quoted in the *Oregonian*, 10 June 1999.

[54] For a theoretical inquiry into "the energies of places" and "modes of experiencing them," see Walter, *Placeways*, 5.

[55] Kirby, *The Countercultural South*, 3.

[56] See John Helmick, "Letter from Idaho," *The Nation* (1 March 1986): 238-39.

[57] All of the quotations and supporting material are in Jeff Kuechle, "The Way We Are," *Northwest Magazine, Oregonian*, 7 June 1987, 7-17.

[58] Sherry Stripling, "Northwest Natives: Friendly, Conservative, and Transplanted," *Seattle Times*, Pacific Section, 8-11.

[59] Robert Borrow, "Oregon: A 97,000-Square-Mile Cure for that Stuffy Feeling," *Oregonian*, 5 August 1973; Griffith, "The Pacific Northwest," 50-51. For the life of Tom McCall, see the superb biography by Brent Walth, *Fire at Eden's Gate: Tom McCall and the Oregon Story* (Portland: Oregon Historical Society Press, 1994). Classic "western" writer Ernest Haycox observed in 1948 that people in the Northwest were "as good an example of middle-class society as could be found." They were neither bawdy nor boisterous, there was none of the "exaggerated electrical energy which belongs to the Texan," and there was no "mass enthusiasm which sets apart the California man. . . . Few zealots and reformers come out of the Northwest." See Ernest Haycox, "Is There a Pacific Northwest?" in *Northwest Harvest: A Regional Stocktaking*, ed. V. L. O. Chittick (New York: Macmillan Co., 1948), 41, 43.

[60] Kuechle, "The Way We Are," 17.

[61] Timothy Egan, "Northwest Noir," *Oregonian*, 22 July 1991; Curt Hopkins, "The Last Weird Place," *Old Oregon* (Spring 1993): 17-21.

[62] Hopkins, "The Last Weird Place," 19; Egan, "Northwest Noir," *Oregonian*, 22 July 1991.

[63] Edwin R. Bingham, "Pacific Northwest Writing: Reaching for Regional Identity," in Robbins et al., *Regionalism and the Pacific Northwest*, 166-67.

[64] Ferris, "Region as Art," 19; Jordan, "The Concept and the Method," 11.

[65] Jordan, "The Concept and the Method," 15, 20.

[66] Sack, *Homo Geographicus*, 2.

[67] I made this argument in "The Historical and Cultural Meaning of Salmon," *OHS Spectator*, no. 1 (July 1999), 25.

Notes on the Authors

❦

Katrine Barber holds a postdoctoral position at the Center for Columbia River History in Vancouver, Washington and teaches at Portland State University. She recently earned her Ph.D. in American Studies at Washington State University.

Keith Benson is professor of history of science, technology, and medicine at the University of Washington and the author and coauthor of several books, including *William Keith Brooks (1848—1908): A Case Study in Morphology and the Development of American Biology* (1979) and, with Jacques Roger, *The Life Sciences in Eighteenth-Century French Thought* (1997).

Stephen W. Haycox is professor of history at the University of Alaska, Anchorage, where he has taught for thirty years. His published work addresses culture, Native people, and law and politics in the history of the American West, Alaska, and the Canadian North.

William L. Lang is professor of history at Portland State University and director of the Center for Columbia River History. His most recent books include *Confederacy of Ambition: William Winlock Miller and the Making of Washington Territory* (1996) and *Great River of the West: Essays on the Columbia River* (1999).

David Laskin is a Seattle writer and the author of two cultural histories of weather, *Braving the Elements: The Stormy History of American Weather* (1993) and *Rains All the Time: A Connoisseur's History of Weather in the Pacific Northwest* (1997).

Kathleen Dean Moore is professor of philosophy at Oregon State University and the author of several books, including *Riverwalking: Reflections on Moving Water* (1995) and *Holdfast: At Home in the Natural World* (1999).

Jeremy Mouat teaches history at Athabasca University in Alberta, Canada. He has published several books and articles on resource development in western Canada and other regions. He is currently writing a biography of the mining financier Whitaker Wright.

Thomas Michael Power is professor and chair in the Economics Department at the University of Montana. His most recent books include *Lost Landscapes and Failed Economies: In Search of Value and Place* (1996) and *Environmental Protection and Economic Well-Being: The Economic Pursuit of Quality* (1996).

William G. Robbins is Distinguished Professor of History at Oregon State University and the author of *Colony and Empire: The Capitalist Transformation of the American West* (1994) and *Landscapes of Promise: The Oregon Story, 1800—1940* (1997).

Quintard Taylor Jr. is Scott and Dorothy Bullitt Professor of American History at the University of Washington and the author of *The Forging of a Black Community: Seattle's Central District from 1870 through the Civil Rights Era* (1994) and *In Search of the Racial Frontier: African Americans in the American West, 1528—1990* (1998).

Gail Wells grew up in Coos Bay, the heart of Oregon's timber country. She is a writer and editor at Oregon State University and is the author or *The Tillamook: A Created Forest Comes of Age* (1999).

Index